Going Native

Indians in the American Cultural Imagination

SHARI M. HUHNDORF

Cornell University Press
Ithaca and London

First published 2001 by Cornell University Press
First printing, Cornell Paperbacks, 2001

Printed in the United States of America

Library of Congress Cataloging-in-Publication Data

Huhndorf, Shari M. (Shari Michelle), 1965–

    Going native : Indians in the American cultural imagination / Shari M. Huhndorf.
      p. cm.
    Includes bibliographical references and index.
    ISBN 0-8014-3852-2 (cloth : acid-free paper) — ISBN 0-8014-8695-5 (pbk. : acid-
free paper)
    1. Indians of North America—Public opinion. 2. Public opinion—United States.
3. Nationalism—United States. 4. Indians in literature. I. Title.
    E98.P99 H85 2001
    973.04'97—dc21   00-010814

Cornell University Press strives to use environmentally responsible suppliers and
materials to the fullest extent possible in the publishing of its books. Such materials
include vegetable-based, low-VOC inks and acid-free papers that are recycled, to-
tally chlorine-free, or partly composed of nonwood fibers. Books that bear the
logo of the FSC (Forest Stewardship Council) use paper taken from forests that
have been inspected and certified as meeting the highest standards for environmental and social responsibility. For further information, visit our website at
www.cornellpress.cornell.edu.

Cloth printing   10 9 8 7 6 5 4 3 2 1
Paperback printing   10 9 8 7 6 5 4 3 2

For my parents,
Roy and Charlene Huhndorf,
and my sister,
Charlsie Huhndorf Arend

The Indian Wars have never ended in the Americas.

—Leslie Marmon Silko, *Almanac of the Dead*

Indians, the original possessors of the land, seem to haunt the collective unconscious of the white man and to the degree that one can identify the conflicting images of the Indian which stalk the white man's waking perceptions of the world one can outline the deeper problems of identity and alienation that trouble him....Underneath all the conflicting images of the Indian one fundamental truth emerges—the white man knows that he is an alien and he knows that North America is Indian—and he will never let go of the Indian image because he thinks that by some clever manipulation he can achieve an authenticity that cannot ever be his.

—Vine Deloria, Jr., "American Fantasy"

Contents

Illustrations

Acknowledgments

THIS BOOK OWES a great deal to the support of friends and colleagues, whose thoughts, suggestions, and careful readings have vastly improved my work. It is a pleasure to thank them here. Richard Sieburth, Arnold Krupat, Fred Myers, and Andrew Ross gave invaluable guidance during the early stages of this project, while conversations with Dean Bear Claw, Harriett Skye, Chris Eyre, and Meg McLagen helped to formulate the book's central questions and made me believe the research was worthwhile. Others have helped in substantial ways by offering suggestions, providing materials, reading chapters, or otherwise engaging (and often challenging) my ideas. I am particularly grateful to Joseph Fracchia, Olakunle George, Roland Greene, Garrett Hongo, Jeffrey Ostler, Beth Hege Piatote, Scott Pratt, Emelia Seubert, James Tarter, Pimone Triplett, and Elizabeth Wheeler. I owe special debts to Karen J. Ford and Dalia Kandiyoti, who have sustained me with their friendship, intellectual engagement, and careful attention to my writing. Timothy Reiss has provided support of various kinds for many years, and his efforts enabled me to undertake this research. My most profound debt, however, is to Patricia Penn Hilden. As a dear friend and generous adviser, she has shaped my thinking in critical ways, and her tireless attention during all phases of this project has improved my work in every respect. Without her, this book could not have been written.

Other kinds of support have also been important. Funding from the Ford Foundation, the Woodrow Wilson Foundation, the University of Oregon, and New York University provided the necessary time to concentrate on research and writing. I have presented parts of this project at several institutions where audiences have offered useful ideas and criticisms, but the Annual Conference of Ford Fellows has been especially helpful. Numerous fellows have commented on my work and influenced me with their own. At Cornell University Press, I am grateful to Bernhard Kendler for his careful attention and guidance. Kenneth Roemer and a second reader for the Press, who remains anonymous, improved this work immensely with their insightful criticisms. Jordana Dolowich provided valuable research assistance during a critical stage.

Some sections of *Going Native* have appeared in other publications. A much earlier version of part of Chapter 1 was published in *As We Are Now: Mixblood Essays on Race and Identity*, ed. William Penn (University of California Press, 1997). Part of Chapter 2 appeared in *Critical Inquiry* (fall 2000).

My deepest gratitude and admiration belong to the dedicatees. My parents, Roy and Charlene Huhndorf, and my sister, Charlsie Huhndorf Arend, have inspired me with their lives. Their unwavering love and support have enabled me to imagine and ultimately to complete this book.

Going Native

"If Only I Were an Indian"

IN HIS HIGHLY ACCLAIMED 1990 box-office hit, *Dances with Wolves*, the director, Kevin Costner, tells the story of Lieutenant John Dunbar, a disillusioned Civil War hero "gone native."[1] The film opens with the young hero, just decorated for an unintended act of heroism (actually a failed suicide attempt), being given the opportunity to relocate to another military post. To the disbelief of his officers and fellow soldiers, Dunbar (played by Costner) chooses the furthermost post, located on the Plains—in other words, in "hostile" Indian country. The character is, in part, fleeing to the edges of civilization from a European-American world apparently gone mad in the bloody Civil War. Deranged officers and soldiers populate the gory early scenes of the film, seemingly bent on their own destruction or the senseless slaying of their brothers. But it is not only the desire to escape from this "bloody slaughter" which draws Dunbar to the frontier. He is also compelled by a nostalgic desire to experience the freedom of life on the Plains "before it's all gone." His subsequent solitary life at the downtrodden post, surrounded only by vast seas of prairie and endless skies, fulfills these fantasies. There, for a short time, he lives the self-sufficient existence of the mythical frontiersman, his only companions his loyal horse and a curious stray wolf.

His solitude is short-lived, however. The post is, after all, located in the territory of unconquered and reportedly malevolent Indians, whose visits soon shatter his peaceful existence.[2] Although these encounters

"If Only I Were an Indian" is the title of a documentary of a Czech "Indian" tribe, a striking example of the phenomenon described in this study. See John Paskievich, dir., *If Only I Were an Indian* (Zimma Pictures with the National Film Board of Canada, 1995).

[1] Kevin Costner, dir., *Dances with Wolves* (Orion Pictures, 1990).

[2] I need to explain at the outset my use of the terms "Native" and "Indian" throughout the book. Although this fact is frequently overlooked, Native America comprises Indians and other groups of indigenous peoples as well, including Alaskan Eskimos, Canadian Inuit, Aleuts, and Native Hawaiians (all non-Indians). "Native" can refer to all or any one of these groups, while "Indian" is a more specific term. It is important to note, however, that each of these terms originated in the experiences of conquest and colonization, and each encompasses multiple groups with distinct histories, languages, and cultures.

initially inspire the defenseless Dunbar with utter terror, he comes to realize that these particular Indians, the Sioux, are not the bloodthirsty savages of popular lore. They are, instead, a "magnificent" and noble race of peaceful people, whose society constitutes a stark counterpoint to a white world gone mad. "I'd never known a people so eager to laugh," Dunbar later writes in his journal, "so devoted to family, so dedicated to each other, and the only word that came to mind was harmony." So noble are these Indians, in fact, that the lieutenant, renamed "Dances with Wolves" by his new friends, eventually abandons his post and joins the tribe. He thus enacts a widespread European-American (frequently male) fantasy. He dons feathers and Sioux clothes, hunts buffaloes, and fights the savage Pawnees. In this way, he fulfills his (heretofore unknown) "true" identity: "As I heard my Sioux name being called over and over, I knew for the first time who I really was." Physical transformations also accompany the character's peculiar metamorphosis, revealing the extent to which race is signified by its physical markers. His light skin, blond hair (now grown long), and, most remarkably, even his blue eyes, darken. Dunbar's resolve to abandon corrupt, degenerate European-American society completely and to remain with the Indians strengthens when he views the decaying carcasses of countless buffaloes ruthlessly slaughtered for their hides and tongues. "Who would do such a thing?" he queries, "Only a people without value and without soul.... It was clear it could only be white hunters." The Sioux, by contrast, are a peaceful and wise people incapable of such ruthless and rapacious exploitation. It thus seems natural that Dunbar should choose to renounce his white identity, at least for a time, and "go native."

Over the last century, going native has become a cherished American tradition, an important—even necessary—means of defining European-American identities and histories. In its various forms, going native articulates and attempts to resolve widespread ambivalence about modernity as well as anxieties about the terrible violence marking the nation's origins. These concerns are clearly central in *Dances with Wolves,* a fact that helps to explain its popularity. Not only did the film prove a tremendous box-office success, it also earned widespread critical acclaim and counted among its numerous prizes the 1991 Academy Award for best picture. As a result, Costner's career skyrocketed. In the eyes of many of its viewers, the film was not just a touching story beautifully told, it was also a long-overdue departure from Hollywood's characteristic depictions of bloodthirsty, scalp-taking Indians, popularized in countless other Western films over many decades (although these "savage" Indians, too, found their places in the film embodied in the murderous Pawnees). Organizers of the Academy Award presentations ensured that Costner's benevolence was not lost on its viewers by continually focusing the program's cameras on the faces of the film's Indian actors.[3] *Dances with Wolves,* the movie industry claimed with pride, was an original, Hollywood's first successful attempt to render justice to these Indians through Costner's sympathetic telling of their proud history. This claim attests to one of the primary impulses behind going native: European Americans' desire to distance themselves from the conquest of Native America.

Yet the politics of *Dances with Wolves* are more complicated than its reception suggests. On closer examination the film seems neither original nor a radical departure from conventional depictions of Native Americans. Like earlier Westerns, it tells a story that leaves stereotyped visions of Native life intact and the radically unequal relations between European Americans and Native Americans unquestioned. Although its primary Native characters are overwhelmingly wise and virtuous, they are nevertheless as unrealistic as the bloodthirsty savages populating other narratives. In any case, they remain more or less incidental to the story. Their primary importance resides in their relation to Dunbar, who is the film's hero and center of consciousness. Not only does this white character retain center stage in the drama, he soon proves himself superior to his Native counterparts. Although he has just recently attained the status of a Sioux warrior, the entire tribe depends upon him for their welfare because he is the most skillful buffalo hunter and warrior. After Dunbar's first hunt, tribal members ask him to regale them over and over with tales of his heroic exploits. In short, he quickly becomes a self-described "celebrity."

Dances with Wolves, in other words, actually reinforces the racial hierarchies it claims to destabilize, and it thus serves another primary function of going native. Although the film manifests some sympathy toward Indians, its primary cultural work in fact is the regeneration of racial whiteness and European-American society. Not only does Dunbar's character ironically demonstrate white superiority even as he goes native, his foray into the Indian world also redraws the boundaries separating racially marked Native American and European-American societies. The narrative, for example, carefully skirts the threat of

[3] Dedicated in part to a discussion of the making of *Dances with Wolves,* Victor Masayesva's documentary *Imagining Indians* (IS Productions, 1992) shows that relations between the filmmaker and the actors were less than idyllic. Other salient critiques of the film include Ward Churchill, "Lawrence of South Dakota: *Dances with Wolves* and the Maintenance of American Empire," in *Fantasies of the Master Race: Literature, Cinema and the Colonization of American Indians* (Monroe, Maine: Common Courage Press, 1992), 243–47; and David Seals, "The New Custerism," *Nation,* 13 May 1991, 634–39.

miscegenation posed by such encounters by having Dunbar falling in love with and then marrying Stands with a Fist, a white woman gone native. The match, in one character's words, "makes sense" because "they are both white." Moreover, the film leaves the integrity and power of European-American society unchallenged. At the end of story, the Sioux (like virtually all other movie Indians) disappear, thus eliminating any threat their presence poses to white privilege. In the film's closing scenes, the military redirects its efforts to the conquest of Indians. An epilogue instructs audiences about the fate of Dunbar's noble companions in the years following the end of the Civil War: "Their homes destroyed, their buffalo gone, the last band of free Sioux submitted to white authority at Fort Robinson, Nebraska. The great horse culture of the plains was gone, and the American frontier was soon to pass into history." The film's end, then, is elegiac. Though regrettable, the Indians' fate, it seems, is inevitable in the face of white settlement.

Predictably, though, Dances with Wolves does not share the fate of "his" tribe. The final scene shows him, leading his probably pregnant wife on horseback, ascending into the mountains. The scene carries heavily Biblical overtones. It recalls illustrations of Joseph leading the mule bearing a pregnant Mary, in search of a place for the birth of Christ, redeemer of a fallen world. Redemption plays a key role in Dances with Wolves. The film implies that these two characters, cleansed of the corruption of European-American life by adopting Indian ways, hold the promise of a new and better white world. It is, in fact, the regeneration of white society that proves the ultimate goal of Dunbar's journey into the primitive.[4] But the narrative serves another purpose. It starkly evokes the conquest of Native America, the precondition of the birth of the white nation, only to assuage the guilt stemming from that painful history. By going native, Dunbar sheds the culpability associated with his official army duties as an "Indian fighter." Significantly, because his perspective provides the film's narrative center and thus the white audiences' point of identification, it also symbolically purges white America of its responsibility for the terrible plights of Native Americans, past and present. It thus assures contem-

---

[4] Importantly, critics' readings of the film often reiterate this purpose of European American regeneration. See, for example, Jane Tompkins's significantly titled essay, "Saving Our Lives: *Dances with Wolves, Iron John,* and the Search for a New Masculinity." Tompkins's argument is remarkable because it ignores the stunning sexism of the film and overlooks its treatment of Native peoples, thus suggesting that this latter problem is unimportant as long as its message "saves *our* [European-American] lives." Patricia Penn Hilden discusses the role of gender in the story in *When Nickels Were Indians: An Urban, Mixed-Blood Story* (Washington: Smithsonian Institution Press, 1995), 182–83.

porary European Americans (including Costner, who reaped vast profits from the film) of the legitimacy of their power and possessions. Because real Indians were destined to disappear, European Americans
are the proper heirs of "Indianness" as well as of the land and resources
of the conquered Natives.

*

This phenomenon of going native, illustrated in *Dances with Wolves* and
countless other cultural expressions produced during the last century,
is the subject of this book. Although Costner received a good deal of acclaim for his originality, the story he told, down to its smallest detail, is
actually a very old one. Like throngs of would-be Natives since the end
of the nineteenth century, Dunbar sees in noble Indian life a means of
escaping a degenerate and corrupt white world. Escape is not his ultimate goal, however. By adopting Indian ways, the socially alienated
character uncovers his own "true" identity and redeems European-
American society. Similarly, throughout the twentieth century, going
native has served as an essential means of defining and regenerating
racial whiteness and a racially inflected vision of Americanness. It also
reflects on the national history by providing self-justifying fantasies that
conceal the violence marking European America's origins. The politics
of going native, then, are extremely complex. Exhibiting profound ambivalence about America's past as well as about modernity, forms of
going native also support European-American hegemony.[5] While those
who go native frequently claim benevolence toward Native peoples,
they reaffirm white dominance by making some (usually distorted) vision of Native life subservient to the needs of the colonizing culture.

Yet, despite the importance of this phenomenon, scholars of Native
America have to date paid little attention to the significance of going native in the forms I describe here. This is the case in part because much
scholarship in the field tends to view Native America in isolation from
the dominant, colonizing culture. In addition, studies that do analyze
the role of Native America as both symbolic and historical presences
within the broader American culture have generally focused on how
European Americans have differentiated themselves from Native

---

[5] In foregrounding the extent to which going native functions as part of larger
process of social domination, I am disagreeing with several key works that insist on
the liberatory aspects of cross-racial impersonations such as Marianna Torgovnick's
Primitive Passions: Men, Women, and the Quest for Ecstasy and Susan Gubar's
Racechanges: White Skin, Black Face in American Culture. As my analyses show, it
is possible to entertain such positive interpretations of this phenomenon if one attends only to its effects on the dominant European-American society.

Americans. Roy Harvey Pearce's seminal text *Savagism and Civiliza-tion,* for example, argues that "the Indian became important for the En-glish mind, not for what he was in and of himself, but rather for what he showed civilized men they were not and must not be."[6] Throughout the era of conquest, Pearce contends, "civilized" European-American iden-tities took shape in contradistinction to particular images of Indians, the detested embodiments of "savagery." Work such as Pearce's is critically important because it shows the relationship between representations of Indians as reviled others and the material process of conquest. As Pearce observes, imagining Indians in this way has historically pro-vided a necessary justification for colonization, including the annihila-tion of countless societies and cultures to make way for European set-tlement in the Americas. More recently, a new generation of scholars has begun to analyze a different (but related) phenomenon: the degree to which many mainstream Americans have also envisioned Native peoples as idealized versions of themselves, as the embodiments of vir-tues lost in the Western world.[7] Part of the larger dynamic of primitiv-ism, this impulse serves most often as a form of cultural critique, and it helps to explain European Americans' desire to go native.[8] Both kinds of representations are present in the earliest European descriptions of America's Natives—in, for example, Columbus's distinction between the peaceful (noble) Arawaks and the bloodthirsty, man-eating (savage) Caribs. In many respects, these visions are two sides of the same coin. Each one serves as a means of defining Western identities (either indi-vidual or collective) against an other, figured alternately as superior or inferior to oneself.

In the twentieth century, going native has become even more im-portant than these other phenomena as a means of constructing white identities, naturalizing the conquest, and inscribing various power rela-tions within American culture. However, the extent to which European-American identities, institutions, and practices depend upon Native im-

[6] Roy Harvey Pearce, *Savagism and Civilization: A Study of the Indian and the Amer-ican Mind* (Berkeley: University of California Press, 1988), 5. Pearce's ground-breaking work, originally published in 1953 as *The Savages of America,* set the stage for other important works on the historical roles and representations of Na-tives in American culture. These include Robert F. Berkhofer, Jr., *The White Man's Indian: Images of the American Indian from Columbus to the Present* (New York: Alfred A Knopf, 1978), and Richard Drinnon, *Facing West: The Metaphysics of Indian-Hating and Empire-Building* (Minneapolis: University of Minnesota Press, 1980).
[7] See, for example, Leah Dilworth, *Imagining Indians in the Southwest: Persistent Visions of a Primitive Past* (Washington, D.C.: Smithsonian Institution Press, 1996).
[8] Marianna Torgovnick's *Gone Primitive: Savage Intellects, Modern Lives* (Chicago: University of Chicago Press, 1990) is one of the most important recent analyses of primitivism, although it does not discuss Native America.

ages and, in some cases, the emulation of Native practices has been largely overlooked in current scholarship on race and American culture. This is a critical omission. Interestingly, this oversight does not extend to analyses of the roles of other racially marked groups. Recently, for instance, scholars have begun to attend to the complex roles African Americans have played in the broader American culture. Toni Morrison, to cite only one prominent example, has argued that "through significant and underscored omissions, startling contradictions, heavily nuanced conflicts, through the way writers peopled their work with the signs and bodies of this presence—one can see that a real or fabricated Africanist presence was crucial to their sense of Americanness."[9]

Yet this assertion is even truer of the Native presence. As the original inhabitants of the continent and the first victims of European Americans, Native peoples figure heavily in the American cultural imagination. To date, however, only one book-length study has analyzed the ways in which European Americans have imitated Natives to construct their individual and collective identities. In his seminal work *Playing Indian*, Philip J. Deloria contends that from the colonial period to the present American "national definitions have engaged racialized and gendered Indians in curious and contradictory ways," through such events as the Boston Tea Party, hobbyists' Native preoccupations, and Indian-inspired communes.[10] An activity similar but not identical to going native in the forms I analyze in this book, playing Indian—temporarily donning Native costume and emulating Native practices (real or invented)—has historically aided European Americans in various quests for identity and authenticity since the Revolutionary Era. A number of other important works, including analyses of captivity narratives and James Fenimore Cooper's novels, examine the related phenomenon of

[9] Toni Morrison, *Playing in the Dark: Whiteness and the Literary Imagination* (Cambridge: Harvard University Press, 1992), 6. Many books have also explored the significance of African Americans in constructing European-American identities through minstrelsy, blackface, and other activities. These include Gubar, *Racechanges;* Eric Lott, *Love and Theft: Blackface Minstrelsy and the American Working Class* (New York: Oxford University Press, 1993); and Michael North, *The Dialect of Modernism: Race, Language and Twentieth-Century Literature* (New York: Oxford University Press, 1994).

[10] Philip J. Deloria, *Playing Indian* (New Haven: Yale University Press, 1998), 5. Articles that analyze impersonations of Indians include Robert Baird, "Going Indian: Discovery, Adoption, and Renaming toward a 'True American' from *Deerslayer* to *Dances with Wolves,*" in *Dressing in Feathers: The Construction of the Indian in American Popular Culture,* ed. S. Elizabeth Baird (Boulder: Westview, 1996), 195–209; Rayna Green, "The Tribe Called Wannabee: Playing Indian in America and Europe," *Folklore* 99 (1988): 30–55; George Lipsitz, "Mardi Gras Indians: Carnival and Counter-Narrative in Black New Orleans," in *Time Passages:*

individual European Americans who have gone native from the earliest days of contact.[11]

By contrast, the instances of going native I describe arose specifically in response to late-nineteenth-century events, and they involve the more widespread conviction that adopting some vision of Native life in a more permanent way is necessary to regenerate and to maintain European-American racial and national identities. Going native as a collective phenomenon with these particular dimensions, as I explain in Chapter 1, expressed a widespread ambivalence about modernity, and it is in relation to modernity's ills that these Native representations took shape. The other major historical factor that contributed to this particular fascination with Native life was the completion of the military conquest of Native America during the same period. The conquest enabled the romanticization of Native life and impelled European Americans to explain this history in self-justifying ways. Indeed, the historical relations between European America and Native America, particularly the nature of the conquest, play a determining role in the forms that going native has taken during the last century. At the same time, these events refigure this violent history in a way that supports social structures that oppress Native peoples. In exploring the complex relations between European and Native Americans and in foregrounding the dynamics of colonization, I am situating myself in a long line of Native American scholars preoccupied with the same questions (though not the same phenomenon).[12] Yet the significance of going native extends well beyond the relations between European Americans

---

Collective Memory and American Popular Culture (Minneapolis: University of Minnesota Press, 1990), 233–56; and Jay Mechling, "'Playing Indian' and the Search for Authenticity in Modern White America," in *Prospects 5*, ed. Jack Salzman (New York: Burt Franklin, 1980), 17–34. Susan Scheckel analyzes the role of the Indian in early-nineteenth-century American nationalism in *The Insistence of the Indian: Race and Nationalism in Nineteenth-Century American Culture* (Princeton: Princeton University Press, 1998).

[11] See, for example, Richard Drinnon's discussion of Thomas Morton in *Facing West*. More recently, June Namias has described how European-American captives often opted to remain with their Native captors; see *White Captives: Gender and Ethnicity on the American Frontier* (Chapel Hill: University of North Carolina Press, 1993). James Axtell also discusses the phenomenon of English settlers voluntarily joining Native communities in "The White Indians," in *The Invasion Within: The Contest of Cultures in Colonial North America* (New York: Oxford University Press, 1985), 302–27.

[12] D'Arcy McNickle, as I have argued elsewhere, focused in his writing on the complex dynamics of the colonization of Native America and the relation of Native peoples to the broader American society. Originally published between the 1930s and the 1970s, McNickle's work is voluminous, but see especially *Native American*

and Native Americans. Often, these representations and events not only articulate and attempt to resolve anxieties about history and modernity, they reflect upon other power relations within the broader society, including the advent of overseas imperialism, changing gender ideals, and the devastating histories of African Americans in the United States.

Yet, regardless of the immense historical and cultural importance of Native America in the broader American culture, the field of American studies has nonetheless been structured to overlook its importance. Despite much work on the role of race in U.S. culture, challenges to conventional notions of American identity and mainstream accounts of the nation's history remain rare. José David Saldívar has remarked upon the extent to which "narrow national ideologies" underlie scholarship in the field, manifesting themselves in an Anglocentric notion of America itself. America, he contends, citing here Sacvan Bercovitch, can no longer be regarded as an "over-arching synthesis, *e pluribus unum.*" What's needed is "to articulate a new, trans-geographical conception of American culture—one more responsive to the hemisphere's geographical ties and political crosscurrents."[13] An overly narrow vision of Americanness, moreover, is both created and reinforced in part by the widespread denial in both popular and academic culture of the violence characterizing the nation's history. As Amy Kaplan has observed, American exceptionalism, including the notion that America never had an empire and that American experience is in fact "antithetical to the historical experience of imperialism," remains unchallenged even by much contemporary work in American studies. Imperialism,

---

Tribalism: Indian Survivals and Renewals (New York: Oxford University Press, 1973), *The Surrounded* (1936; reprint, Albuquerque: University of New Mexico Press, 1992), and *Wind from an Enemy Sky* (1978; reprint, Albuquerque: University of New Mexico Press, 1995). Laura Cornelius is another seminal but often overlooked figure in Native American intellectual history who explored similar questions; see *Our Democracy and the American Indian* (Kansas City, Mo.: Burton Publishing, 1920). More recently, the scholar and activist Vine Deloria, Jr., has published several books on Native rights, Indian philosophy, and the role of Native America in mainstream American culture. Although his works are numerous, the text that most directly addresses my particular concerns here is *Custer Died for Your Sins: An Indian Manifesto* (Norman: University of Oklahoma Press, 1988). Leslie Marmon Silko, whose *Gardens in the Dunes* I discuss in Chapter 4, is also fundamentally concerned with colonial processes, most obviously in her later work.

[13] José David Saldívar, *The Dialectics of Our America: Genealogy, Cultural Critique, and Literary History* (Durham, N.C.: Duke University Press, 1991), xi–xii. See also George Lipsitz, "The Possessive Investment in Whiteness: Racialized Social Democracy and the 'White' Problem in American Studies," *American Quarterly* 47, 3 (1995): 369–87.

she says, "has been simultaneously formative and disavowed in the foundational discourse of American studies," a critical omission that can be remedied only by attending to "the multiple histories of continental and overseas expansion, conquest, conflict, and resistance which have shaped the cultures of the United States."[14]

Importantly, however, even work that attends to these multiple histories as well as to the dynamics of conquest and resistance usually ignores the history of America's internal colonialism, and often the presence of Native America itself. The following passage taken from an important discussion of postcolonial literatures, *The Empire Writes Back,* is unfortunately symptomatic:

> We use the term 'post-colonial'... to cover all the cultures affected by imperial process from the moment of colonization to the present day. This is because there is a continuity of preoccupations throughout the historical process initiated by European imperial aggression.... The literature of the USA should also be placed in this category.... What each of these [post-colonial] literatures has in common beyond their special and distinctive regional characteristics is that they emerged in their present form out of the experience of colonization and asserted themselves by foregrounding the tension with the imperial power, and by emphasizing their differences from the assumptions of the imperial centre. It is this which makes them distinctively post-colonial.[15]

With characteristic blindness, these authors ignore the fact that European America has itself functioned—and continues to function—as a colonial and imperial power. Such an oversight supports the myth of American exceptionalism. The denial of the dispossession and slaughter of millions of Native peoples, a process one historian has labeled the "American holocaust,"[16] characterizes both academic scholarship and popular understandings of history.[17] The factors that compel these de-

---

[14] Amy Kaplan, "'Left Alone with America': The Absence of Empire in the Study of American Culture," in *Cultures of United States Imperialism,* ed. Amy Kaplan and Donald E. Pease (Durham, N.C.: Duke University Press, 1993), 4–5.

[15] Bill Ashcroft, Gareth Griffiths, and Helen Tiffin, *The Empire Writes Back: Theory and Practice in Post-Colonial Literatures* (New York: Routledge, 1989), 2. I have suppressed a paragraph break.

[16] See David E. Stannard, *American Holocaust: The Conquest of the New World* (New York: Oxford University Press, 1992).

[17] Ward Churchill labels this tendency "holocaust denial" in *A Little Matter of Genocide: Holocaust and Denial in the Americas 1492 to the Present* (San Francisco: City Lights Books, 1997).

nials and omissions are obvious. Acknowledging this terrible past contests the imaginary unity of America and undermines the ideal of a free and democratic nation. It also raises a series of challenging, perhaps unthinkable, questions about the defensibility of European-American political dominance, past and present, and even the legitimacy of European Americans' presence on the continent. Moreover, the conquest of Native America, which took hundreds of years to complete, cannot be dismissed as an anomaly. Rather, it is the foundational event in American history. As such, it has been built into the nation's narratives, though in distorted and obfuscatory ways. The above passage from the *Empire Writes Back* not only repeats these errors by ignoring the historical and contemporary presence of Native America, it goes a step further. By identifying European America as the victim of colonial domination, it reinforces the illusion of the nation's historical innocence.

These fundamental contradictions in American identity and history—the tension between the ideal of a free and democratic nation and the reality of racial hierarchies, the discrepancy between the myth of peaceful expansion and the history of bloody conquest—reemerge again and again in the cultural imagination. It is, perhaps, for this reason that European Americans have always been obsessed with stories of the nation's origins, repeatedly retelling and refiguring their collective past in self-justifying ways. This obsession manifests itself in seemingly insignificant as well as in highly visible forms. Daily, for instance, American children articulate these stories by playing games in which cowboys are pitted against savage Indians, performances that articulate the cant of conquest.[18] Another example, this one staged on a grander scale, is also telling. In 1991, when the National Museum of American Art organized a mildly revisionist exhibit about the nation's colonial history, the displays immediately elicited public cries for censorship. Titled "The West as America: Reinterpreting Images of the Frontier, 1820–1920," the exhibit rewrote conventional understandings of the "settling" of the West in minor ways which nevertheless did not fundamentally challenge European America's self-serving vision of its history. The outcry that ensued had rapid effects: Congress threatened to withhold the museum's funding. Organizers quickly changed the exhibit, diluting its message until it was little more than yet another celebration of American colonial history.[19] These events unequivocally

[18] The phrase is Francis Jennings's. See *The Invasion of America: Indians, Colonialism, and the Cant of Conquest* (Chapel Hill: University of North Carolina Press, 1975).
[19] See, for example, Mary Panzer, "Panning 'The West as America': or, Why One Exhibition Did Not Strike Gold," *Radical History Review* 52 (winter 1992): 105–113.

show the white nation's inability to acknowledge its violent beginnings. Throughout the twentieth century, going native has also served as an important means of articulating these same anxieties. This book analyzes how particular visions of the nation's history have become dominant and how their inherent contradictions both conceal and betray white America's colonial past and its hegemonic aspirations.

If *Going Native* deals with the complex relations between cultures that give rise to the processes of domination and resistance, it is also concerned with the intersections between disciplines and cultural practices implicated in these processes. In my analyses, culture serves as a key site for articulating and resisting the power relations that characterize American society. As I use it here, "culture" includes but is not limited to "high" culture in the sense Matthew Arnold used the term. I rely instead on a cultural studies conception of culture comprising, in the words of Stuart Hall, "the actual grounded terrain of practices, representations, languages and customs of any specific historical society."[20] Moreover, I am particularly concerned with how culture operates, including the interrelations of various cultural practices (ranging from world's fairs and fraternal organizations to films and literary texts) and their complex interactions with other social processes. Culture, as Antonio Gramsci contended, does not reflect or arise from social relations in any simple sense. Rather, it functions as a "material force," one means by which hegemony—the cultural, intellectual, and political dominance of a particular social group—is established and maintained. In terms of colonial and imperial relations, culture and social dominance are related in two ways. First, as Edward Said has observed, both colonialism and imperialism "are supported and perhaps even impelled by impressive ideological formations that include notions that certain territories and people *require* and beseech domination, as well as forms of knowledge affiliated with domination."[21] Culture, to the degree it articulates these "ideological formations," serves as a means of creating the necessity for dominating other groups even as it justifies this dominance. But hegemony, as Gramsci argued, cannot operate without at least the partial consent of the subordinated groups, and culture—particularly popular culture—also serves as a means of reeducating and reforming subordinated classes to accept (indeed, even to support) their own domination.[22] Culture accomplishes

---

[20] Stuart Hall, "Gramsci's Relevance for the Study of Race and Ethnicity," in *Stuart Hall: Critical Dialogues in Cultural Studies*, ed. David Morley and Kuan-Hsing Chen (London: Routledge, 1996), 439.
[21] Edward W. Said, *Culture and Imperialism* (New York: Alfred A. Knopf, 1994), 9.
[22] See Stuart Hall, "Notes on Deconstructing 'the Popular,'" in *Cultural Theory and Popular Culture*, ed. John Storey (London: Harvester Wheatsheaf, 1994), 455.

this in part by shaping the ways we understand social relations, histories, and our places within them.

Ultimately, though, the operations of culture are more complex than this. While culture never lies outside the realm of social domination and coercion, its function cannot be completely determined by these dynamics. Because culture operates as "a force field of relations shaped, precisely, by these contradictory [political] pressures and tendencies," struggles over cultural meanings comprise part of broader struggles for power in society.[23] Popular culture in particular is characterized by a "double movement of containment and resistance." It is a site where "the struggle for and against a culture of the powerful is engaged," an "arena of consent and resistance."[24] This conception of culture dictates that critics look for multiple and contradictory meanings that articulate social struggles. It also compels us to recognize subordinated groups as cultural and political agents rather than simply as victims. *Going Native* focuses primarily on European-American performances and representations of nativeness, thus engaging in a process of ideology critique. At the same time, however, it also attends to these moments of resistance, to the ways in which Native peoples contest the definitions imposed upon them or actively utilize them for their own subversive purposes. While presenting these voices of resistance is a secondary goal of this book, it is an important one because it shows that the dominant culture's ways of seeing are by no means natural or inevitable.

Recognizing that there are other, non-hegemonic ways of seeing also suggests the possibility of social change. As Tony Bennett contends, commenting here on Gramsci's class-based conception of power relations,

the bourgeoisie can become a hegemonic, leading class only to the degree that bourgeois ideology is able to accommodate, to find some space for, opposing class cultures and values. A bourgeois hegemony is secured not via the obliteration of working-class culture, but via its *articulation* to bourgeois culture and ideology so that, in being associated with and expressed in the forms of the latter, its political affiliations are altered in the process. As a consequence of its accommodating elements of opposing class cultures, "bourgeois culture" ceases to be purely or entirely bourgeois.[25]

[23] Tony Bennett, "Popular Culture and 'the Turn to Gramsci,'" in *Cultural Theory and Popular Culture,* ed. Storey, 224.
[24] Hall, "Notes on Deconstructing 'the Popular,'" 456, 466.
[25] Bennett, "Popular Culture and 'the Turn to Gramsci,'" 225. I have suppressed a paragraph break.

Acts of going native certainly reveal white America's aspirations to hegemony, most specifically through that society's attempts to obliterate Native peoples, cultures, and histories. At the same time, though, other questions arise. To what extent does evoking "nativeness" destabilize the notions of race, gender, and history which the dominant culture seeks to naturalize? Do these complex workings of culture reveal the conflicts and fissures at the heart of an Americanness imagined as *e pluribus unum?* If so, perhaps in these contradictions lies the potential for decolonizing knowledge and accomplishing social change.

*

Going native in its modern manifestations originates in the relations between two simultaneous late-nineteenth-century events: the rise of industrial capitalism, with its associated notions of linear historical progress, and the completion of the military conquest of Native America. During that period, anthropological theories inspired in good measure by social Darwinism equated industrial capitalism and technological advancements with white racial dominance and social progress. At the same time, however, the vast changes sweeping a rapidly modernizing American society created a nostalgia for origins, now embodied in the cultural imagination in the "primitive." Idealizing and emulating the primitive, modernity's other, comprised in part a form of escapism from the tumultuous modern world. Consistently, throughout the twentieth century, going native has thus been most widespread during moments of social crisis, moments that give rise to collective doubts about the nature of progress and its attendant values and practices. Each of the chapters that follow explores one such historical period: the turn of the century; the years following World War I; the turbulent 1960s and 1970s, which spawned the counterculture and a series of civil rights movements; and the so-called New Age of the Reagan era. Ultimately, however, escapism is not the most fundamental goal of going native. Ironically, even as they articulate anxieties about modernity, these representations and events also reaffirm the racialized, progressivist ethos of industrial capitalism.

Going native is shaped by and refigures another phenomenon as well: the completion of the military conquest of Native America. Throughout the twentieth century, this event (or, more accurately, this series of events concluding in North America in the late nineteenth century) has also proved a source of collective anxiety, as persistent denials of the nature of American history attest. Going native constitutes a series of cultural rituals that express and symbolically resolve this anxiety about the nation's violent origins. At the same time, however, forms of going native reflect the changing relationship of the dominant, colonizing culture to Native America in the twentieth century. One of the arguments of this book is that the conquest did not end with white America's military triumph. Rather, throughout the twentieth century, white America has repeatedly enacted rites of conquest to confirm and extend its power over Native America, and these racial dynamics continue to shape contemporary American life. This power has taken a variety of forms. Whereas Native land and resources have long comprised the primary objects of the dominant culture's desires, more recently, Native cultures and even identities have provided newer domains of conquest. Changing forms of going native map these transitions and link these events to better-known expressions of colonialism. Furthermore, as the book shows, going native articulates and supports other forms of imperial, gender, and racial domination within the broader American culture as well.

The following chapters are thus organized both thematically and chronologically. Their primary subject is the way the act of going native both reflects the changing relationships between Native America and European America and intersects with other social structures and historical events. Each chapter represents a kind of case study, designed to reflect the broader social dynamics during a particular historical moment. While all of the materials I analyze have been massively influential in that they have attracted large audiences and shaped popular perceptions, often other examples could have supported these arguments just as effectively. Indeed, one of my contentions is that going native, in the forms I describe it, is a pervasive phenomenon manifested daily in mainstream American culture.

Chapter 1 sets the stage by mapping the way Native Americans figured in the European-American cultural imagination as the military conquest drew to a close. In particular, it demonstrates that after the conquest, European Americans rewrote this history in a self-justifying manner by redefining Native Americans as part of their own past. This chapter shows European America going native by claiming Indianness as part of its own collective identity. Two landmark events—the Philadelphia Centennial Exposition of 1876 and the World's Columbian Exposition of 1893—mark this transition and reveal its relation to the completion of the military conquest. For late-nineteenth-century audiences, these representations both obfuscated the history of the conquest and reflected on other critical debates and power struggles in the broader American culture. More specifically, this new model of Americanness—so curiously based on a mythic version of a conquered people—ironically privileged middle-class Anglo-Americans in the controversies over national identity that stemmed in part from the labor and immigration crises of the period. The elision of white American identities and Native history and practices becomes even clearer in Frederick Jackson's Turner's renowned frontier thesis speech, which was initially delivered at the 1893 fair. At the same time, these Native representations served a different, yet complementary purpose as they provided a precedent for and justified America's imperial debut overseas. This role becomes obvious in another influential form of going native analyzed in the chapter's final section: the emergence of nationalist (and masculinist) fraternal organizations with Indian themes which aimed to combat the enervating effects of civilized life. Chapter 1 thus explores a series of interrelated questions: How did popular images of Native peoples change in the latter part of the nineteenth century? How did middle-class white America define itself during these tumultuous years? How did the stories Americans told themselves about the nation's origins relate to U.S. domestic crises and controversies surrounding imperialism abroad? How do race and nation intertwine in these stories? Finally, what do these stories reveal—or conceal—about America's bloody colonial past, a past built upon the conquest of Native America?

While Chapter 1 shows European America rewriting the military conquest of Native America by going native, Chapter 2 analyzes different forms of going native during the high point of the colonization of another frontier: the Arctic. Colonization of this region began in earnest during the early part of the twentieth century, and it intensified after World War I. The war years, however, challenged turn-of-the-century celebrations of masculinity, social progress, and imperialism, and going native (in this case, going Eskimo) served to conceal the relationship of this new colonial enterprise to earlier expansionism. But many Western men "went Eskimo" for other reasons as well. In popular images, arctic life provided an escape from the industrial capitalist world that, ironically, also confirmed its core values. During the interwar years, then, going native served contradictory purposes as it both challenged and reinscribed the values and practices of the modern West, including colonialism. Chapter 2 analyzes this preoccupation with Eskimo life by focusing on the following questions: How did knowledge about the Arctic provide a rationale for colonial expansion? Conversely, how did colonialism and the nature of life in the newly urbanized industrial capitalist world shape the knowledge Westerners produced, even the ostensibly value-free language of science and documentary? How did changing gender roles affect these representations? Finally, how and for what purposes did these texts rewrite the repressed history of Western interventions in the Arctic? To answer these questions, this chapter analyzes early- and mid-twentieth-century travel accounts along with Robert Flaherty's landmark 1922 film, *Nanook of the North*. The chapter concludes by discussing the figure of Minik, a young Eskimo captive raised in New York whose words and life challenge these arctic imaginings.

Westerners' desires to escape the industrial capitalist ethos and to deny their violent history become even clearer in Chapter 3, which analyzes a particularly striking instance of going native, the case of Forrest Carter's highly acclaimed "autobiography," *The Education of Little Tree.* Originally published in 1976, the book was presented as the "Native" author's autobiographical remembrances of his boyhood in the Tennessee hill country where he was raised by his Cherokee grandparents. *The Education of Little Tree,* however, is a forgery: Forrest Carter is actually the pseudonym of Asa Carter, a former Ku Klux Klan leader and anti–civil rights activist. Carter's "transformation" from a rabid white supremacist to an "Indian" seems puzzling and has led most observers to conclude that it marks a genuine change in the author's racist attitudes. Yet, upon closer examination, it becomes clear that Carter's autobiography actually complements and extends his earlier Klan activities. Going native, in this case, serves to reassert white dominance even as it conceals a profoundly racist project. Carter, in fact, penned two works that show their protagonists going native. The first one, a novel called *Gone to Texas,* tells the story of a Confederate outlaw who bonds with Indians. This novel rewrites Reconstruction history to create the illusion of white Southerners' innocence with regard to the oppression of Natives and African Americans even as it narrates the regeneration of whiteness in the postbellum era. In eliding the figures of the outlaw and the Indian, the novel sets the stage for *The Education of Little Tree,* the text that shows Carter himself going native. *The Education of Little Tree* extends the ideological work of *Gone to Texas* in another way as well by applying the earlier novel's vision of white racial dominance to the civil rights era. At the same time, both works respond to another historical context, specifically the counterculture's discontents with modernity, and in this respect they mark yet another transition in European Americans' views of Natives. Like Eskimos during the interwar years, Natives still seemed to embody an alternative to modernity, this time in the form of a renewed connection to the land and the possibility of spiritual regeneration. Carter's texts thus show a newer form of white Americans' desires for Native things as culture itself becomes an object of appropriation.

Quests for a connection to the land, spiritual regeneration, and other forms of Native culture also motivate the New Age movement, the context of the book's final chapter. Compelled by the conviction that the world has gone awry in spiritual, racial, economic, and ecological terms, many New Agers turn to Natives in an effort to remedy modernity's ills. Thus, across the country, these spirit seekers go native by forming "tribes," participating in "traditional" Native rituals, and emulating Indian practices in other ways. In the New Age, then, we seem to have come full circle in our story. If the late nineteenth century typically celebrated technology, materialism, and a masculinist vision of imperial conquest, the New Age, by contrast, seems intent on replacing these values with Native-inspired alternatives. In fact, though, the New Age movement bears a more complicated relationship to America's past because it also relies upon the logic of industrial capitalism and its colonialist impulses. One emblematic text, Lynn Andrews's *Medicine Woman,* provides a case in point. This faux autobiography, like Carter's, shows its white author going native, this time by narrating its protagonist's transformation into an Indian "medicine woman." *Medicine Woman*'s narrative clearly reveals the complicity of the author (and, by implication, the New Age movement) in the history of Native conquest. Its form is important as well. Strikingly, this text utilizes the conventions of that most starkly colonial of genres, the captivity narrative. When one compares Andrews's text with the best-known account of Indian captivity, Mary Rowlandson's seventeenth-century narrative *The Soveraignty and Goodness of GOD*, one sees undeniable similarities between white/Indian relationships in the New Age and those in the colonial period. But this comparison also reveals a key difference that reflects the particular dynamics of conquest in the contemporary era: New Agers do not just appropriate Native things as their predecessors did, they even attempt to occupy Native identities. Yet the New Age is not without Native voices of resistance, and this fact reflects the failure of the colonizing culture to own Nativeness completely. In her novel *Gardens in the Dunes,* for instance, Leslie Marmon Silko refigures the conventions of the captivity narrative for anticolonial purposes as she shows both the destructive effect of going native on Native peoples and its complicity in other, more obvious forms of conquest.

What these chapters show, then, is the extent to which going native comprises a cherished national ritual, a means by which European America figures and reenacts its own dominance even as it attempts to deny its violent history. In the Conclusion, which briefly discusses one of the 1994 opening exhibits in the National Museum of the American Indian's Heye Center (the newest addition to the Smithsonian, that most American of institutions), I demonstrate that these rites remain an integral part of European America's national identity. I also suggest that white America's failure to come to terms with its terrible past destines it to repeat the violence marking its origins.

CHAPTER ONE

Imagining America: Race, Nation, and Imperialism at the Turn of the Century

IN 1907, J. W. SCHULTZ published *My Life as an Indian*, a story that anticipates the one told by Kevin Costner in *Dances with Wolves* decades later and marks a transition in the representation of Native peoples in American culture. Set in the mid-nineteenth century, just before European-American invasions into the region reached their highest point, Schultz's book celebrates his years on the frontier living as a member of the Blackfoot tribe. Inspired by the painter George Catlin's romantic depictions of vanishing Indian life and by Lewis and Clark's accounts of their transcontinental explorations, Schultz was drawn to the Plains by his "love of wild life and adventure." "I hated the conventions of society," he wrote, referring to life in his native New England town. "[I] thought so much of the Indians, and wanted to live with them."[1] When he reached adulthood, he fled his New England home and the confinement of "civilized occupations" to travel West. Eventually, he settled with the Blackfoot Indians, grew his hair long, donned buckskin clothing, married a Native woman, and lived in every way "as an Indian." With evident nostalgia, *My Life as an Indian* describes the time its author spent learning from medicine men and warriors, hunting buffalo, and going on the warpath against the tribe's enemies. These days of freedom and adventure were not to last, however. Schultz lived on the Plains during the final years before the successful military conquest of North America reached the lands of the Blackfoot and neighboring tribes. The closing pages of the book narrate the annihilation of the buffalo herds, the confinement of the Indians on reservations, and their cruel fate at the hands of corrupt government agents. Sadly, by the turn of the century, the romantic Plains Indian life depicted by Schultz (as well as by Catlin and others before him) was a mere memory, a casualty of the forward march of history.

---

[1] J. W. Schultz, *My Life as an Indian* (1907; reprint, New York: Fawcett Columbine, 1981), 9–10.

By the early twentieth century, such idealized portraits of bygone Plains Indian life as well as stories of white men "gone native" were increasingly common. When Schultz penned *My Life as an Indian,* however, they had only recently become popular. Indeed, a few decades earlier, the thought of living with Indians would have inspired most European Americans with unspeakable terror and disdain. Although some settlers had idealized Native peoples from the earliest days of contact, they comprised a distinct minority.[2] Throughout the era of conquest, as Roy Harvey Pearce has argued, most colonists imagined the Native inhabitants of North America as "the worst of Satan's creatures," obstacles to "civilized progress westward," or as savages, living antitheses of civilization.[3] "The Indian, in his savage nature," Pearce writes, "stood everywhere as a challenge to order and reason and civilization."[4] Literature provided one (but certainly not the only) medium for articulating these sentiments. Until the mid-nineteenth century, captivity narratives describing the horrifying fates of noble settlers, often women, at the hands of violent savages typified accounts of European-American interactions with Natives. Later, dime novels adapted these conventions, titillating vast audiences with stories of Indian brutality inflicted upon hapless settlers. Beginning around the turn of the century, Western novels and films—the self-aggrandizing tales that mainstream Americans told themselves about the nation's origins—supplied further opportunities for Indian-hating, justifying Europe's bloody conquest of the Americas with fictions of Native peoples' aggression and inherent malevolence.

As the nineteenth century progressed, however, the conquering culture began to reimagine the objects of its conquest. Popular images of Native peoples, though never monolithic, grew increasingly ambivalent. Indians continued to serve as civilized society's inferior "other," but more and more often European Americans looked to Native America to define themselves and their nation. The reasons were partly historical. During this period the military conquest of Native America drew to a close. Lured by the prospect of gold and free land, white settlers arrived in the West en masse during the middle years of the century with the U.S. military in tow. The relentless conquest, begun with Columbus's arrival, thus commenced in earnest in the West. The Indians' days of independence were numbered. The Battle of the Little Bighorn on 25 June 1876 marked the last Indian military triumph, a victory over

[2] For one important and very early example of this response, see Richard Drinnon's discussion of Thomas Morton in *Facing West.*

[3] Pearce, *Savagism and Civilization,* 31, 41. See also Berkhofer, *White Man's Indian.*

[4] Pearce, *Savagism and Civilization,* 6.

Custer's Seventh Cavalry which soon cost the Sioux and Cheyenne dearly. Although the bloody U.S.-Indian wars in the West wound down in the 1870s, the Wounded Knee massacre of 1890 usually signals the end of the military conquest of Native America. At Wounded Knee, a reconstituted Seventh Cavalry avenged Custer's 1876 defeat by slaughtering around three hundred unarmed Lakota Sioux, mostly women, children, and old people.[5] With them died any serious threat Native peoples posed to the consolidation of colonial power on the continent. No longer a challenge to white civilization, Native peoples thus began to play a more ambivalent role in the American cultural imagination. Going native, as the following analyses show, expresses European America's anxiety about the conquest and serves in part to recast this terrible history by creating the illusion of white society's innocence. At the same time, these events also assert white dominance. In this regard, Schultz's story is symptomatic. By identifying with the Blackfoot, who conveniently "vanish" at the end of the narrative, Schultz concealed his complicity in the conquest. And his use of Native America as a playground or tourist destination of sorts, a means of escaping confining "civilized occupations," betrays a privilege predicated on white dominance.

The military conquest of Native America was not the only historical factor that reshaped popular images of Native peoples, however. Key conflicts within the dominant society also contributed to these changes. Vast territorial expansion throughout the century had brought together not only diverse geographical regions but culturally and linguistically different populations as well, a fact that complicated the question of "Americanness." For this reason and others, by the latter half of the nineteenth century European America found itself in a period of rapid social change. The divisiveness of the Civil War shattered the fragile political unity of Europe's more established settlements in the eastern part of the country. In the decades that followed, urbanization, political turmoil, and industrial progress further transformed the postbellum landscape. Strikes and violent class conflicts, fed in part by a series of crippling economic depressions, began to plague urban centers. Meanwhile, massive immigrations from Asia as well as from Eastern and Southern Europe threatened Anglo-American hegemony. In all these conflicts, race loomed large. By the end of the century, mainstream America thus confronted critical problems: What was the nature of American national identity? How could the Anglo-American middle classes retain power in this rapidly changing society? And was it possible to reconcile a history

---

[5] Though problematic, James Mooney's *The Ghost-Dance Religion and the Sioux Outbreak of 1890* (Chicago: University of Chicago Press, 1965) remains the classic account of the events leading up to the Wounded Knee massacre.

marred by slavery and colonial violence, not to mention the advent of imperialism abroad in the 1890s, with the quintessentially "American" ideals of freedom, equality, and democracy?

Mounting social change led many European Americans to "remember" Native American life with nostalgia. Indians, now safely "vanishing," began to provide the symbols and myths upon which white Americans created a sense of historical authenticity, a "real" national identity which had been lacking in the adolescent colonial culture. This new model of Americanness, curiously based on a mythic version of a conquered people, related in complex ways to the power structures within the nation as well as to its imperial debut overseas. In this first chapter I ask a series of interrelated questions: How did middle-class white America define itself during these tumultuous years? How did the stories Americans told themselves about the nation's origins relate to U.S. domestic crises and the nascent controversies surrounding imperialism abroad? How do race and nation intertwine in these stories? How did popular images of Native peoples change during this period? Finally, what do these stories reveal—or conceal—about America's bloody colonial past, a past built upon the conquest of Native America?

Inevitably, popular culture became a critical site for staging debates surrounding what—and, perhaps more important, *whose*—experiences constituted the nation's history and identity. Two emblematic events, the 1876 Philadelphia Centennial Exposition and the 1893 World's Columbian Exposition, manifested particularly clearly the complicated intersections of race, nationalism, and imperialism during this transitional moment in American history. These two world's fairs provided opportunities for the dominant American culture to tell stories of its own origins to vast audiences, through both visual displays and performances like Frederick Jackson Turner's famed frontier thesis speech, delivered at the World's Columbian Exposition. Marking a key historical transition from the last Indian military victory in 1876 to the end of the conquest in 1890, these events expressed critical changes in the place Native peoples occupied in the American cultural imagination. By siting Native America in European America's past, they show white America going native in part to conceal its violent history. After the conquest, representations of this troubling history reflected on other conflicts and power relations within the broader American society. Visions of Native America, now identified with European America, both articulated and reinforced white dominance at home and abroad, frequently in contradictory ways, during this period of rapid social change. Later, going native in turn-of-the-century fraternal organizations (including the Boy Scouts) would employ and refigure these changing representations of Native peoples, relating them specifically to America's nascent imperial ventures overseas. As the following chapters show, these images and the emergent phenomenon of going native have shaped popular understandings of Native America throughout the twentieth century.

TELLING STORIES: VISIONS OF AMERICA AT THE 1876 AND 1893 WORLD'S FAIRS

Toward the end of the nineteenth century, Michael Kammen writes, "American memory began to take form as a self-conscious phenomenon."[6] The production of memory and the creation of tradition during this era, prompted in part by the dislocations and losses of the Civil War, showed the dominant American culture struggling to define itself as a unified entity. Questions of national identity focused primarily on unresolved issues that had preoccupied European Americans since the Revolutionary era: Was colonial American culture merely an extension of its European (particularly Anglo) roots? If not, what made America unique? But it was not only the nation's relationship to Europe that posed a problem. The history of America, a nation born from the genocide of Native peoples and built on slave labor, undermined the values of liberty and equality the nation claimed to hold dear. A presence that haunted (and continues to haunt) the American cultural imagination, Native America challenged Europeans' occupancy of the continent and, thus, threatened the legitimacy of the nation itself. In telling the nation's story, then, European Americans had to explain this part of their past. What, exactly, was the relationship between European America and Native America? And how could white Americans tell the story of a bloody conquest in a way that justified their presence as well as their privileges?

To answer these questions, the dominant culture first had to recognize that European America had a particular history. In 1895, a government report urging the protection of antiquities, titled "What the United States Government Has Done for History," began by lamenting that "it was not till about 1875 that the Government and people of the United States seemed to realize that our country has a history."[7] The manifestations of this new realization included increasing numbers of public historical displays as well as large-scale

[6] Michael Kammen, *Mystic Chords of Memory: The Transformation of Tradition in American Culture* (New York: Vintage Books, 1991), 100.
[7] Ibid., 185. This history of "our" country obviously—indeed, pointedly—excluded precolonial Native history.

commemorations of the white nation's foundational events. These were accompanied by a renaissance of patriotism and a growing interest in American music, folk art, and colonial architecture. In the latter part of the nineteenth century, world's fairs also provided key opportunities for the dominant culture to tell stories about the nation and its origins to large audiences. These fairs showcased what their organizers (all leaders in industry, academia, and government who thus represented the white middle classes) defined as an authentic, uniquely American identity.

International expositions, in the words of one important critic, comprised "symbolic universes," "triumphs of hegemony" that "propagated the ideas and values of the country's political, financial, corporate, and intellectual leaders."[8] Because nineteenth-century world's fairs were the first mass culture events, their influence was monumental, and they both shaped and reflected a white, middle-class ethos. Admissions to the Philadelphia Centennial Exposition in 1876 totaled ten million, nearly one-fifth of the nation's population. Over twenty-seven million attended the World's Columbian Exposition sixteen years later, making it the first event in the United States to draw such large crowds.[9] The messages these events conveyed also made their way into other popular culture venues. Although U.S. fairs advertised that their primary purpose was to increase global trade and to promote American technology, they also served as an important means of asserting American superiority and imperial might.[10] Both these goals played against a background of European competition, a competition the "new" United States was intent on winning over the "old" nations of Europe. In the expositions, notions of race, progress, nation, and empire intertwined in fundamental ways. In these "symbolic universes," technology signified progress, a notion which defined America and rendered it different from (even superior to) its European counterparts. In addition, progress—equated with technological advances—justified Western paternalism toward its "less developed" neighbors, a sentiment that paved the way for imperial expansion

[8] Robert Rydell, *All the World's a Fair: Visions of Empire at American International Expositions, 1876–1916* (Chicago: University of Chicago Press, 1984), 2–3.
[9] The significant cost of attending these fairs (including travel, lodging, meals, and admission fees) suggests that most visitors were of the middle classes. Organizers, however, attempted to attract working-class visitors, even designating a "poor man's day" with reduced admission fees, as part of an effort to reshape the perspectives of strikers and labor organizers. See Rydell, *All the World's a Fair,* 32–33.
[10] For a discussion of the origins and functions of world's fairs, see Paul Greenhalgh, "Origins and Conceptual Development," in *Ephemeral Vistas: The Expositions Universelles, Great Exhibitions and World's Fairs, 1851–1939* (Manchester: Manchester University Press, 1988).

at the close of the century. While they attempted to create a unified vision of Americanness, though, these narratives and events were fraught with contradictions. They thus reveal the massive social conflicts which fractured fin-de-siècle American society.

*

Self-conscious articulations of "Americanness" became increasingly audible at the Philadelphia Centennial Exposition of 1876. For a nation united by neither race nor history, the question of American tradition was complex. In some respects the attempt to define a national identity during this era was an effort to refigure the country's problematic past and to resolve problems raised by the diversity of its population. At the fair, U.S. displays provided an opportunity for middle-class Anglos to define their own story as the history of America.[11] The exposition thus commemorated the birth of the white nation, while its vision of a unified America hid the massive racial and class conflicts which plagued the United States during the late nineteenth century. As the place where Anglo-Americans had declared their independence from England a century earlier, Philadelphia provided the perfect site for staging this vision; the city was, as organizers frequently declared, the "nation's birthplace." Having defined independence from England as the nation's originary moment, the exposition thus celebrated "the first centennial of American freedom and national unity" in 1876, the nation's 100th "birthday."[12] While the issue of how to define Americanness engendered some controversy among the exposition's racially homogeneous group of planners, when the exposition opened "three ideas had already been identified with the national character: the Pioneer Spirit, Republicanism (incorporating democracy) and Progress." These three themes subsequently served as signifiers of "Americanness" in each of the fairs of the following several decades.[13]

"Progress," in fact, was the most fundamental theme of the exposition, the one that gave meaning to white America's history and institutions. At the fair, the development of industrial technology provided evidence of the nation's progress. The exposition itself opened on 10 May

[11] Priscilla Wald writes that race was a crucial part of the process of constructing "Americanness" in legal terms as well. See her discussion of the Cherokee Nation (1831) and Dred Scott (1857) Supreme Court decisions in *Constituting Americans: Cultural Anxiety and Narrative Form* (Durham: Duke University Press, 1995), chap. 1.

[12] See Frank H. Norton, ed., *Frank Leslie's Illustrated Historical Register of the Centennial Exposition 1876* (New York: Frank Leslie's Publishing House, 1877), 10–11.

[13] Greenhalgh, *Ephemeral Vistas*, 127.

1876 with a technological exhibition. In Machinery Hall, the center-piece of the fair that occupied an expansive fourteen acres of floor space, President Grant ignited the Corliss Steam Engine. "The steam was on," one guidebook proclaimed, "the engine was in motion...hundreds of machines of all descriptions were in operation, and the International Exhibition of 1876 was at that instant thrown open to the world."[14] U.S. displays throughout the fairgrounds followed this lead by showing "a complete panorama of American industrial progress during the past century,"[15] an objective mandated in 1871 when Congress created the United States Centennial Commission: "It is deemed fitting that the completion of the first century of our national existence shall be commemorated by an exhibition of the natural resources of the country and their development, and of its progress in those arts which benefit mankind, in comparison with those of older nations."[16]

In keeping with these goals, American inventions occupied center stage at the exposition with exhibits of the telephone, the telegraph, the sewing machine, and other examples of national ingenuity. In Machinery Hall, even the machines fueling the event themselves became objects of display.[17] The order of these displays was also carefully conceived. Planners categorized exhibits into ten departments ranging from raw materials to manufacturing to industry and the arts.[18] The sequence demonstrated "as nearly as possible in the order of their development, the result of the use of these materials, placing at the end the higher achievements of intellect and imagination." Exhibits were "designed to carry the spectator through the successive steps of human progress."[19] Raw materials for production came first, followed by fabric, furniture, and other manufactured goods. Technology, including machines, motors, and transportation, occupied the next higher rung on the ladder. The arts and objects designed for "the improvement of the physical, intellectual, and moral condition of man" completed the displays. As one commentator claimed, articulating the prevailing sentiment, it was "progress" that "rendered possible the mechanical triumphs of the present day, in which seem to be attained the acme of speed and the perfection of workmanship."[20]

[14] J. S. Ingram, *The Centennial Exposition, Described and Illustrated* (Philadelphia: Hubbard Bros., 1876), 97.
[15] Norton, *Frank Leslie's Register,* 10.
[16] Cited in ibid., 11.
[17] R. Reid Badger, *The Great American Fair: The World's Columbian Exposition and American Culture* (Chicago: Nelson Hall, 1979), 17.
[18] Rydell, *All the World's a Fair,* 20–21.
[19] William Phipps Blake, quoted in ibid., 20.
[20] Ingram, *Centennial Exposition,* 224.

If the displays at the Philadelphia Centennial Exposition equated progress with technology, they also naturalized technological progress as the universal "law of life."[21] Inevitably, measures of progress not only pivoted on the competition between Western nations but also drew explicit comparisons between the accomplishments of different races. In the displays, industrial progress was thus clearly linked to scientific racism, particularly as manifested in theories of social evolution. Exhibits of "primitive" technologies such as weapons and tools highlighted the (white) nation's achievements by showing how far civilization had evolved in relation to "less developed" (usually a synonym for nonwhite) peoples, civilization's still living ancestors.

Indeed, Native American exhibits at the Philadelphia Centennial Exposition, like those of other non-Westerners, contrasted starkly with the boastful displays of Western technology. The U.S. Department of the Interior exhibit devoted most of its space to a vast array of "Indian specimens" including "a superb collection of bows, arrows, and other weapons of war, some very curious wooden idols from British Columbia, head-dresses, jewelry, and ornaments; various skins and robes are manufactured into garments; buckskin hunting-shirts, trimmed with wampum; women's dresses of sheepskin and wampum; ax-heads and arrowheads of flint and other stone."[22] Weapons, in fact, outnumbered all other Native objects exhibited.[23] Their dominance likely aimed to demonstrate the savagery of their makers. But one clear effect of the exhibition was to portray primitive, weapon-making Indians as inevitably vanishing peoples whose significance and fate lay in their obvious inferiority to (white) civilization.[24] Thus, just as the planners intended industrial technology to reflect on the state of civilized societies, so too did displays of "primitive" objects indicate the level of advancement, the character, and the fate of their makers.

Comparisons between Native and Western technologies, and by implication Native and Western societies, were inevitable. Bows and arrows obviously appeared primitive in relation to the Gatling guns, torpedoes, and other Western weapons on display. The organization of the displays also encouraged such comparisons. Planners extended the hierarchical system which classified materials from "raw" to "finished" in the other exhibits to the displays of Indian artifacts organized by the

[21] Ibid., 21.

[22] Norton, *Frank Leslie's Register,* 106.

[23] Robert J. Trennert, Jr., "A Grand Failure: The Centennial Indian Exhibition of 1876," *Prologue,* summer 1974, 28.

[24] Spencer Baird, secretary of the Smithsonian and organizer of the fair's Indian exhibits, announced that within a century Indians would cease to exist as such and would "be merged in the general population." See Rydell, *All the World's a Fair,* 24.

Smithsonian in the Government Building. Native objects were arranged in "evolutionary sequence" from the least to the most technologically advanced.[25] In addition, the background art in these displays confirmed the impression that Native peoples were primitive. Objects and mannequins stood against a background of "wild and picturesque [Western U.S.] scenery" and "geological formations," thus associating Native peoples with the raw materials that served as the foundation of industrial progress.[26] The contrast was clear: "The central conception underlying the Indian exhibit at the Centennial, in short, was that Native American cultures and people belonged to the interminable wasteland of humanity's dark and stormy beginnings. The Indians' worth as human beings was determined by their usefulness as counterpoint to the unfolding progress of the ages."[27]

These displays clearly reflected and reinforced emerging scientific notions of race and culture, represented most notably in the United States in the work of the anthropologist Lewis Henry Morgan.[28] In *Ancient Society, or Researches in the Lines of Human Progress from Savagery through Barbarism to Civilization,* published in 1877, Morgan wrote that human societies inevitably progressed through the various stages of savagery and barbarism before finally breaking through into civilization. "The slow accumulations of experimental knowledge," Morgan asserted, constituted "a natural as well as necessary sequence of progress." In tracing the earliest stages of this "progress of knowledge," he devoted particular attention to the modes and tools of subsistence, since the task of mastering the methods of subsistence, in his theory, characterized the existence of "primitive" peoples.[29] Morgan's

[25] Rydell, *All the World's a Fair,* 25. Cultural differences between the various Native groups were ignored. Artifacts originating in diverse cultures from throughout the Americas were all deemed representative of a monolithic, primitive "Indianness" that contrasted with the advancement of Western civilization.

[26] Ingram, *Centennial Exposition,* 150.

[27] Rydell, *All the World's a Fair,* 24–25.

[28] Lewis Henry Morgan, *Ancient Society, or Researches in the Lines of Human Progress from Savagery through Barbarism to Civilization* (New York: Henry Holt, 1878). See also Edward Burnett Tylor, *Primitive Culture* (1873; reprint, New York: Harper and Row, 1958), whose celebrated arguments influenced Morgan's theories. Although Morgan's seminal work was not published until after the closing of the Philadelphia Centennial Exposition, similar understandings of culture (all influenced by Darwinism) gained popularity years before. Clearly, the Smithsonian scientists who organized the Native exhibits at the fair shared similar views. Morgan, however, was among the first scientists in the United States to develop these ideas systematically. It is for this reason, as well as because of the monumental influence of his work, that I cite him here.

[29] Morgan, *Ancient Society,* 3, 8.

FIGURE 1. The Indian Department in the U.S. Government Building, re-printed from Frank H. Norton, ed., *Frank Leslie's Historical Register of the United States Centennial Exposition, 1876* (New York: Frank Leslie's Publishing House, 1877).

theory thus carried dual implications. On the one hand, it presented a unified vision of humankind. Differences, he argued, were a product of various stages of universal human development rather than of autonomous histories. Thus, he wrote, "in studying the conditions of tribes and nations in these several ethnical periods we are dealing, substantially, with the ancient history and condition of our own remote ancestors."[30]

[30] Ibid., 18.

On the other hand, by embracing this vision of human progress, he assigned relative values to these differences. Non-Western peoples were "primitive" and their societies were less fully developed than those of Westerners, who embodied the pinnacle of progress. In Morgan's terms, the "primitive," in contrast to the white European, stood "at the bottom of the scale" of development, "a child in the scale of humanity."[31] Displays of objects in exhibits such as those mounted by the Smithsonian in Philadelphia seemed to establish the validity of this theory of culture very effectively. By siting objects (both Western and non-Western) on a universal scale of social evolution, organizers "proved" by implication the superiority of technologically advanced societies.

This distinction between "primitive" Native societies and technologically superior Western "civilization" was not lost on visitors to the Philadelphia Centennial Exposition. The Indian exhibit, in the words of one reporter, provided "the strongest imaginable contrast to the mechanical progress of the present." In fact, by providing a point of contrast, the Native displays served to glorify the accomplishments of a technologically inventive European society celebrated throughout the fair. Charles Rau, supervisor of the exhibit, announced that "the extreme lowness of our remote ancestors cannot be a source of humiliation; on the contrary, we should glory in having advanced so far above them, and recognize the great truth that *progress* is the law that governs the development of mankind."[32]

Yet the "primitiveness" of Indians carried various and sometimes conflicting associations. Carved totem poles, buckskin clothing, beadwork and pottery usually evoked images of a rather backward and quaint, but likely harmless, people. Other exhibits, however, communicated an even stronger and more frightening meaning. The prevalence of Native weapons, for example, suggested a fiercer brand of savagery. Some displays were explicitly threatening. The Department of the Interior exhibit boasted a grotesque series of stuffed papier-mâché Indian "braves" adorned in red face paint and feather headdresses—the accouterments, in other words, of war. Some of these mannequins even represented real-life warriors. The figure of the Cheyenne warrior Tall Bull, killed in 1869 at the Battle of Summit Springs, reportedly wore the very clothing taken from the warrior's dead body. The Sioux leader Red Cloud also appeared in this array, ominously posed with a raised tomahawk in one of his hands and a string of scalps dangling from his waist. An object of intense fascination for many fairgoers, he was, in the words of one local newspaper, a "re-

[31] Ibid., 37.
[32] Rydell, *All the World's a Fair,* 24.

pulsive looking" figure who appeared "ready to pounce on some unsuspecting victim."[33]

For most viewers, these displays carried profound political implications reflecting on the relations between Native American and European America. In the 1870s, European America remained immersed in wars of conquest in the West. To those few who questioned the justice of this conquest, the exposition promised that the dominance of (white) civilization over (Native) savagery was an inevitable part of the "universal law of progress," the "manifest destiny" of white Americans. By indicating that progress (rather than European-American acquisitiveness) underlay the conquest, the exhibits also conveniently deflected difficult ethical questions about centuries of slaughter of Native peoples and usurpation of their resources. The Indian displays, then, complemented the story of America celebrated at the Philadelphia Centennial Exposition. European-American history was the true history of the continent, and certainly the only one worth remembering. Writing about the fair in the *Atlantic Monthly*, William Dean Howells expressed the derision with which many fairgoers viewed Indians: "The red man, as he appears in effigy and in photograph in this collection, is a hideous demon, whose malign traits can hardly inspire any emotion softer than abhorrence."[34] Howells articulated the sentiments of many observers who saw in the Indians' "inevitable" fate a cause not for sorrow but for celebration.

But as Americans were soon reminded, in 1876 the military conquest of Native America was not yet a fait accompli. Only a few weeks after the exposition opened on 25 June 1876, Custer's Seventh Cavalry met its demise at the Battle of the Little Bighorn. Confident of their own superiority, many Americans were surprised to learn that Indians still posed a threat to the white nation's dominance. The displays at the fair provided assurances for these viewers as well. While the exhibits frequently raised the specter of Native savagery, they also quelled viewers' fears by promising them that "progress" would soon render the Indian threat meaningless. The impressive displays of American weapons in Machinery Hall, for example, overwhelmed the primitive bows and arrows showcased in the Indian exhibit. Moreover, the absurdity of the stuffed papier-mâché constructions allayed the terror evoked by such figures as the tomahawk-wielding Red Cloud. Although apparently different from these savage figures, a series of romantic images depicting bygone Native life similarly reassured fairgoers that white America would overcome the Indian threat. Photographs of Hopi

[33] Trennert, "A Grand Failure," 128.
[34] Quoted in ibid., 127.

villages in Arizona and other scenes depicted Indians "as if they were no longer living, which greatly undermined their humanity and living dynamism."[35] Even the spatial location of the Indian displays in the Department of the Interior section of the Government Building suggested that Indians were literally contained by the federal government. Indian objects (and, by implication, Native peoples), it seemed, now "belonged" to white America.

The planners of the exposition did not simply highlight the differences between Native America and European America, however. They also strove to show that these groups were fundamentally alike. This objective first became clear during the planning phase of the exposition. Initially, Spencer F. Baird, the assistant secretary of the Smithsonian Institution responsible for collecting the objects displayed, proposed exhibiting live Indians. In choosing representatives of various tribes, he applied a complicated set of criteria. The more "civilized" tribes—those who had intermarried extensively with whites and adopted European practices—were immediately ruled out. They did not show the stark contrast between savagery and civilization that the planners sought to represent. Significantly, though, Baird also excluded the least assimilated tribes and individuals. His thirteen-point checklist included the following requirements: "The individuals selected had to be more [racially] white than Indian. Each family had to be influential among the tribe, speak English, have a pleasant disposition, be the 'cleanest and finest looking,' and have a clean child, a dog, and a pony."[36] But in the end, these plans for live Indian displays fell through. However, the exhibits did contain other evidence of Indians' likeness— or potential likeness—to whites. An exhibit on Indian education, for example, showcased "specimens of chirography, patchwork, and other efforts made by the Wyandot children." The Wyandots, long a racially mixed tribe, thus displayed in one observer's words "a very creditable advancement, and [held] out good encouragement for the [Interior] department in prosecuting these attempts at Indian education."[37]

These presentations of Natives' similarity to Europeans complemented the ideological work performed by the displays contrasting Indian savagery and white civilization. By primitivizing Native peoples, the exposition's planners defined Americanness in a way that privileged European America. In the "symbolic universe" of the Philadelphia Centennial Exposition, progress—which defined Americanness—equaled industrial technology, and industrial technology was an achievement of

[35] Ibid., 129.
[36] Ibid., 125.
[37] Norton, *Frank Leslie's Register,* 103.

white America. The framework of social evolution thus explained white dominance as a consequence of the "universal" law of progress. At the same time, however, Native Americans (and, by implication, other races) could not differ from European America fundamentally without upsetting the illusion of national unity and this construction of racial hierarchies. In the same way that Morgan's racial theories united humanity by explaining differences as varying levels of progress, these exhibits strove to create a picture of a unified America by placing racial others in the white nation's past. In the imaginary world of the exhibition, Native peoples thus posed no threat either to the presence of Europeans in the Americas or to the hegemony of middle-class white society. As the Indian education exhibit attempted to show, these "primitive" people would inevitably—and naturally—become like Anglo-Americans or disappear.

In fact, Native Americans embodied white America's historical past in explicit ways. The displays symbolically resolved centuries-old conflicts between Native America and European America—conflicts being played out in the wars in the West—by transforming Native peoples into "our" (white America's) Indian history. One of the most celebrated objects at the exposition provides an apt example. The "century vase," cast in solid silver, intertwined the nation's narrative with the story of universal human progress that constituted the primary organizing principle of the exposition:

> The Pioneer and the Indian represent the first phase of civilization; groups of fruit, flowers, and cereals, the natural products of the soil. The slab of polished granite signifies the unity and solidity of the government, on which rest the thirty-eight States. The band of stars, thirty-eight encircling the piece, thirteen in front, represent the present and original number of States in the Union. ...The medallion on the [back] side is the Genius of Philosophy and Diplomacy, with one hand resting on the printing-press, and with the other holding a portrait of Franklin....The front panel of the vase represents Genius ready to inscribe on the tables the progress made in literature, science, music, painting, sculpture, and architecture. On the reverse panel, Genius is ready to record the advancement in commerce, agriculture, mining, and manufactures....[T]he central figure, America, is inviting and welcoming all nations to unite with her in celebrating the triumph of her centennial year.[38]

[38] Ingram, *Centennial Exposition,* 306–9.

FIGURE 2. The celebrated century vase on display at the Philadelphia Centennial Exposition, reprinted from J. S. Ingram, *The Centennial Exposition, Described and Illustrated* (1876; reprint, New York: Arno, 1976).

Not only did the vase represent the stages of progress from raw materials to manufacturing and technology to the arts, it also interpreted the nation's history in these terms. Note, for example, the equivalence of Indians with "natural products of the soil" in the first phase of civilization. The more advanced stages of progress predictably leave Indians behind. Note also the equivalence of the Indian and the pioneer in this first phase. Together, they constitute the white nation's foundations. The narrative unfolded on the century vase thus conceals the conflicts, past and present, between Indians and Europeans in order to represent an image of "unity and solidity." But the narrative served another purpose as well. Not only did it naturalize European-American dominance by placing Native peoples in the historical past, it also contributed to a conception of American identity that differentiated it from its European roots. White America "owned" Native America; it appropriated Native

America for its national past. In 1876 this myth of America gone native at once made the nation unique and shielded it from criticisms of its violent history.

Over the years, as the memory of the conquest grew more distant, the image of Native America as the white nation's past became increasingly important. As the Indian wars wound down in the 1870s, and particularly after the Wounded Knee massacre of 1890, Native America no longer seemed to challenge the political power of European Americans. Meanwhile, during these years, middle-class whites began to confront challenges from other sources. Ironically, after 1890, images of Native America—reimagined as European America's native history (a move foreshadowed by the Philadelphia exposition)—helped Anglos retain their power and their status in a series of domestic and international conflicts. During this transitional period in representations of Native America, European Americans began identifying with Natives on a large scale. Although images of savage Indian others still found their place in twentieth-century American culture, Native peoples also figured as an integral part of white America's identity. While this shift manifested itself throughout American culture, it was at the next great American fair, the World's Columbian Exposition of 1893 (opening three years after Wounded Knee), that this change became startlingly obvious.

*

On 1 May 1893, nearly sixteen years after the Philadelphia Centennial Exposition closed, the World's Columbian Exposition opened in Chicago during a period of rapid cultural change. While questions of American cultural identity had also preoccupied the planners of the Philadelphia fair, these issues had become increasingly vexed in the intervening years. Only days after the Chicago exposition commenced, the nation plunged into a deep economic depression, one that would persist well beyond the duration of the fair. The economic downturn worsened problems begun years before when the ranks of the urban working classes started to swell. Nearly half of these workers lived near or below the poverty line, and virtually all of them endured harsh working conditions. Strikes grew more and more common through the 1880s and early 1890s, frequently claiming casualties during the ensuing violence. The Populist revolt, too, gained momentum during this period. Often, as in the case of the 1886 Haymarket Riot, these conflicts hit Chicagoans close to home. Responding to widespread fears that strikers' violence would escalate into full-scale class warfare, the United States government built hundreds of armories between 1880 and 1910. Meanwhile, the country's increasing ethnic and racial diversity complicated these class divisions. Non-Anglos comprised an increasingly greater proportion of the working classes as new groups of immigrants flooded the country and large numbers of former slaves sought employment in urban centers.[39] The "race problem," moreover, was a national concern, manifested perhaps most obviously in the reestablishment of white supremacy in the post-Reconstruction South and debates over the fate of Native peoples after the end of the Indian wars.[40] The "incorporation of America" also took its toll. Economic changes, combined with swift industrialization and urbanization, "wrenched American society from the moorings of traditional values." Consequently, "controversies over the meaning of America symbolized struggles over reality, over the power to define as well as control it."[41] Thus, when the Chicago fair opened, white Americans' faith in progress and their own dominance, firmly entrenched in 1876, was being shaken.

The planners of the World's Columbian Exposition, then, confronted a different set of questions and challenges than had their predecessors in Philadelphia. These changing circumstances called for different configurations of "Americanness" as well as a different story of the nation's origins. Like the organizers of the Philadelphia exposition, who had responded to questions of American heritage in ways that naturalized the current social order, in particular the conquest of Native America, planners of the Chicago world's fair aimed primarily to "resolve" (at least symbolically) the monumental problems of the moment. Thus, the Chicago exposition was, like other world's fairs, an exercise in "cultural and ideological repair and renewal."[42] For many fairgoers in 1893, the visions staged at Chicago gave order and coherence to their increasingly chaotic social world. These visions also promised observers a more stable future in which middle-class white Americans would retain their dominance at home and wield more power abroad.

---

[39] The immigration crisis was at its peak in 1893. Twenty-five million immigrants arrived between 1865 and 1915, most of them after 1890. Moreover, post-1890 immigration brought in new ethnic types from Central, Eastern, and Southern Europe, a fact which gave rise to profound anxieties about their ability to be assimilated into mainstream society and contributed to the rise of American nativism during this period. See Edwin C. Rozwenc and Thomas Bender, *The Making of American Society*, vol. 2 (New York: Alfred A. Knopf, 1973).

[40] Richard Slotkin's *The Fatal Environment: The Myth of the Frontier in the Age of Industrialization, 1800–1890* (New York: Atheneum, 1985) shows the links between the conquest of Native peoples, the responses to labor unrest, and the reestablishment of white supremacy in the South in the post-Reconstruction era.

[41] Alan Trachtenberg, *The Incorporation of America: Culture and Society in the Gilded Age* (New York: Hill and Wang, 1982), 7–8.

[42] Robert W. Rydell, *World of Fairs: The Century-of-Progress Expositions* (Chicago: University of Chicago Press, 1993), 10.

At Chicago, it was not America's independence from Britain that took center stage. Rather, the 1893 world's fair celebrated the 400th anniversary of Columbus's "discovery" of the "new world." This, too, was a thoroughly European vision of the nation's origins, a triumphant story of expansion in which the millions of Native inhabitants of this "new" world functioned merely as incidental players or, more commonly, as savage obstacles to the inevitable spread of Western civilization. Figures of Columbus were everywhere at the fair. Several statues of the intrepid explorer decorated the grounds. One featured his likeness in a chariot, suggesting both a historical connection with Roman imperialism and a Biblical association that linked conquest with Christian redemption. Replicas of the Niña, Pinta, and Santa Maria—the explorer's fleet—also provided popular attractions. Like the stories of American independence and ingenuity that dominated at Philadelphia, the Columbus story also served to illustrate the progress that planners defined as quintessentially American. The arrival of Columbus, so the tale went, brought enlightenment to a hopelessly backward continent. As one official guidebook put it, "the success of the voyage of the Genoese sailor marked the era of endless and boundless advance of civilization."[43] According to another, "[Columbus's] star will ever remain of the first magnitude in the vision of civilized nations; for it was he who first brought the order of practical discovery out of the chaos of theory and doubt; it was he who first truly opened to the progress and civilization of the Old World the wealth and opportunities of the New."[44] Even as it defined expansion as progress, the exposition thus also linked expansion with plunder. It was progress, it seemed, that guaranteed that Europeans would possess "the wealth and opportunities" of the lands they colonized. At the Chicago exposition, this notion reflected both on European America's history and on its imperial future.

For many Americans, this interpretation of the Columbus story resonated with 1890s concerns. If Columbus had brought progress and civilization to the chaotic Old World, the story implied, so too could the vision of progress at the exposition resolve the fin de siècle chaos of the United States. Other exhibits at the fair replicated this opposition between the backward "Old World" and the progressive new one in ways that carried clear messages about the present. Importantly, like the Philadelphia exhibition, the World's Columbian Exposition delineated the boundaries of the nation in ways that excluded non-Anglos.[45] The fair

[43] *The City of Palaces: Picturesque World's Fair* (Chicago: W. B. Conkey, 1894), 1.
[44] William E. Cameron, ed., *History of the World's Columbian Exposition*, 2d. ed. (Chicago: Columbian History Company, 1893), 5.
[45] The fact that Columbus himself was a non-Anglo immigrant to the Americas presented something of a contradiction, which organizers "resolved" by positioning Anglos as Columbus's rightful heirs to North America (see below).

FIGURE 3. Statue of Columbus taking possession of the New World. The statue was located in front of the Administration Building at the World's Columbian Exposition. Reprinted from William E. Cameron, ed., *History of the World's Columbian Exposition* (Chicago: Columbian History Company, 1893).

thereby swelled the tides of nativism and nationalism that swept American politics in the 1890s. But the myth of Columbus carried other implications as well. By defining his story as the nation's originary moment, planners created a vision of an America born in imperial conquest. This story thus implied a more expansive vision of America's past and its future than had the exhibits at Philadelphia, one that prefigured the heated debates on imperialism that came to the fore at the close of the decade. Both responses served to buoy national confidence in the face of pressing social problems. John Higham writes: "When the troubles of the late nineteenth century raised doubts of the nation's stamina, two short cuts for restoring confidence presented themselves: disunity might be rationalized as a product of foreign influence, or denied by a compensatory demonstration of national virility. One response led toward protective measures at home, such as immigration restriction; the other encouraged an offensive posture abroad."[46] In Chicago, the exhibits offered stories of Americanness that fed both tendencies. Here, not only was America's story the story of white America, it was a story that privileged Anglos over all other Europeans. It thus excluded more recent immigrants. The displays at the fair also presented a vision of the West's "others" that encouraged increasingly widespread expansionist impulses.

Both products of American nationalism, nativism and imperialism depended to some degree on particular conceptions of the white nation's "superiority." Once again, Americans' understandings of their superiority depended upon the linked notions of race and social progress. Like the Philadelphia Centennial Exposition, then, the World's Columbian Exposition served to illustrate "the growth and progress of human endeavor in the direction of a higher civilization" and, more specifically, "the stupendous results of American enterprise...[and the] magnificent evidences of American skill and intelligence."[47] Also reminiscent of the Philadelphia displays, Indians, both as living exhibits and as symbols, provided along with other indigenous peoples from around the world a historical foundation by which to measure American progress. Interpreting the ethnological exhibits, Frederick Putnam, director of Harvard's Peabody Museum and head of the Department of Ethnology and Archaeology at the Chicago fair, reminded fairgoers that "we must never lose sight of the fact that this Exposition is a Columbian Exposition; that its very existence is due to the fact that the voyage of Columbus 400 years ago led to the discovery of America by our race, its subsequent peopling by the Europeans and the consequent development of great

[46] John Higham, *Strangers in the Land: Patterns of American Nativism, 1860–1925* (New Brunswick, N.J.: Rutgers University Press, 1988), 76. As Higham points out, although both were driven by a burgeoning American nationalism, nativism and imperialism worked at cross-purposes. "Nativistic fears of racial pollution," Higham writes, generally countered the expansionist objectives of imperialists (109). See also Walter Benn Michaels, *Our America: Nativism, Modernism, and Pluralism* (Durham: Duke University Press, 1995).
[47] Cameron, *History of the World's Columbian Exposition*, 328.

nations on the continent. This development...has been of a most re-markable character upon this continent." Establishing the superiority of the colonial culture required a point of contrast, and the lowly Indian, now apparently vanishing in the wake of historical progress, provided an ideal example of the inferiority of the West's "others":

> But what will all this amount to without the means of comparison in the great object lesson? What, then, is more appropriate, more essential, than to show in their natural conditions of life the differ-ent types of peoples who were here when Columbus was crossing the Atlantic Ocean and leading the way for the great wave of hu-manity that was soon spread over the continent and forced those unsuspecting peoples to give way before a mighty power, to resign their inherited rights, and take their chances for existence under the laws governing a strange people?...These peoples, as great nations, have about vanished into history, and now is the last op-portunity for the world to see them and to realize what their con-dition, their life, their customs, their arts were four centuries ago. The great object lesson then will not be completed without their being present. Without them, the Exposition will have no base.[48]

Clearly, then, distinct and interdependent racial hierarchies under-pinned the exhibits. In the words of one of the its organizers, the exhi-bition showed that although an Italian discovered America, "it re-mained for the Saxon race to people this new land, to redeem it from barbarism, to dedicate its virgin soil to freedom, and in less than four centuries to make of it the most powerful and prosperous country on which God's sunshine falls."[49]

Nowhere was the contrast between savagism and white civilization starker than in the relationship between the two main exhibition centers, the White City and the Midway Plaisance. A heavily laden symbol and an obvious tribute to racial whiteness, the aptly named White City provided the centerpiece of the event and, by implication, the nation's narrative as well. A monument to industry and the arts, it lauded the technological and intellectual achievements of the West. As was the case in Philadel-phia's displays, technology took center stage, again marking the West's progress and signifying its superiority. The layout of the White City was

[48] Quoted in Curtis M. Hinsley, "The World as Marketplace: Commodification of the Exotic at the World's Columbian Exposition, Chicago, 1893," in *Exhibiting Cultures: The Poetics and Politics of Museum Display,* ed. Ivan Karp and Steven D. Lavine (Washington, D.C.: Smithsonian Institution Press, 1991), 347.
[49] John T. Harris, quoted in Badger, *Great American Fair,* 55.

FIGURE 4. The White City at the World's Columbian Exposition viewed from the Electricity Building, reprinted from William E. Cameron, ed., *History of the World's Columbian Exposition* (Chicago: Columbian History Company, 1893).

also key. Rigid order was its underlying principle. Buildings—most notably the Court of Honor and the Administration Building, and others showcasing machinery, electricity, agriculture, manufactures, and the arts—were arranged symmetrically, interlaced with open plazas and ponds. The neoclassical style dominated.[50] Whiteness, literally, was its most central characteristic. The whitewashed surfaces of the buildings gleamed, an effect augmented after dark by night lighting (itself touted as a major technological achievement). The racial implications were obvious. In a pamphlet protesting the exclusion of a significant African-American presence at the fair and presenting a counterimage of American life to that presented by the exposition, Frederick Douglass and Ida B. Wells labeled the exposition's center a "whited sepulcher."[51]

[50] See Alan Trachtenberg, "White City," in *The Incorporation of America;* and James Gilbert, *Perfect Cities: Chicago's Utopias of 1893* (Chicago: University of Chicago Press, 1991).
[51] Rydell, *All the World's a Fair,* 52.

The White City, in fact, excluded nonwhite peoples in a very literal way. Organizers relegated people of color to the Midway Plaisance, a mile-long, six-hundred-foot-wide stretch of land connecting Washington and Jackson Parks. The Midway provided the most visible racial displays at the World's Columbian Exposition. Though live exhibits were not uncommon in European fairs, the World's Columbian was the first American exposition to display live people in a systematic way. On the Midway organizers constructed a series of seventeen villages showcasing exotic subjects living and working in simulations of their "natural" environments. Nearly half of these scenarios represented villages of Western colonial subjects. They included villages from Lapland, Dahomey, China, and Tunisia, as well as scenes from the "everyday life" of Eskimos and American Indians. All the village displays featured indigenous peoples as representatives of their respective cultures. Organizers employed them to go about their daily lives in these simulated environments for the amusement of onlookers. Less obviously racialized sites on the Midway, including a Hungarian Orpheum and a scene of Old Vienna, frequently depicted scenes from Europe's past. By juxtaposing these displays with the ethnological exhibits, organizers implied that nonwhites belong to humanity's past rather than to the historical present.

Like the Indian exhibits at the Philadelphia Centennial Exposition, the Midway displays drew explicit contrasts between Europeans and non-Westerners. If the White City signified the coherence and order ostensibly characterizing white civilization, the ethnological displays on the Midway evoked pure chaos and savagery. There, horrified fairgoers witnessed natives practicing "weird beliefs" and "ceremonials" destined to "strike pity and disgust upon the minds of enlightened beholders." Dahomey animal sacrifices provided a favored attraction; their aftermath found "celebrants, male and female, grow wild—men, women, and children grovelling in the dirt and revelling in gore." There, too, West Indians performed voodoo ceremonies, Buddhists praised "uncouth clay and wooden monstrosities," and Samoans worshipped fetishes.[52] Descriptions of the Midway's spectacles frequently likened the peoples on display to animals: the Egyptian belly dancers were "lithe as panthers," an Eskimo child looked much like a "seal," and the Samoans were "magnificent animals."[53] But it was not only the peoples and their religious practices that invited comparisons between Westerners and the colonized subjects displayed on the Midway. Technology provided another counterpoint. While the stunning architecture of the White City testified to the West's skill and taste, native peoples' achievements were

[52] Cameron, *History of the World's Columbian Exposition*, 313–16.
[53] *City of Palaces*, 34, 176, 99.

much more modest. In the Java Village, for example, "clever little carpenters" used "the most primitive methods" to construct bamboo huts.[54] Peculiar sounds also augmented the primitive scenes spectators witnessed as "ear-piercing discords [poured] without ceasing up and down the Plaisance." A stark contrast to the White City's vision of the "New Jerusalem," the Midway was instead a frenzied "Tower of Babel." Through this contrast, the displays were designed to demonstrate that the White City (and, by implication, white America) represented "the fullest flower of civilization and Christianity."[55]

An irresistible attraction for most fairgoers, the Midway constituted, in the words of one commentator, "the playground of the multitude" where "they learned much while they ate, drank, stared and were merry."[56] Sited among the native villages and other exotica was the Ferris Wheel. It proved another popular draw for crowds, and it defined the Midway Plaisance (indeed, as its name suggests) as a place for entertainment and carnivalesque revelry. The sideshow atmosphere that characterized these displays is telling. It was, in fact, a source of controversy among its planners. Initially, organizers appointed the Harvard scientist F. W. Putnam along with the anthropologist Franz Boas to design the Midway display under the direction of the Smithsonian Institution. Putnam's racial theories and his Darwinian vision echoed those conveyed in the displays at Philadelphia nearly two decades earlier. He conceived the Midway Plaisance as an anthropological presentation which one of its planners described as "an illustrated encyclopedia of humanity."[57] Arranged sequentially according to their degrees of civilization, the villages were "designed to carry the spectator through the successive steps of human progress."[58] Soon, though, Putnam's "Street of All Nations" took on a more widely appealing carnivalesque quality, and the organizers of the exposition opted to replace the scientist with impresario Sol Bloom. As Bloom tellingly observed many years later, appointing Putnam to design the Midway was like making "Albert Einstein manager of the Ringling Brothers and Barnum and Baily Circus."[59]

Under the flamboyant Bloom, the circuslike qualities of the Midway soon dominated. In fact, though, Bloom's objectives were not as distant from Putnam's as they initially seem.[60] Putnam's racial theories

[54] Ibid., 64.
[55] Cameron, *History of the World's Columbian Exposition,* 313–14.
[56] *City of Palaces,* 15.
[57] Hinsley, "World as Marketplace," 346.
[58] Rydell, *All the World's a Fair,* 20.
[59] See Gilbert, *Perfect Cities,* 87.
[60] Beginning with the first U.S. exposition in New York in 1853, which was organized by P. T. Barnum, American world's fairs generally tended to emphasize

FIGURE 5. A view of the Midway Plaisance at the World's Columbian Exposition, reprinted from *The City of Palaces: Picturesque World's Fair* (Chicago: W. B. Conkey, 1894).

(influenced by Morgan) brought Europeans and non-Europeans into a single, explanatory framework, placing nonwhites on a lower scale of the evolutionary ladder. In a sense, Bloom's displays accomplished similar ideological work. If science demonstrated the inferiority of

---

entertainment to a greater degree than their European counterparts did. This emphasis attests to the complex relationship between "scientific" displays and other spectacles. During the late nineteenth century, there was significant overlap in the displays of freak shows (a main feature of world's fairs), dime museums (sometimes billed as miniature world's fairs), and international expositions. Barnum's primary occupation, in fact, was not the circus but museum work. All of these spectacles claimed to serve the purposes of scientific investigation and education. Symptomatically, by the last quarter of the century, the distinction between tribal peoples and individuals with physical abnormalities collapsed within the context of these types of exhibits, a phenomenon indicative perhaps of the atavistic fears and fantasies of their viewers. See Robert Bogdan, *Freak Show: Presenting Human Oddities for Amusement and Profit* (Chicago: University of Chicago Press, 1988). For a discussion of the rise of dime museums in the United States, see Karl E. Meyer, *The Art Museum: Power, Money, Ethics* (New York: William Morrow, 1979).

these racial others, so too did their status as entertainment. This status, of course, depended upon the fact of conquest. Moreover, the grotesque spectacles staged on the Midway by organizers of the exposition contrasted "savagism" and white "civilization" in an obviously self-aggrandizing manner. White superiority was evident as well in the relationships between performers and (mostly white) spectators. This relationship, in essence, was distinctly colonial, thus enacting the broader dynamics at work in the fair's Columbian theme. On the Midway, nonwhite others were made available for Western consumption in various ways, some more obviously colonial than others. An Alaskan Indian village, for example, showcased the "fast-developing resources" of "*our* vast territory."[61] Prominently displayed furs of sea otter, fox, seal, and mink fed the demands for furs from the region. Gender also figured in many of the Midway displays in ways that enacted colonial consumption. The Egyptian *danse du ventre,* frequently described in heavily erotic terms, numbered among the most popular performances. A beauty pageant featuring women from throughout the world titillated spectators as well, as did the scantily clad women in the village displays. Rumors of prostitution quickly spread. The ostensible availability of these women's bodies for sexual conquest articulated colonial conquest in obvious ways. The Midway's message was clear: the non-West existed for the both the amusement and the development of the West.

Visitors to the Midway understood the convergence of Bloom's circus-inspired spectacle of otherness and Putnam's more scientific vision, as well as their association with colonial conquest. While many viewers stressed the amusement park quality of the exhibits, others read the scientific implications very clearly. The *Chicago Tribune,* for instance, described a stroll down the Midway as an opportunity "afforded to the scientific mind to descend the spiral of evolution, tracing humanity in its highest phases down almost to its animalistic origins."[62] Like the *Tribune* reporter, most viewers also felt contempt and a sense of their own superiority when viewing these exotic peoples. An official account of the Eskimo village reported that it was "an interesting, even though a rather repulsive, place to visit."[63] A handbook to the fair described the village in similar terms: "For a fee of 25 cents one can see the natives, their wolfish-looking dogs, their sledges, spears, stoves, canoes, lamps, etc.

---

[61] *City of Palaces,* 71 (emphasis mine). Alaska was purchased by the United States from Russia in 1867 without the consent of its predominantly Native population.
[62] Rydell, *All the World's a Fair,* 65.
[63] J. W. Buel, *The Magic City: A Massive Portfolio of Original Photographic Views of the Great World's Fair* (Philadelphia: Historical Publishing Co., 1894), unpaginated.

FIGURE 6. Alaskan Indian Village at the World's Columbian Exposition, re-printed from *The City of Palaces: Picturesque World's Fair* (Chicago: W. B. Conkey, 1894).

There are men, women, and children in the village, and their modes of life and the sanitary conditions (or rather the want of them) peculiar to them and their crowded quarters do not 'lade the pulsing air with sweet-est perfumes.'"[64] The parallels with the story of Columbus celebrated at the exposition were unmistakable. The Midway, frequently dubbed "terra incognita," bore distinct similarities to the wild and barbaric land that Columbus had found, at least according to popular myth. In another striking parallel to Columbus's story, references to the Midway as a Tower of Babel (in contrast to the New Jerusalem embodied in the White City) transformed conquest into Christian redemption. It was, most viewers believed, the "white man's burden" to rescue their savage brethren from the grotesque spectacles on the Midway.

Thus, while the Midway displays conspicuously enacted colonial domination and consumption, they also hid the darker side of conquest.

[64] *Handbook of the World's Columbian Exposition* (Chicago: Rand McNally, 1893), 182. The fact that the unsanitary and overcrowded quarters were provided for the Eskimos by the exposition organizers seems to have been lost on fairgoers.

FIGURE 7. "Medicine" and "Plenty Horse," described as Sioux Indian chiefs, on display at the World's Columbian Exposition, reprinted from *The City of Palaces: Picturesque World's Fair* (Chicago: W.B. Conkey, 1894).

Not only did they transform slaughter and domination into entertainment, they justified these brutal acts by explaining them in terms of particular notions of racial and social progress. In addition, the displays instructed viewers that colonized peoples themselves recognized imperial conquest as Western benevolence. Exhibited natives frequently smiled and willingly performed for spectators, often reportedly making fast friends (although in these cases they were usually behaving as their employers instructed them to). Sometimes the message that natives welcomed Western dominance, or at least easily tolerated it, became stunningly explicit. As one observer commented on the displays of "Medicine" and "Plenty Horse," two Sioux "chiefs" (whose people, remember, had just undergone decades of the most brutal conquest which culminated in the slaughter at Wounded Knee in 1890):

> Here were the remnants of some of the greatest tribes upon the continent, tribes whom the whites despoiled of vast regions and whom they almost annihilated...; here, too, were representatives of the great tribes of the Far West, not yet extinct, but rapidly going the way of their Eastern kindred. It was a curious and, in some respects, almost a saddening sight. The Indians themselves did not appear to be much depressed [!] by the fact that their grandfathers were rulers when they themselves were but features of a show for the multitude. They lived placidly in their wigwams, their squaws and papooses about them, played the games in fashion with them, and gave an occasional war dance for the benefit of guests.[65]

While the distinction between the Midway and the White City created illusions of Western superiority that legitimized Western dominance, these exhibits performed other complementary functions as well. Constructions of savage "others" also aimed to create consensus—and thus a coherent citizenry—among white Americans. In *The Birth of the Museum*, Tony Bennett describes how such spectacles contribute to the formation of an apparently homogeneous citizenry and, as a result, national identities. Since the nineteenth century, observes Bennett, museums, exhibitions, and other spectacles have "played a pivotal role in the formation of the modern state" through a mechanism he labels the "exhibitionary complex." Historically, the exhibitionary complex has operated through displays of objects in public institutions "where, through the representations to which they were subjected, they formed vehicles for inscribing and broadcasting the messages of power... throughout society."[66] The apparatus of power, in this way, works on the surveyor as well as the surveyed. In the particular case of exposition displays such as those on the Midway, images of colonized peoples both reflected and reinforced their subjugation to Western colonial power. But these spectacles also transformed Western viewers in part because the very act of seeing conjured a fantasy of

---

[65] *City of Palaces*, 102.
[66] Tony Bennett, *The Birth of the Museum: History, Theory, Politics* (London: Routledge, 1995), 66, 60–61.

their own dominance: "This ambition towards a specular dominance was...evident in the conception of international expositions which, in their heyday, sought to make the whole world, past and present, metonymically available in the assemblages of objects and peoples they brought together and, from their towers, to lay it before a controlling vision."[67] In other words, by allying the white spectator with the colonial power of the state, these displays created an intoxicating illusion that positioned these viewers as the subjects, rather than the objects, of state power. In this way, the exhibitionary complex transformed diverse groups of people into a self-identified citizenry by associating them with the principles of progress and power that defined Americanness. These displays thus specified whiteness as the defining characteristic of the nation. By associating national identity with a transnational notion of progress (culminating in the triumph of industrial capitalism), the exhibitions constructed a white citizenry, "a 'we' conceived as the realization, and therefore just beneficiaries, of the processes of evolution and identified as a unity in opposition to the primitive otherness of conquered peoples."[68] It is important to note, however, that the white public was by no means a homogeneous group. One critical effect of the displays was to underplay class and other divisions. They thereby created the illusion of a unified and homogeneous white American citizenry by glossing over the domestic conflicts that ravaged 1890s society.

The displays at the World's Columbian Exposition thus served a number of intersecting political purposes. They constructed a white citizenry and justified its dominance over the colonial subjects on the Midway, and they also racialized class and ethnic struggles, thereby extending this dominance to a series of domestic conflicts. For instance, the Midway reflected on the immigration crises that obsessed many Americans in the late nineteenth century. In one critic's words, the Midway was "molded by the special problems of Chicago's urban environment: the

---

[67] Ibid., 66.

[68] Ibid., 79. This argument raises the important question, Who is the implied viewer of the displays? While the self-congratulatory messages lauded at the expositions were clearly directed to white viewers, obviously a more diverse public attended the events. Judging by the reactions of various groups of nonwhites, it seems that different viewers in fact identified with the spectacles differently. In 1893, some African Americans, for example, objected to the gory displays in the Dahomey village, recognizing that they were intended to reflect on blacks as a group. Others, including Frederick Douglass, protested the exclusion of African Americans and other minorities from the displays in the White City, clearly recognizing it as a monument to racial whiteness. The fair's organizers in fact underscored the separation between viewers by designating particular days for African Americans to attend.

cultural mixing of the city's vast immigrant populations."[69] Nor was the association between immigrants and the "savagery" represented on the Midway merely implicit. In his speech at the dedication ceremonies in October 1892, New York senator Chauncy M. Depew warned against "those who come to undermine our institutions and subvert our laws."[70] While the Midway articulated the threat posed by these new immigrants, the fact that the orderly White City overshadowed the Midway created the reassuring illusion of "elite control" over unruly immigrant populations. This configuration extended to late-nineteenth-century class conflicts as well. In an era when strikers were frequently dubbed "Indians" or "savages," the associations between workers and nonwhites would have been clear.[71] The White City reassured viewers on this count as well by symbolically resolving these class conflicts. William Dean Howells related a story told by Daniel Burnam, the exposition's director of works: "[He] told me that when he told his mother of the magnificent consensus of wills and aims in the capitalists and artists who created [the White City's] beauty, she saw in it a vision of the New Jerusalem, and a direct leading of the Lord toward 'the wonder that shall be,' when all men work in harmony, and not in rivalry."[72] The fair, in other words, provided white, middle-class viewers with a comforting vision of stability, control, and order in the face of racial, ethnic, and class-based challenges. After Chicago, Robert Rydell writes, "millions of Americans would understand the ensuing decades of social struggle and imperial adventure as an integral part of the evolutionary process that accompanied progress."[73] By defining the racialized White City as the embodiment of progress, the exposition thus assured middle-class white Americans of their continued dominance during this period of rapid social change.

Although the displays on Chicago's Midway constructed the identities of both white civilization and its primitive others through a series of oppositions, apparently contradictory displays of Native peoples (especially Plains Indians) complicated this message. In many of the exhibits, Natives figured much like the other colonized peoples present at the

[69] Gilbert, *Perfect Cities*, 125.
[70] Cited in Trachtenberg, *Incorporation of America*, 209.
[71] In fact, the association of strikers with Indians and other nonwhites became increasingly commonplace during this period. Alex Nemerov writes that the era's popular Western paintings, for example, "come across less as documents of the old-time plains than as allegorical expressions of the urban, industrialized world, circa 1900—a world of strikes and proposed anti-immigration legislation." See Nemerov, "Doing the 'Old America': The Image of the American West, 1880–1920," in *The West as America: Reinterpreting Images of the Frontier, 1820–1920*, ed. William H. Truettner (Washington, D.C.: Smithsonian Institution Press, 1991), 288.
[72] Cited in Gilbert, *Perfect Cities*, 100.
[73] Rydell, *All the World's a Fair*, 71.

fair. Images of savage Sioux warriors, for instance, differed little from those of other "primitive" peoples on the Midway. As they had in Philadelphia, these exhibits also assured fairgoers that the threat posed by these "savages" had been contained by the superior military prowess of the United States. One statue entitled "America" showed "Liberty, or Civilization..., her breast emblazoned with the stars of our States, extending her domain over the wild Indian and the buffalo."[74] In other ways, the exposition explicitly celebrated the conquest of Native America. Colonel George R. Davis, director-general of the exposition, had himself served in the Indian wars, most notably under General Phil Sheridan at the bloody Battle of Washita. His experience inevitably made its way into the exposition. A military parade, led by General Nelson Miles (another notorious Indian killer), helped launch the event. But here, images of the now-conquered Indians that had not so long before inspired terror were transformed into spectacle, even into sources of entertainment. At the parade, Sioux and Crow warriors took up the rear and "trotted past" the cheering crowds. Now, organizers assured the viewers, those "once hostile savages" were "now soldiers of the Government."[75] Similarly, the exhibits proper showed the cabin of Sitting Bull, whose military genius had contributed to Custer's demise in 1876, with a sign that read "War Dances Given Daily."

Assurances that the Indians had been contained were also conveyed by the Indian boarding school exhibit. At the urging of Richard Henry Pratt, mastermind of the devastating Indian boarding school policy begun in 1879 (Pratt's motto was "kill the Indian and save the man"), the Bureau of Indian Affairs organized a showcase of his boarding school experiment as a counterpoint to the exhibits on the Midway. The BIA brought thirty to forty Indian children to Chicago along with their teachers so that fairgoers could witness, as one guidebook put it, "the North American Indian in the character of a student, demonstrating the benefits of civilization." As a point of contrast, the organizers of this show displayed a "red man as a savage wrapped in a blanket."[76] Both

---

[74] *City of Palaces*, 79.

[75] Cameron, *History of the World's Columbian Exposition*, 218.

[76] *A Week at the Fair Illustrating the Exhibits and Wonders of the World's Columbian Exposition* (Chicago: Rand McNally, 1893), 111. See also H. H. Bancroft, *The Book of the Fair: An Historical and Descriptive Presentation of the Columbian Exposition at Chicago in 1893*, vol. 1 (reprint, New York: Bounty Books, n.d.), 122. Pratt found the plans for Indian displays on the Midway objectionable, and he agreed to stage the boarding school exhibit as a more worthwhile counterimage of Native peoples. The Smithsonian had originally solicited Pratt to plan the ethnological displays on Indian customs and life intended for the Government Building. Pratt declined for ideological reasons; the exhibits, he believed, were "contrived by the two government bureaus [as] calculated to keep the nation's attention and the Indian's energies

kinds of exhibits—the Indian as savage and the assimilable Indian as beneficiary of civilization—assured viewers of their own superiority and justified their power. Indeed, the very fact that the government could organize exhibits of conquered peoples attested to the military might of the United States. In many respects, then, the impressions rendered by Chicago's Indian displays were reminiscent of those at Philadelphia: in the startling contrast between the exhibits on the Midway and the displays constituting the White City, Americans found evidence of the inferiority of the indigenous inhabitants of the continent, justification of the conquest, and confirmation of the progress of civilization.

Yet Native peoples figured in other, more complicated ways that upset the constructions of nation and race based on the simple antithesis of savagism and civilization. Interestingly, in other displays and events at the World's Columbian Exposition, Indians served not as the counterpoint to white America but rather as a symbol of quintessential Americanness. Although white America was literally built on the destruction of Native America, the stories European Americans told about themselves as the century drew to a close also depended upon the symbolic resurrection of the Indian as the originary figure of the nation, a role foreshadowed by the contradictory images embedded in the displays in both Philadelphia and Chicago. This configuration responded to late-nineteenth-century American anxieties about the conquest and contemporary social upheavals while gesturing more strongly to the nation's imperialist future. Perhaps the most critical and influential expression of these dual notions of the Indian's relation to white Americanness was Frederick Jackson Turner's frontier thesis speech. Delivered at one of the academic conferences organized in conjunction with the World's Columbian Exposition, the speech told yet another story of the nation's origins, one with vastly important messages about the vexed intersections of race, nation, and imperialism in turn-of-the-century American culture.

*

If the 1893 World's Columbian Exposition compelled fairgoers to consider the nation's present turmoil and promised resolutions to these crises, it also provided an opportunity for reflecting on America's colonial past as well as its imperial future. As we have seen, conquest delineated the cul-

---

fixed upon his valueless past, through the spectacular aboriginal housing, dressing, and curio employments it instituted" (see Badger, *Great American Fair,* 105). While Putnam and Boas, who agreed to take on the task Pratt shunned, showed pre-Columbian artifacts untainted by the influences of civilization, Pratt argued that it was only this "civilizing" process that was worthy of display.

tural landscape of the fair. By commemorating Columbus's "discovery" of the Americas in 1492, planners made imperial conquest the defining moment in the nation's past. But the 1893 fair went beyond the mere retelling and memorializing of European America's beginnings. These stories promised audiences that the white race would triumph despite the trials of the present. In a paper delivered at one of the congresses organized in conjunction with the exposition, one speaker announced: "This westward march of empire and freedom during the ages comes to an abrupt end.... The Columbian Exposition of 1893 celebrates both the beginning and the end of the Columbian epoch of characteristic modern Western Civilization and the beginning of a new epoch in which the race is again to be tested."[77] It was, however, the speech of the historian Frederick Jackson Turner delivered on 12 July 1893 that most famously described the nature of the "Columbian epoch" just ended and pointed toward new beginnings. Here, too, race proved critical. "The Significance of the Frontier in American History" painted a picture of American history that complemented the story of Columbus celebrated at the exposition. For many, the figure of Columbus resonated with a more recent hero of American culture, the pioneer. Columbus, in one critic's words, "could be seen as the original prototype of the American adventurer/hero who, like Boone or Crockett or Carson, blazed trails into an unknown wilderness so that others might follow and begin building the American Empire."[78] It was this pioneer whom Turner celebrated in his speech. The question of American empire—past and future—figured prominently in his narrative as well. He composed an exalted tale of (male, European) trailblazers driven westward into unknown lands, compelled by a force the nineteenth century labeled "manifest destiny," and in the process creating "America." His story, then, like the one told by the World's Columbian Exposition, concerned the nature of European America's identity and its history. Like the story of Columbus, Turner's tale has attained the status of myth, long dominating both academic and popular cultural versions of America's origins.[79]

[77] James Skelton, cited in Badger, *Great American Fair,* 100.

[78] Badger, *Great American Fair,* 43.

[79] Many contemporary Western historians have taken issue with Turner's concept of the frontier and with the centrality of the frontier idea in Western historical studies. Critiques of Turner's frontier include Jack D. Forbes, "Frontiers in American History and the Role of the Frontier Historian," *Ethnohistory* 15 (spring 1968): 203–35; Patricia Nelson Limerick, "The Adventures of the Frontier in the Twentieth Century," in *The Frontier in American Culture,* ed. James R. Grossman (Berkeley: University of California Press, 1994), 66–102; Limerick, *The Legacy of Co ———·····*
The Unbroken Past of the American West (New York: W.W. Norton, 1987`
generation of historians and writers has also begun telling the story c
from other points of view, most notably those of conquered peoples. F
cal perspective on pioneer settlement, see Janet Campbell Hale's *?*
Bloodlines: Odyssey of a Native Daughter (New York: HarperPerenr

Although it celebrated the pioneers' achievements in settling the "Great West," Turner's story was also profoundly ambivalent about where the United States stood. "The Significance of the Frontier in American History" declared that the frontier had closed, thus defining the 1890s as a watershed in American history. At the beginning of his speech, Turner, citing the 1890 census bulletin, announced that the unsettled "frontier line" had been so broken by "isolated bodies of settlement" that the frontier itself—as the boundary between civilization and the wilderness—no longer existed. For Turner, this fact proved critical for a number of reasons. The nation's history, from his perspective, had been "in a large degree the history of the colonization of the Great West," a process that had been completed by 1890 (significantly, the year of the Wounded Knee massacre, the event that marks the end of the military conquest of Native America, although Turner himself did not explicitly make this connection). But it was not just the westward movement of the American colonies that was key for the historian. Even more critical were its effects. For Turner, the most important product of the frontier experience was Americanness itself. "The existence of an area of free land, its continuous recession, and the advance of American settlement westward," he argued, "explain American development."[80] The "growth of nationalism," the "evolution of American political institutions" (49), and even the American character grew out of the frontier experience: "The frontier is productive of individualism. Complex society is precipitated by the wilderness into a kind of primitive organization based on the family. The tendency is anti-social. It produces antipathy to control, and particularly any direct control.... The frontier individualism has from the beginning promoted democracy" (53). The close of the frontier, then, constituted a monumental crisis. The question was obvious: if the frontier experience, the process of colonizing the land and its people, created the nation's identity (its history, its institutions, and its character), what would happen now that European Americans had settled the "Great West"? The very essence of America, it seemed, was at stake.

The issue of what constituted Americans and Americanness was fundamental for Turner, and in this regard his thesis was at once backward looking and speculative about the nation's future. Importantly, by defining the nation and its history as the movement of (predominantly Anglo) pioneers westward, the frontier thesis, like other national narratives, performed particular exclusions. Turner's vision obviously ig-

[80] Frederick Jackson Turner, "The Significance of the Frontier in American History (1893)," in *Rereading Frederick Jackson Turner*, with commentary by John Mack Faragher (New York: Henry Holt, 1994), 31. Hereafter cited by page number in the text.

nored the histories of Native Americans and other nonwhite inhabitants of the West. It was, at best, a partial story. In one scholar's words, "the cartography that so inspired Turner, it turns out, was less a work of science than of the imagination."[81] Shaped, perhaps, less by objective facts than by a collective cultural imagination, the speech is important in part because of the way it responded to the crises the Anglo-American middle-class confronted at the end of the nineteenth century. The story Turner told about the nation was *their* story. "Our early history," he claimed, "is the study of European germs developing in an American environment" (33).[82] For Turner, however, it was not simply these roots that produced Americans. Rather, it was the frontier experience that transformed and unified these immigrants into the modern nation, in part by severing their ties to their homelands. "The frontier," he asserted, "is the line of most rapid and effective Americanization," a process that became more and more effective the further West the immigrants traveled. "Moving westward, the frontier became more and more American....Thus the advance of the frontier has meant a steady movement away from the influence of Europe....And to study this advance...is to study the really American part of our history" (33–34).

Turner's vision of America, then, was in good measure a transformation and renewal of its European roots that pointedly excluded the separate—and older—histories of Native peoples, as well as the histories of other nonwhite peoples. Nevertheless, the roles that Indians play in Turner's account generate the most resonant tensions in the frontier thesis speech. These apparent contradictions suggest some of the most profound dilemmas confronting America in the 1890s. For Turner it was in part the European immigrants' complex relationships with Native Americans that rendered them *true* Americans. Often, Native peoples are simply absent from his imaginary landscape, which appears empty and unpopulated, the proverbial "virgin land" of conventional colonial discourse (his definition of the frontier, in fact, pivoted on sparse populations). At other times, however, Indians embody a savagery to be conquered along with the wilderness (here, he repeated the messages of many of the displays at the World's Columbian Exposition). "The Indian was a common danger" along the frontier line, he claimed, a force that unified the frontier settlements in defense against this savage otherness.

---

[81] John Mack Faragher, "'A Nation Thrown Back upon Itself': Frederick Jackson Turner and the Frontier," in *Rereading Frederick Jackson Turner*, 6.

[82] Turner's vision, though, was selective even in its description of European settlement. He ignored the colonial histories of the Spanish, the French, and the Russians; none of these groups followed the east-to-west trajectory Turner defined as "universal history." Nor do women play any significant role in the frontier thesis.

These constructions similarly relied upon common colonial tropes. What was new and striking about Turner's formulations, however, was the way that he also defined Indians not in opposition to Americanness but rather as predecessors of Turner's quintessential American, the pioneer:

> The wilderness masters the colonist. It finds him European in dress, industries, tools, modes of travel, and thought. It takes him from the railroad car and puts him in the birch canoe. It strips off the garments of civilization and arrays him in the hunting shirt and moccasin. It puts him in the log cabin of the Cherokee and Iroquois and runs an Indian palisade around him. Before long he has gone to planting Indian corn and plowing with a sharp stick; he shouts the war cry and takes the scalp in orthodox Indian fashion. In short, at the frontier the environment is at first too strong for the man. He must accept the conditions which it furnishes, or perish, and so he fits himself into the Indian clearings and follows the Indian trails.... [H]ere is a new product that is American. (33–34)

In other words, Turner envisioned the frontier process as one in which colonists succumbed to the wilderness and regressed temporarily into the "savage" state of the Indian. In Turner's view, by "going native"—in a limited way and for a limited time—the colonists were thus inculcated with an Americanness in the making. It is important to remember, however, that this regression into savagery was not an end in itself. Although the passage conceals their agency and denies their mastery ("the wilderness masters the colonist"), Turner's colonists in fact went native in order to overcome savagery, in order to establish their dominion over the Indians and the wilderness—in other words, to further the course of colonial progress.

Turner, then, saw the Indian as a predecessor of the pioneer and, hence, of civilization. This formulation clearly shows the influence of emergent social evolutionary conceptions of race, specifically those of Morgan, which similarly placed "primitive" peoples in civilization's past. It also reflected nineteenth-century notions of progress on which social evolution depended. Progress, in fact, underlay Turner's vision of the frontier experience, and this was why, for him, the experience created American identity. On the frontier, "complex European life" met "the simplicity of primitive conditions" (37). This return to the primitive marked a process of "perennial rebirth," a series of new beginnings in which Americans on the frontier relived the process of "social development"—a progressive model that in itself defined Americanness (32). In his speech, Turner traced these stages quite clearly. This "record of social evolution" began with "the Indian and the hunter" and was followed by the trader, the rancher, and finally the farmer. The advent of the "manufacturing organization with city and factory system" completed the cycle (38). Turner's white audiences, figured here as the heirs of the pioneers, could thus pride themselves in having reached the pinnacle of progress and in having overcome the savagery of both the primitive Indians and the wilderness.

Turner's narrative thus refigured both the nature of progress and the Indians' relationship to Americanness as defined in most of the Philadelphia Centennial Exposition's displays. While the organizers of the Philadelphia fair usually depicted Native peoples as the antitheses of civilization, Turner by contrast positioned Indians as a necessary stage in the development of civilization. In the speech, it was in fact pioneers' encounters with "savagery," including the process of going native, that constituted social progress. Without these encounters (in other words, without white Americans enacting the stages of progress), American civilization threatened to disintegrate. But even as Turner's thesis relied on Morgan's concept of social evolution, it modified Morgan's arguments. For Turner, it was the actions of individuals (in this case, individual pioneers) engaged in historical processes, rather than the development of the race as a whole, that enabled civilization to advance. Turner's thesis thus develops social evolutionary theory by emphasizing competitive individualism and also articulates the ideology of industrial capitalism. This emphasis foreshadows the forms going native would take during the twentieth century.

But Turner's delineation of stages culminating in the modern industrial moment was not the only part of his speech that envisioned America's history as linear and progressive. The often startling metaphors he employed to describe the frontier reinforce his vision of progress as the driving force in American history. He began the speech with a strikingly Darwinian description of the "evolution" of American institutions and "the *rise* of representative government; the *differentiation* of *simple* colonial governments into *complex* organs; the *progress* from primitive industrial society, without division of labor, up to manufacturing civilization" (32, emphases mine). By depicting American history as a rise from primitivism to civilization, Turner explicitly evoked an evolutionary notion of progress. Also remarkable are his organic metaphors, including references to the "differentiation" of the simple to "complex organs" of governments. American history, "this progress from savage conditions," he maintained, was a topic for the "evolutionist" (41). At times in the essay, inanimate objects and historical processes, in fact, seem to take on a life and an agency of their own. The frontier, in particular, not only provides the "vital forces that call these organs into life" (31), it actually seems to progress westward of its own volition: "As the frontier had leaped over the Alleghanies, so now it skipped the Great Plains and Rocky Mountains; and...the advance of the frontiersman beyond the Alleghanies had caused the rise of important questions of transportation and internal improvement....Railroads, fostered by land grants, sent an increasing tide of immigrants into the Far West" (36). As the frontier "leaped" and "skipped" in its relentless movement westward, giving rise in the process to advancing technology, it appeared to meet little resistance. "Gifts of free land," he absurdly claimed, readily "offer[ed] themselves" (59) to these westering frontiersmen. Meanwhile, the narrative both literally and metaphorically displaced Indians, both by removing them from the land and disappearing them from history.

These images of the frontier, which implied that westward expansion and conquest were both natural and inevitable, reframed American history. Responsibility for a massive and bloody conquest no longer lay with human agents. Rather, it was the "disintegrating forces of civilization [that] entered the wilderness," creating "fissures" in Indian societies. In Turner's vision, in fact, this conquest was at times not a conquest at all, a view that clearly shows anxieties about the violence characterizing white America's history. "Long before the pioneer farmer appeared on the scene, primitive Indian life had passed away" (40), he declared, apparently forgetting the Indian battles that he mentioned in passing in other places in his account. Native peoples, apparently, were casualties of progress rather than of violence. But Turner's narrative contains another significant contradiction. Indians, in his model, were not simply the antitheses of civilization, a presence that had to disappear to make way for white society. Rather, Indians actually "pioneered the way for civilization": "The buffalo trail became the Indian trail, and this became the trader's 'trace'; the trails widened into roads, and the roads into turnpikes, and these in turn were transformed into railroads" (40). Defining Indians as the necessary forerunners of civilization carried a number of critical implications. By figuring the conquest as an inevitable part of the march of progress, Turner located Indian life solely in the past, leaving no place for Native peoples in the contemporary world. This maneuver was, in a sense, appropriative; Natives became part of America's past, constituting "our Indian history." Their "disappearance"—the result of the abstract force of progress rather than human acts of conquest—thus negated the challenges Native America posed to European-American hegemony and rendered the colonists the legitimate heirs of Indian lifeways and land. As George R. Davis, director-general of the Chicago exposition, proclaimed during the dedication ceremonies, "what we are and what we possess as a nation, are not ours by purchase, nor by conquest, but by virtue of [our] heritage."[83] Remarkably, "The Significance of the Frontier in American History" thus maintained a vision of the nation's innocence in the Columbian era, a vision that upheld the quintessential American values of "freedom" and "democracy" for all its citizens. The speech also refigured the nature of American identity. By rendering Native Americans the predecessors of the pioneers, Turner bestowed the status of "true" Americans (the status, in other words, of the native) on contemporary white men, the heirs of these pioneers. His thesis thus symbolically resolved the challenges that the influx of immigrants posed to the political dominance of these men, settled questions surrounding the status of former slaves, and dealt with other upheavals of the postbellum era.

Turner's thesis was not the only event at the World's Columbian Exposition where fairgoers found such contradictory representations of Native peoples. Turner's vision of American history, which positioned Indians both as an enemy of civilization and as the predecessor of contemporary Anglo-Americans, also informed some of the displays. A vexed symbol throughout the fair, Indians appeared in the White City and on the Midway to different effects. While Indians embodied a controlled savagism on the Midway, in the White City some displays alluded to the Indian's essential Americanness. Most notably, a prominent statue generically dubbed "The Indian" adorned the area outside the centrally located Transportation Building. The statue was inspired by the Sioux leader Red Cloud. While at the Philadelphia Centennial Exposition the papier-mâché likeness of the tomahawk-wielding warrior had instilled fear, this figure affected fairgoers much differently. Along with its counterpart, a statue called "Cowboy," the warrior on horseback conveyed an image "thoroughly American" in theme and manner.[84] Buffalo Bill's Wild West show, which attached itself to the fair, also described Indians for the first time in 1893 not as violent savages but rather as "The Former Foe—Present Friend—the *American.*"[85] Moreover, the fair and the events associated with it both reflected and contributed to perceptions in the larger American culture. For instance, near the end of the century Indian images became associated with two other key markers of "Americanness": as baseball became the "national pastime," many teams selected Indian names;[86] and a nameless,

[83] Cameron, *History of the World's Columbian Exposition,* 222.
[84] *City of Palaces,* 141.
[85] See, for example, Richard Slotkin, *Gunfighter Nation: The Myth of the Frontier in Twentieth-Century America* (New York: Atheneum, 1992), 78–79.
[86] For a discussion of the rise of participatory sports in the late nineteenth century and its implications for changing conceptions of masculinity, see Michael S.

FIGURE 8. Statue of "The Indian" near the Transportation Building in the White City at the World's Columbian Exposition, reprinted from *The City of Palaces: Picturesque World's Fair* (Chicago: W. B. Conkey, 1894).

generic Indian joined the ranks of presidents as a figure on American currency.

This shift in the role Indians occupied in the cultural imagination depended both on the changing needs of the dominant society and on the historical situation of Native peoples. After the military conquest of Native America was complete, the federal government launched a series of policies designed to assimilate Natives into mainstream American society. The boarding school policy celebrated in the Chicago displays provided one tool for decimating Native cultures. The General Allotment Act (or Dawes Act) of 1887 supplied another. The act mandated that reservation land be divided into individual parcels, thus effectively shattering traditional social structures and attempting to transform Natives from communal occupants of collective property into individual farmers (in other words, into Western proprietors). Agents then further

Kimmel, "Baseball and the Reconstitution of American Masculinity, 1880–1920," in *Cooperstown Symposium on Baseball and the American Culture (1989)*, ed. Alvin L. Hall (Westport, Conn.: Meckler Publishing, 1991), 281–97.

reduced tribal landholdings by opening vast tracts of "surplus" reservation land to white settlement. Although neither the boarding school policy nor the General Allotment Act completely destroyed Native societies as they were intended to do, their aggressive attempts to assimilate Native peoples certainly diminished the ideological challenge Native America posed to the dominant culture by undermining the cohesiveness of communities and traditions. Since most observers believed that "authentic" Natives no longer existed as a historical presence, moreover, Indians came to be regarded as disembodied symbols (and, ironically, symbols of white American identity). The disparity between the Indian as symbol and as historical presence is underscored by the fact that even as Indians began to signify white Americanness, Native peoples as a whole had not yet attained the status of American citizens themselves.[87]

While Turner's narrative contributed to the oppression of Native America by rewriting U.S. history in a way that belied the violence of (indeed, even the fact of) conquest and by redefining citizenship in ways that privileged Anglo-American men, it also carried critical implications for the nation's future. If American identity, in his thesis, lay in the *process* of westward movement and the qualities that encounter, struggle, and conquest inculcated in the West's inhabitants, the only way to ensure the continuity of "Americanness" was continued movement westward.[88] Indeed, it seemed, this was the destiny of (white male) Americans. Since, by the time Turner delivered his speech, Anglo-American settlement had long since reached the westernmost part of North America, the only areas left for expansion were overseas. The frontier thesis speech thus prefigured the debates on U.S. imperialism that would come to the fore only a few years later.

The question of empire played a key role in other events at the World's Columbian Exposition. Indeed, since the middle of the century, international expositions had stimulated imperial aspirations in numerous ways, and this fair proved no exception. In 1893 Columbus himself, of course, was the quintessential imperial figure. A prominently displayed statue of the explorer, sword in hand, taking possession of the New World obviously resonated with America's late-nineteenth-century imperial ambitions.[89] The "ceaseless, resistless march of

[87] After 1887, Indian males who accepted the terms of the General Allotment Act were granted citizenship, but Native peoples as a group were not made American citizens until 1924. It is important to note that many Natives did not, and do not, desire American citizenship, considering it yet another effort to assimilate Native peoples and to undermine the political autonomy of Native communities.

[88] See Limerick, *Legacy of Conquest.*

[89] See *City of Palaces,* 57.

civilization, westward, ever westward," it seemed, was a fact both of the past and of the future as well.[90] While an impressive naval review in New York harbor celebrated the opening of the fair on the East Coast, extensive weapons displays throughout the Chicago fairgrounds also demonstrated America's capability for expansion. Clearly, Americans saw themselves in competition with other imperialist nations.[91] These messages were not lost on observers. "As Columbus discovered America," asserted one speaker at the congresses organized in conjunction with the fair, "so must Americans find a true religion for the whole world, and show the people of all nations a new religion in which all hearts may find rest."[92] The rising American nationalism that fed U.S. imperial ambitions became concrete in 1898 when the United States took possession of the Philippines, parts of the Caribbean, and Hawaii, adding these territories to a host of small Pacific islands acquired in the middle of the century. Several regions of Central and South America also became possessions or protectorates. By the early part of the twentieth century, America numbered among the world's major imperial powers.

From the beginning, though, American imperialism sparked intense controversy. Americans, in the opinion of many, had themselves overthrown one imperial regime; what right had they to create another? Moreover, imperialism ran counter to the values of freedom, equality, and democracy—the myth of American exceptionalism—that white Americans believed defined their nation. These objections were clearly somewhat disingenuous, however, or at best misguided. Mainstream Americans' visions of themselves denied that their nation was literally built on the conquest of Native peoples and the enslavement of Africans and Indians. Nor was the expansionism unprecedented. In the middle of the century, the United States had dramatically increased its territory in a war of conquest against Mexico. Conquest, then, was not an anomaly. Rather, it formed the white nation's foundations.

The disjunction between the facts of history and the way Americans saw themselves lent particular significance to the Indian images in Turner's speech and in the World's Columbian Exposition's exhibits. These images too embodied important contradictions. On one hand, Indians in Turner's narrative served as the savage objects of conquest, as counterpoints to the "true" American culture, a formulation that echoed the messages staged at the Philadelphia Centennial Exposition seventeen years earlier. In addition, the process of conquest so central to

[90] Cameron, *History of the World's Columbian Exposition*, 222.
[91] See Greenhalgh, *Ephemeral Vistas*, 76.
[92] Quoted in Badger, *Great American Fair*, 126.

Turner's narrative reflected on the present by providing a historical precedent for American imperialism abroad. By identifying his pioneers with Indians, however, Turner also obfuscated the facts of history as well as the dynamics of contemporary American expansionism. And by eliminating a substantial Native presence from his narrative and refiguring the colonists' relations to Indians, he concealed the violence of and motivations underlying colonial expansion, past and present. Progress, it seemed, dictated expansion as well as the disappearance of Native peoples, thus making it inevitable that Europeans would assume their places. His narrative, then, both justified European-American expansionism before and after 1893 while maintaining the illusion of colonial innocence.

Turner's speech, moreover, was not the only noteworthy event to link America's expansionist past and its future. A decade later, the implications of America's "ceaseless movement westward," including the relationship between Natives and America's other colonized peoples, became much more explicit. At the St. Louis Louisiana Purchase Exposition in 1904, the nation celebrated its new status as a major imperial power. The event, in one organizer's words, comprised "the largest and finest colonial exhibit ever made by any Government."[93] In St. Louis, the Philippines Reservation, temporary home to 1,200 Filipinos, recast the bloody U.S. campaign against the islands which had ended only two years earlier. From the earliest days of overseas expansion, the links between America's imperial wars abroad and the conquest of Native America had been clear. Not only did soldiers and officers who had been stationed on the frontier participate in expansionist campaigns overseas (these included General Nelson Miles, a famous Indian fighter and leader of one of the military parades at the World's Columbian Exposition), the nation's earlier conquest of "savagery" seemed to justify white Americans' struggles for dominance abroad. As one officer wrote: "If we decide to stay [in the Philippines], we must bury all qualms and scruples about Weylerian cruelty, the consent of the governed, etc., and stay. We exterminated the American Indians, and I guess most of us are proud of it, or, at least, believe the end justified the means; and we must have no scruples about exterminating this other race standing in the way of progress and enlightenment, if it is necessary."[94] Apparently, just as America controlled "its" Indians, so had it a right—perhaps even a duty—to govern other natives as well. Theodore Roosevelt, a strident advocate of expansionism and a champion of the conquest of Native America, gave this response to the protests of

[93] Cited in Rydell, *World of Fairs*, 20.
[94] Cited in Drinnon, *Facing West*, 314.

anti-imperialists: if white Americans were "morally bound to abandon the Philippines, we were also morally bound to abandon Arizona to the Apaches."[95] Given the nature of U.S. history, imperialism, it seemed, was natural and inevitable.

*

Despite the triumphant vision of white Americanness created in its displays and at its conferences, however, the World's Columbian Exposition offered only illusions. Moreover, these were extremely ephemeral illusions that shattered only months after the fair opened. While the White City, in particular, sought to create the appearance of a unified America and to suppress the fact that class, racial, and ethnic antagonisms plagued late-nineteenth-century society, it soon fell victim to these same conflicts. Shortly after the fair closed, vandals defaced the pristine structures comprising the fairgrounds with graffiti. As the national economic panic worsened, growing numbers of homeless people settled into the abandoned buildings. Finally, in July 1894, during the Pullman Strike, arsonists reduced the White City to rubble. Yet while the White City soon faded into memory, its ideals did not. In the following years, as the nation realized its imperial ambitions, many still clung to the visions of triumphant whiteness that the fair's organizers had offered to eager audiences. As time went on, images of Native peoples remained critical to the way white Americans imagined themselves. If anything, Natives became increasingly important. At Philadelphia in 1876, Natives had served primarily as a counterpoint to white American civilization, while at Chicago in 1893 they also figured importantly as part of European America's past. In the following years, the links the World's Columbian Exposition forged between America's colonial past and the nation's nascent imperialist campaigns grew more obvious. Around the turn of the century, this connection became increasingly explicit as mainstream Americans identified with Native peoples in ways that recast the dynamics of American expansion. Most notably, in the countless men's organizations that emerged during this period, men actually began performing "Indianness" as a means of creating new visions of the nation and bolstering its imperial ventures.

[95] Cited in Eric Breitbart, *A World on Display: Photographs from the St. Louis World's Fair, 1904* (Albuquerque: University of New Mexico Press, 1997), 43. Roosevelt, of course, was an outspoken champion both of the conquest of Native America and overseas imperialism. See especially Roosevelt, *The Winning of the West*, 4 vols. (New York: G. P. Putnam's Sons, 1889–96).

On countless evenings all across America in the late nineteenth century, groups of men gathered in locations known only to themselves to perform secret rituals. During this period, an increasingly widespread fascination with ritual—frequently inspired by particular perceptions of Indian life—found an outlet in the activities of many of these groups. The Improved Order of Red Men, one such fraternal organization founded in the 1860s, required the following initiation rite for its new members:

> Slowly the young man walks toward the sacred campfire. He hesitates, and glances back at the tribal elders, who urge him forward. Thunder rumbles in the distance and lightning pierces the darkness, revealing tribesmen seemingly asleep by a teepee. As the youth approaches, the tribesmen leap to their feet, bind him with a rope, and carry him into the bushes. There they give him a ritual loincloth and moccasins and smear dyes on his face. Several nights later he is brought back to the camp and bound to a log.... Suddenly, an elder, knife in hand, rushes toward the bound figure and subjects him to an ordeal. The tribesmen and elders then gather round, eager to embrace the newest member of their secret society.[96]

This "Indian" ritual, created and performed by a society of white men, actually took place in a lodge room, and used lamps, gaslights, and a gong for its effects. Despite the peculiarity of its rituals, the Improved Order of Red Men was by no means unique. Indian-inspired men's and boys' clubs began to spring up around the middle of the nineteenth century and proliferated in the decades that followed. One commentator, writing in 1897, even described the last third of the century as the "Golden Age of Fraternity." During that period, up to one-fifth of all adult males belonged to one or more of the seventy thousand fraternal lodges in the United States, many of which had Indian themes or sponsored Indian-type activities.[97] By the end of the century, American fraternal organizations collected a combined annual income of up to $2 billion (a figure matching the amount spent on federal defense during the same period),[98] a fact underscoring their popularity and cultural importance.

---

[96] Mark C. Carnes, *Secret Ritual and Manhood in Victorian America* (New Haven: Yale University Press, 1989), 1.

[97] Idem.

[98] Mark C. Carnes, "Iron John in the Gilded Age," *American Heritage*, September 1993, 42.

While this particular fascination with Native life reached a crescendo around the turn of the century, it was by no means new. As early as 1842, Lewis Henry Morgan had founded the Grand Order of the Iroquois, a secret society of men dedicated to collecting data on Iroquois life. In their gatherings, which were opportunities to "shed inhibitions and live, if only for an evening, the life of the 'noble savage,'" members would "dress in Indian regalia and utter the 'war whoop.'" The organization also provided Morgan with a chance to outline his theories on progress and the development of civilization. Unpublished papers of the society anticipated the argument Morgan made famous in the 1870s: that Anglo-American advancement made the Indians' disappearance inevitable. In the words of one member, the "superiority both mental and physical of the Anglo-Saxon race orders [the Indians'] continual existence as a separate and distinct people, impossible." Indeed, the fact that a group of Anglo-American men could play Indian in this fashion seemed to demonstrate that "a new order of things is to take place," that whites would literally take the places of Native Americans.[99] The groups that emerged later in the century were founded on similar understandings of the relations between European America and Native America. The Order of the White Crane, for example, "named for White Crane, the Hereditary Chief of the Ancient Tribe of Ojibway Indians," required that its members be either "royal descendants of Aztec or Toltec kings, or else of colonial settlers who had arrived prior to 1783. Potential members without royal Indian blood had to be of 'Aryan' stock."[100] The first, obviously impossible criterion for membership suggests that in the minds of most observers Indians now firmly occupied a place in white America's past, along with the nation's other progenitors (colonial settlers and pioneers). In addition, the preoccupation of these hobbyists with Indians resonates with the spectacles of racial otherness staged on the Midway: both reflected and enacted the colonial dominance of white America.

Turn-of-the-century fraternal organizations complemented the ideological work performed by late-nineteenth-century world's fairs in other ways. Largely an urban and middle-class phenomenon, these groups concerned themselves with creating a "cohesive, hard-working citizenry—patriotic, disciplined, and conventional in values."[101] In this respect, the work of these groups paralleled the efforts of other reform-

[99] James Bush and Clinton Rogers, cited in Robert E. Bieder, "The Grand Order of the Iroquois: Influences on Lewis Henry Morgan's Ethnology," *Ethnohistory* 27, 4 (1980): 349–50.
[100] Kammen, *Mystic Chords of Memory*, 249.
[101] David I. Macleod, *Building Character in the American Boy: The Boy Scouts, YMCA, and Their Forerunners, 1870–1920* (Madison: University of Wisconsin Press, 1983), 130.

ist movements during the Progressive Era. Their values, clearly, reflected those of the Protestant middle classes, and they functioned in some respects as a tool of social control over increasingly diverse and unruly populations. They also frequently answered nativist anxieties (note, for example, the Order of the White Crane's requirement that members be descended from "colonial settlers who had arrived prior to 1783"). By making race a criterion for membership, these groups provided Anglo-American men with a privileged social space sheltered from the threats posed by newer immigrants, nonwhites, and women.

In other respects, however, the fraternal organizations that emerged near the end of the century responded to a set of problems unique to that era, and in this way they differed from the Indian-inspired groups and other Native representations of earlier years. Progress—embodied in the linking of social Darwinism and technological achievements—now proved a source of ambivalence, an increasingly widespread response to changes in American life as the century drew to a close. If Morgan's thesis in the 1870s had manifested a firm faith in the value of material advancement and thus the inevitable social dominance of European Americans, many now found these convictions doubtful. While the 1876 and 1893 world's fairs had celebrated technology as a triumph, now the specter of degeneration haunted the nation's urban landscapes. A stark contrast to the pristine White City, the realities of modern industrial life often were poverty, crime-ridden ghettos, arduous working conditions, and widespread disease. The nature of modern life, then, no longer seemed clearly to demonstrate the superiority of the white race. To explain and justify their dominance, European Americans had to look elsewhere.

Consequently, while Morgan had found evidence of European-American superiority in technological advancement, turn-of-the-century observers often looked instead to individual achievements. In particular, many drew analogies between the national body and individual male bodies.[102] Physical regeneration increasingly seemed to hold the promise of national regeneration. In the 1890s, health became almost an obsession, one that could best be indulged in the outdoors, as far as possible from the decay of urban life. Physical health and the flight to nature thus represented a new model of virility. "Masculine hardiness and power," as one critic explains, "suddenly seemed an absolutely indispensable remedy for the artificiality and effeteness of late nineteenth-century

---

[102] See Mark Seltzer, *Bodies and Machines* (London: Routledge, 1992), esp. part 5, "The Love-Master," as well as Amy Kaplan, "Romancing the Empire: The Embodiment of American Masculinity in the Popular Historical Novel of the 1890s," *American Literary History* 3 (December 1990): 659–90.

life."[103] Physical strength became linked to racial superiority as well: "Around the turn of the century, Americans were obsessed with the connection between manhood and racial dominance.... [M]iddle-class Americans found [a multitude of ways] to explain male supremacy in terms of white racial dominance and, conversely, to explain white supremacy in terms of male power.... [A]s white middle-class men actively worked to reinforce male power, their race became a factor which was crucial to their gender."[104] The political implications were obvious. What physical strength accomplished for the individual, imperialism (as a form of physical and racial dominance) accomplished for the nation. "The acquisition of empire," in one historian's words, "reinforced the self-confidence, the economic power, and the cultural authority of a bourgeoisie which felt threatened by internal decay and lower-class discontent."[105]

Theodore Roosevelt is perhaps the best-known advocate of this "strenuous life." Time spent on western ranches engaged in hunting and other physically demanding activities had strengthened the young Roosevelt and cured his physical ailments. This regime, he believed, could similarly benefit other men. In "The Strenuous Life," an 1899 speech to a Chicago men's group, Roosevelt denounced a life of "ignoble" and "slothful" ease in favor of "the life of toil and effort, of labor and strife." "The over-civilized man," he continued, had "lost the great fighting, masterful virtues," which could be regained only through a life of physical hardship and strife.[106] As a means of providing these experiences, Roosevelt founded the Boone and Crockett Club (named, incidentally, for two notorious Indian killers) for men in 1888. Its sanctioned activities included the killing of large animals and the exploration of unknown lands, activities which, many believed, could combat the deleterious effects of civilized life on masculinity. Roosevelt's program for individual self-transformation, he hoped, would transform and toughen the nation as well. Whereas individual men could exert their "masterful virtues" through physical strength and dominance over women, their fellow men, and nature, the nation could achieve great-

[103] John Higham, "The Reorientation of American Culture in the 1890's," in *The Origins of Modern Consciousness,* ed. John Weiss (Detroit: Wayne State University Press, 1965), 29.

[104] Gail Bederman, *Manliness and Civilization: A Cultural History of Gender and Race in the United States, 1880–1917* (Chicago: University of Chicago Press, 1995), 4–5. I have suppressed a paragraph break.

[105] T. J. Jackson Lears, *No Place of Grace: Antimodernism and the Transformation of American Culture, 1880–1920* (Chicago: University of Chicago Press, 1981), 117.

[106] Theodore Roosevelt, "The Strenuous Life," in *The Roosevelt Book: Selections from the Writings of Theodore Roosevelt* (New York: Charles Scribner's Sons, 1914), 26–27.

ness through imperial conquest, the exercise of "dominance over the world." Roosevelt believed that individuals engaged in manly occupations like soldiering and manual labor would build a masterful nation. For the economically privileged unlikely to engage in "a life of toil" or to enlist as soldiers in the imperial wars, he advocated "the field of exploration and adventure" as an appropriately strenuous (and imperialist) occupation.[107]

Roosevelt also enthusiastically supported many turn-of-the-century fraternal organizations. Their concerns echoed his own, as they too attempted to inculcate strength and military ideals in American men. Somewhat ironically, Indians frequently provided a model for accomplishing these goals. Although these fraternal organizations served men of all ages, the most mainstream and influential Indian-inspired clubs were those that emerged in the context of turn-of-the-century youth movements in the United States, most notably the Boy Scouts. Significantly, the Boy Scouts was born in Britain during a moment of imperial crisis. Lieutenant-General (later Lord) Robert Baden-Powell, founder of the organization, drew inspiration for the movement from his experiences during the Boer War. When serving as an officer in the British Army, Baden-Powell had found the quality of recruits and the nature of their training inadequate for combat situations. British men, he feared, had become too "soft" to defend their nation or exercise their military muscle abroad. Consequently, he devised a system designed to remedy these failures. He completed his "Aids to Scouting" in 1899 during the siege of Mafikeng. Returning to England in 1903, he adapted his program to meet the needs of young boys. He published the first edition of the Boy Scout handbook, *Scouting for Boys,* in 1908, launching what would quickly become an international movement.

As the group's name suggests, militarism took center stage in the Boy Scouts. Military clothing inspired the scout uniform, and boys learned martial as well as survival skills in their training. Baden-Powell, in fact, used "A Handbook for Instruction in Good Citizenship" as the subtitle for *Scouting for Boys.* Nationalist and imperialist themes dominate the text. Articulating contemporary fears about the decline of civilization, Baden-Powell evoked the specter of the fall of the Roman Empire as a warning about the fate of his own nation: "People say that we have no patriotism nowadays, and that therefore our Empire will fall to pieces like the great Roman Empire did, because its citizens became selfish and lazy.... [But] I am sure that if you boys will keep the good of your country in your eyes *above everything else* she will go all right." In a subsequent chapter devoted entirely to the subject of empire, he explicitly defined manliness as

[107] Ibid., 22–23.

a means of fortifying national and imperial strength: "Remember that the Roman Empire...fell at last, chiefly because the young Romans gave up manliness."[108] Baden-Powell's concerns about the deterioration of individual, nation, and empire intertwined. For him, individuals formed the fabric of society; they were the "bricks in the wall" of the nation, and their strength or weakness in turn dictated the state of national health. He envisioned the Boy Scout movement as a means of combating national problems not through social programs but instead by training individual boys in manliness. Manliness, in this case, meant more than the acquisition of military skills. Health also became critically important. Only the physically fit had the vigor to repel the nation's enemies.[109] Boys trained in this way, Baden-Powell believed, would ensure domestic order and maintain imperial control abroad. As the Boy Scout handbook instructed its young readers, "A scout practises self-control, for he knows that men who master problems in the world must first master themselves."[110] Self-mastery, in other words, facilitated world-mastery.[111]

Americans became quick converts to Scouting. The movement spread to the United States in 1910, only two years after it was launched in Britain. Soon, it became the country's largest youth organization. Over the next thirty years, sales of Baden-Powell's *Scouting for Boys* in the United States ranked second only to sales of one other book, the Bible.[112] The appeal to Americans was obvious, even overdetermined. American concerns about nation and empire paralleled those of England, and Baden-Powell had taken his primary influences from the pages of American history books. Two rival groups, the Woodcraft Indians and the Sons of Daniel Boone, each claimed to have inspired the Boy Scouts. The Woodcraft Indians, founded by Ernest Thompson Seton, aimed "to discover, preserve, develop, and diffuse the culture of the Redman" through recreational activities for young boys.[113] Wood-

[108] Sir Robert Baden-Powell, *Scouting for Boys* (London: C. Arthur Pearson, 1924), 28–9, 281.
[109] Baden-Powell thus articulated changing popular conceptions of gender ideals that associated manliness with virility. During this era of women's suffrage, this ideal of manliness provided an arena in which women could not compete. See Bederman, *Manliness and Civilization,* 14.
[110] *Boy Scouts of America: The Official Handbook for Boys,* 15th ed. (Garden City, N.Y.: Doubleday, Page, 1916), xi.
[111] See Allen Warren, "Citizens of the Empire: Baden-Powell, Scouts and Guides and an Imperial Ideal, 1900–40," in *Imperialism and Popular Culture,* ed. John M. MacKenzie (Manchester: Manchester University Press, 1986), 232–56.
[112] Roderick Nash, *Wilderness and the American Mind* (New Haven: Yale University Press, 1982), 148.
[113] Ernest Thompson Seton, from the 1906 edition of *The Birch Bark Role,* quoted in Michael Rosenthal, *The Character Factory: Baden-Powell and the Origins of the Boy Scout Movement* (New York: Pantheon Books, 1984), 27.

crafters formed "tribes," camped in tipis, donned feather headdresses, "scalped" each other (one's "scalp," a tuft of horse hair, could be lost in competitive games), counted coup, and smoked peace pipes. The Sons of Daniel Boone, by contrast, drew inspiration from the myth of the pioneer. Its founder, Daniel Carter Beard, relied more heavily on techniques for outdoor survival in his plans for young boys. Camping, fishing, and similar activities formed the basis of the group's activities.

In the American context, it is symptomatic that these two movements came together in the Boy Scouts. In the United States, as in Britain, Scouting quickly became "a new element in a symbolic system whose concern [was] the creation and preservation of an ideal national history."[114] Indeed, in the United States as well as in Britain, the movement quickly attained the status of a national symbol, a position supported by its patriotic ideals. By the turn of the century, due in part to the world's fairs of recent decades, both pioneers and Indians had become central figures of American nationalism. In the words of one movement leader, the "work and attributes of backwoodsmen, explorers, and frontiersmen" would make boys "true American citizens, physically fit and of high character." Blessings from political leaders augmented the Boy Scouts' status in the United States and secured its nationalist associations. President Herbert Hoover, for example, celebrated the movement for "reviving the lore of the frontier," while Scout enthusiast Theodore Roosevelt agreed to become an honorary vice president.[115] On more than one occasion the Boy Scouts of America received the blessings of political leaders. The organization won a Congressional Charter in 1916, which, among other provisions, exempted it from legislation prohibiting civilians from wearing military-type uniforms.[116]

Scouting's choice of pioneers and Indians as role models, however, generated important contradictions as well. Clearly, in the Boy Scout movement, the effort to reinscribe white racial dominance underpinned its agenda of class and national regeneration as well as imperial expansion. In a sense, then, the choice of Indian role models seems curious. If Scouting aimed to create a coherent citizenry based on middle-class Protestant values and white dominance, in what ways could Indians serve as models? Moreover, how could the now-conquered Natives, as very recent victims of colonial domination, support the movement's imperialist leanings? Articulating these

[114] Robert H. MacDonald, *Sons of the Empire: The Frontier and the Boy Scout Movement, 1890–1918* (Toronto: University of Toronto Press, 1993), 178.
[115] William D. Murray, *The History of the Boy Scouts of America* (New York: Boy Scouts of America, 1937) 419–20.
[116] See Macleod, *Building Character in the American Boy,* 156–57.

contradictions, Indians occupied conflicting roles in Boy Scout lore. If Boy Scouts were to perform the work of army scouts, pioneers, and explorers,[117] this work entailed fighting "savages." In the historical mythology of the movement, "savages" clearly denoted Indians. Indeed, "Indian fighters" such as Kit Carson, Buffalo Bill, and Daniel Boone numbered among the movement's official heroes, and it was the very act of fighting Indians that made them manly men.[118] It was, in fact, this experience that Scouting intended to replicate and to replace. In the words of one of the movement's popularizers, every family "should possess *Scouting* in default of the chance of going on the warpath with a Red Indian."[119] The Scouts' celebration of those who "have cleared the wilderness and planted wheat where forests once grew, who have driven back the savage, and have fostered civilization in the uncultivated places of the earth" also clearly resonated with more contemporary imperial concerns (much as Turner's frontier thesis speech and the theme of the World's Columbian Exposition had).[120] Evoking and reenacting white America's previous racial conquests gave contemporary imperial endeavors a history and seemed to assure their success.

In Boy Scout lore, however, Indians stood for much more than the conquered objects of colonial and imperial ventures. Boy Scouts not only (symbolically) conquered Indians but emulated them as well. Like their predecessors, the Woodcraft Indians, Boy Scouts frequently enjoyed camping out in tipis, donning feather headdresses, practicing archery, and engaging in Indian-inspired games. At times, Indians even served as official figures in the movement. Several Boy Scout Association publications, for example, displayed Indian designs on their covers. One illustration, sketched by Baden-Powell himself and entitled "Genesis of Scouting," showed a warrior hunting buffalo. Another depicted a "brave...kneeling protectively behind a Boy Scout on a hillside" as together they looked "into a rosy future."[121] If men and boys regenerated themselves by fighting Indians, apparently they thrived by playing Indian as well.

---

[117] *Boy Scouts Official Handbook,* 4–5.

[118] See, for example, Percy Keese Fitzhugh, *The Boys' Book of Scouts* (New York: Thomas Y. Crowell, 1917).

[119] Charlotte Mason, cited in MacDonald, *Sons of the Empire,* 23.

[120] *Boy Scouts Official Handbook,* 334.

[121] See MacDonald, *Sons of the Empire,* 143. MacDonald explains that, predictably, the Indian proved a controversial figure in the Boy Scout movement. Baden-Powell was particularly ambivalent about the use of Indians as models for young boys, in part because of the conflicting images of Natives that remained prevalent in popular culture.

FIGURE 9. Stereoscope titled "playing Indian." Part of the caption reads: "Long ago before there were any white people or cities here, our country was the home of Indians. The Indians lived outdoors. That is why they were so strong. They had to go hunting and fishing for their meat.... The 'pretend' Indians in this picture are learning to be strong." Published by the Keystone View Company (n.d.).

How can we account for this puzzling contradiction? Its partial source was the increasingly widespread ambivalence about social progress, which accounted in some measure for the popularity of the Boy Scouts and other fraternal organizations of the period. Seton, for example, articulated common concerns about modern society when he asserted that Americans had grown "degenerate." "We know money grubbing, machine politics, degrading sports, cigarettes...false ideals, moral laxity and lessening church power, in a word '*City rot*' has worked evil in the nation."[122] Firmly established as an earlier (and, it now appeared, more vital) stage of social development, Indians seemed to provide a way of rejuvenating an increasingly degenerate white society. Now that individual men enabled social development through

[122] Cited in Macleod, *Building Character in the American Boy,* 32.

physical strength and virility, playing Indian accomplished important cultural work. By emulating Natives, boys reenacted the stages of prog- ress outlined earlier in the century by Morgan and echoed by Turner, thus ironically affirming racialized conceptions of social development and their own superiority.

In the 1890s the American psychologist G. Stanley Hall formalized these notions of the relationship between the individual and social prog- ress in his revolutionary and widely celebrated theories on childhood development, most notably the "recapitulation theory." According to Hall, children repeat the epochs of human history in the process of their development. Following Morgan's idea that culture proceeds through a fixed series of stages before culminating in (white, middle-class, West- ern) civilization, Hall contended that children enact savage patterns of behavior in the successful maturation process. Just as "most savages in most respects are children," he asserted, so too are children like sav- ages: "The child is in the primitive age. The instinct of the savage sur- vives in him." [123] Boys' attraction to the habits of feral men such as fron- tiersmen and savages, therefore, was natural and should be encouraged.

This regression into savagery, however, was not an end in itself but instead a means of playing out and finally overcoming boys' savage in- stincts as they grew into manhood, a process that paralleled and af- firmed white society's rise to civilization. Ultimately, Hall's concern was with the maintenance of this civilization, which weak men could only fail to sustain. He believed that the failure of adolescents to live out their instincts would result in the "retrogression, degeneracy, or fall" both of the individual and, ultimately, of civilized society. [124] In one critic's words, "By taking advantage of little boys' natural reliving of their ancestors' primitive evolutionary history, educators could 'inoculate' them against the weakness of excessive civilization....By shoring up the collective masculine power of the civilized races, Hall believed he could not only save civilization from degenerating; he could help move civilization to- ward a millennial perfection." [125] Key to the notion that a dose of sava- gism could regenerate civilization was Hall's idea that the "lower races" were "almost everywhere far healthier as well as more recuperative

[123] G. Stanley Hall, quoted in Bederman, *Manliness and Civilization*, 111, 78.
[124] Hall, quoted in Macleod, *Building Character in the American Boy*, 99. For a dis- cussion of Hall's theories and their relationship to youth movements, see especially Macleod, "Adolescence and Gang-Age Boyhood: An Ideology for Character Build- ing," in ibid., chap. 6; also Bederman, "'Teaching Our Sons to Do What We Have Been Teaching the Savages to Avoid': G. Stanley Hall, Racial Recapitulation, and the Neurasthenia Paradox," in *Manliness and Civilization*, chap. 3; and MacDonald, *Sons of the Empire*, 132–35.
[125] Bederman, *Manliness and Civilization*, 94.

from injuries or operations than civilized man." Thus, he contended, the "best of the lower races represent that most precious thing in the world,—stocks and breeds of men of a new type, full of new promise and potency for our race."[126] Such ideas fit squarely with the gendered nature of popular Plains Indian images of the period. Inspired by the memory of the recently conquered Plains warrior, these representations showed Indians as both hardy (a result of the "natural life") and warlike. (These images also indicate the change in popular representations since the Philadelphia Centennial Exposition in 1876, where the displays assured viewers of the superior military power of white America. Because the Natives no longer posed a significant military threat, they could now serve as a military ideal for the dominant culture.) In the words of one historian: "It was an imperial habit of mind to divide non-Europeans into martial and non-martial races: the martial races kept their virtues sharp by war, the non-martial races were soft and 'over-civilized.'"[127] Playing savage, then, by providing the strength and skills civilized boys needed to overcome "real" savages on the imperial frontier, was in fact intrinsic to Western progress.[128] In this way, Hall's theories completed the refiguring of Morgan begun by Turner. For Hall, it was not racial progress or historical processes that rendered white society dominant. Rather, by enacting the stages of progress, individuals established the superiority of both their race and their nation.

The contradiction between the progressivism of the Boy Scouts and its nostalgic tendencies, then, is only apparent. Like its imperialist inclinations, the movement's vision of intrepid pioneers and savage warriors inhabiting a world where manliness remained unchallenged can be explained by the desire for social dominance. Now established as the site of the white nation's origin story, as the place where civilization initially overcame savagery, the frontier provided a framework for articulating other forms of power relations: "People seemed to thrive upon the backward glance, not so much for purposes of escapism, though that inclination certainly existed, but because the creative consequences of nostalgia helped them to legitimize new political orders, rationalize the adjustment and perpetuation of old social hierarchies, and construct acceptable new systems of thought and values."[129]

[126] Hall, "Civilization and Savagery," in *Proceedings of the Massachusetts Historical Society*, 2d ser. (Boston: Massachusetts Historical Society, 1903), 10–11.
[127] MacDonald, *Sons of the Empire*, 135.
[128] This was, in fact, a familiar paradigm in colonial narratives. Richard Slotkin, for example, describes the importance of "the man who knows Indians" and even verges on "savagery" himself in the process of conquest. See *Fatal Environment* and *Gunfighter Nation*.
[129] Kammen, *Mystic Chords of Memory*, 295.

Around the turn of the century, the "new political order" in question was overseas imperialism. Historical tales of pioneers and Indians provided a precedent for domination and conquest in the present. Moreover, by showing Indians' superior military prowess, these narratives reversed the terms of history in a way that concealed white aggression and justified these newer campaigns against other "savages." At the same time, by focusing on and locating authentic Native life in the past and by redefining Indianness in terms useful to the dominant culture, these stories both enacted and concealed a contemporary colonial relationship with Native America.

The work of these narratives ultimately proved more complex than this, however. A means of celebrating dominance, they also betrayed some degree of ambivalence about the fact of conquest. Renato Rosaldo explains:

> Curiously enough, agents of colonialism—officials, constabulary officers, missionaries, and other figures...—often display nostalgia for the colonized culture as it was "traditionally" (that is, when they first encountered it). The peculiarity of their yearning, of course, is that agents of colonialism long for the very forms of life they intentionally altered or destroyed.... Imperialist nostalgia revolves around a paradox: A person kills somebody, and then mourns the victim. In more attenuated form, someone deliberately alters a form of life, and then regrets that things have not remained as they were prior to the intervention.[130]

Thus, imperialist nostalgia also acts as a form of historical "mystification," concealing both the facts of conquest and the complicity of colonial culture (past and present) in "often brutal domination."[131] Similarly, by "going native," Boy Scouts professed Indian sympathies while actually performing colonial relationships. Just as Schultz in *My Life as an Indian,* as I observed at the beginning of this chapter, simultaneously performed and denied colonial dominance in the process of going native, so too did the Boy Scouts enact and obfuscate the dynamics of American colonialism and imperialism. In both cases, "playing Indian," identifying with the victims rather than with the conquerors, provided a means of denying responsibility for brutal domination.[132]

---

[130] Renato Rosaldo, "Imperialist Nostalgia," in *Culture and Truth: The Remaking of Social Analysis* (Boston: Beacon Press, 1989), 69–70. I have suppressed a paragraph break.

[131] Ibid., 70.

[132] For a discussion of this denial in the context of American historiography as well as contemporary American studies, see Kaplan, "'Left Alone with America,'" 3–21.

Indeed, Boy Scout publications explicitly contributed to the illusion of American innocence. Early handbooks published by the Boy Scouts of American included a final chapter on "Patriotism and Citizenship" focusing on the territorial acquisitions of the United States since the American Revolution. Predictably, though, the handbooks remained conspicuously silent about the conquest of Native America. "We have come into possession of our territory," the chapter begins, "through treaty, purchase, and annexation."[133] The remainder of the section offers a similarly obfuscating account of U.S. expansion. The Mexican-American War, for example, it describes as the rescue of Texans from a "barbaric" and "despotic" Mexican government—an action, moreover, that was "welcomed and encouraged by the Mexicans" themselves.[134] Similarly, it explains the origins of the Spanish-American war of 1898 in the following terms: "The war with Spain was not of this country's seeking. The island of Cuba, whose distress had aroused the sympathy of the whole world, was our near neighbor, and to sit idly by and witness the inhuman treatment practiced by the Spanish soldiery upon the helpless islanders would hardly be a part creditable to any people. It was not our intention at first to do other than to relieve the suffering and distress of Cuba." Although the outcome of this war was not only "the freedom of Cuba" but the U.S. acquisition of Puerto Rico, Guam, and the Philippines, the handbook assured its young readers that "there is no country in the world less warlike than ours, and no country in the world that more potently argues for universal peace."[135] Imperial acquisition, it appeared, thus numbered among the "good deeds" that comprised a scout's duty.

This ambivalence about the nation's origins, manifested in events which simultaneously celebrate and deny white America's history of conquest, characterizes Native images in the twentieth century as well. Going native is thus more complicated than it seems, and its cultural work extends beyond European America's relation to Native America. As was the case in fin-de-siècle America, throughout the twentieth century going native has also served to articulate other forms of racial and gender domination in the broader society. As we shall see, a vast range of conflicts have come to bear symbolically on the Indian, the original victim of European-American conquest.

*

[133] *Boy Scouts Official Handbook*, 423.
[134] Ibid., 432–33.
[135] Ibid., 438–39.

Like the closing of the Western frontier, the end of World War I marked a watershed in American history. For the Boy Scouts as well as for the rest of the Western world, the war proved catastrophic. Countless Scoutmasters and former Boy Scouts met their fates in the trenches in what would later be dubbed the "slaughterhouse of Europe." As a result, as the 1910s drew to a close, the Boy Scouts became decidedly less militaristic.[136] Imperialism, too, grew increasingly suspect, as did social progress manifested in modern industrial capitalism. Americans' enthusiasm for going native, however, only heightened in the postwar years, although it took different (but related) forms. After the war, American men found a new and gentler object of fascination and emulation, one who inhabited another—perhaps the last—colonial frontier and seemed to embody an alternative to (rather than an earlier stage of) the modern industrial world. This time, in an effort to reinvent themselves yet again, many American men turned to the Eskimos.

[136] See Macleod, *Building Character in the American Boy,* 139.

CHAPTER TWO

Nanook and His Contemporaries: Traveling with the Eskimos, 1897–1941

IN THE FALL OF 1897, the ship *Hope* docked in a New York City harbor; its arrival changed forever the lives of its passengers and captivated an entire nation. Onboard were six Polar Eskimos—one woman (Atangana), three men (Qisuk, Nuktaq, and Uisaakassak), and two children (Minik and Aviaq)—brought by the arctic explorer Robert Peary at the behest of anthropologist Franz Boas and other officials of the American Museum of Natural History.[1] Encouraged by the stunning popularity of the live human exhibits at the World's Columbian Exposition in Chicago four years earlier and undeterred by the high mortality rate of the people exhibited for fairgoers' amusement, Boas had asked the explorer to collect a live "specimen" for scientific study on his next journey north. But not even Boas could have foreseen the public sensation these Eskimos caused. On a single day following the *Hope*'s arrival, twenty thousand people visited the ship, anxious to glimpse the Natives who, despite the stifling heat, were dressed in the elaborate furs expected by curiosity seekers. Nor did New Yorkers' attention soon wane. Housed in the basement of the museum, the Eskimos drew throngs of eager visitors who crowded around a ceiling grate installed above their living quarters.

---

[1] I should like to note at the outset the reasons for my use of the term "Eskimo," as opposed to "Inuit," throughout most of this chapter. In 1977, participants in the Inuit Circumpolar Conference officially rejected "Eskimo" and adopted the Native term "Inuit" as the preferred designation for all Eskimo peoples. This decision was both a recognition of the politics of naming and part of a political platform aimed at self-determination. "Eskimo," it is widely believed, carries pejorative connotations, and in any case is a designation initially used by hostile outsiders. In spite of this, I have opted to use "Eskimo" in this essay for two reasons. First, when not employing the more specific designations of "Yup'ik" or "Inupiat," Native Alaskans continue to use "Eskimo" to identify themselves. In addition, this chapter is concerned with images; the term "Eskimo," which has been used for centuries, evokes images and carries associations conventionally (though often erroneously) associated with Eskimo peoples which "Inuit" does not. For a brief etymology of "Eskimo," see David Damas, introduction to *The Arctic*, ed. Damas, vol. 5 of *Handbook of North American Indians*, ed. William E. Sturtevant (Washington: Smithsonian Institution Press, 1984), 1–7.

Both the exhibition and the scientists' investigations were ill-fated, however. Like virtually all Natives displayed for viewing throughout the centuries of conquest, these quickly fell sick. Yet even this turn of events proved a source of entertainment, as one journalist reported: "One of the most amusing forms of entertainment consisted in an illustration of the manner in which the Eskimos attempt to conjure away illness. This in their opinion can only be accomplished by rubbing the sides of the body and singing a weird sort of a lullaby that with all its peculiarities is not absolutely discordant."[2] Within months, four of the Eskimos died of pneumonia, and even in death they endured prying Western eyes. The anthropologist Alfred Kroeber painstakingly documented the intimate displays of grief and the death rituals of the survivors as, one by one, their companions and family members perished.[3] Despite the relatives' vociferous protests, the museum then removed the brains of the dead for study and retained their bones for display. Eventually, embarrassed by the fate of the four Eskimos, museum officials returned the sole surviving adult, Uisaakassak, to Greenland in July 1898. Nevertheless, they opted to keep the eight-year-old Minik, placing him in the care of an Anglo-American family as an experiment in cultural assimilation. Since he was no longer quaint or "primitive," the public soon lost interest in his plight. Not until many years later did another side to this story emerge when the adult Minik expressed sharp criticism of Peary, Boas, and the museum itself. His accounts of these events challenge the

[2] Quoted in Kenn Harper, *Give Me My Father's Body: The Life of Minik, the New York Eskimo* (Iqaluit, N.W.T., Canada: Blacklead Books, 1986), 37. Harper has written a detailed and moving account of these events focusing on the tragic life of Minik, the only child survivor. Reconstructed from press reports and oral histories, Harper's is the only book-length account of Minik's story. As this book goes to press, there is a resurgence of interest in Minik's story. In spring 2000, Steerforth Press reissued Harper's account, which immediately outsold the publisher's estimates and went into its second printing. Shortly thereafter, actor Kevin Spacey optioned the film rights, promising to reintroduce the life of Minik and the history of Arctic exploration into American popular culture.

[3] Like Boas, Alfred Kroeber was apparently inured to the tragic results of these experiments in studying and displaying live humans. Kroeber is widely known for his later involvement with Ishi, the last surviving member of the Yahi tribe. Alone and starving, Ishi wandered into a slaughterhouse in a small California town in 1911. The police soon placed him in the care of University of California anthropologists, a team eventually headed by Kroeber. Ishi lived out the remainder of his days as a resident of the Phoebe Apperson Hearst Museum on the Berkeley campus where he frequently served as a live exhibit. He, too, quickly succumbed to disease. The best-known (but utterly uncritical) account of these events has been written by Theodora Kroeber, wife of the anthropologist. See *Ishi in Two Worlds: A Biography of the Last Wild Indian in North America* (Berkeley: University of California Press, 1961).

FIGURE 10. Minik, posed in Eskimo clothing shortly after his arrival in New York, reprinted from Kenn Harper, *Give Me My Father's Body: The Life of Minik, the New York Eskimo* (Iqaluit, N.W.T., Canada: Blacklead Books, 1986).

conventional colonial perspectives on such encounters. I shall return to his saga, nearly lost to history, at the end of this chapter.

Despite (or perhaps in part because of) their tragic fates, the arrival of these Polar Eskimos rekindled America's enduring fascination with arctic Natives, an interest that soon manifested itself in both high and low culture and grew in intensity through the 1930s. Peary's 1897 journey north was one of several voyages he made to the Arctic during that and the following decade in his quest to be the first white man to reach the North Pole. He frequently returned with objects that further ignited public interest and funded his future ventures: Eskimo corpses and bones, artifacts, animal specimens, and, on this particular voyage, the famed Cape York meteorite. In the first two decades of the twentieth century, the Polar controversy captivated the nation. Both Peary and his archrival, Frederick Cook, claimed the distinction of "capturing" the Pole, and the ensuing debate, which was often heated, drew in such luminaries as Theodore Roosevelt, the National Geographic Society, the New York Explorer's Club, and a host of other political and scientific figures. World's fair exhibits, frequent throughout these boastful years of Western expansion, also underscored the importance of the Arctic by staging live exhibits. The 1904 St. Louis Louisiana Purchase Exposition and Seattle's 1909 Alaska-Pacific-Yukon Exposition featured Eskimo villages which took the form of *faux* ice structures inhabited by fur-clad Natives and their sled dogs. By the time Robert Flaherty released his widely acclaimed and now classic documentary *Nanook of the North* in 1922, the American public was hooked on tales of Eskimos and arctic life. *Nanook* became a watershed, after which no imagining of the Far North could free itself from the panoply of stereotypes born in the late nineteenth and early twentieth centuries and brought to fruition in Flaherty's work. The film also spawned what one prominent observer has labeled "Nanookmania," a marketing craze that produced dozens of trademarks including "Eskimo Pie" ice cream.[4] A few years later, two major Hollywood studios capitalized on the Eskimos' popularity, producing two feature films with arctic themes: Universal's *Igloo* (1932) and MGM's *Eskimo* (1934). The interwar years also marked the high point of anthropological research on the Arctic.[5] Amateurs had their day as well. Countless travel accounts document the voyages of both explorers and ordinary citizens (virtually always male) who journeyed north seeking the experiences promised by these scientific and popular narratives.

[4] See Asen Balikci, "Anthropology, Film and the Arctic Peoples," *Anthropology Today* 5, 2 (1989): 7.
[5] For key sources, see Damas, introduction to *The Arctic*; and Henry B. Collins, "History of Research Before 1945," in *The Arctic*, ed. Damas, 1–16.

Yet over the course of these years, from the 1897 visit of Peary's Eskimos to New York to the 1922 release of *Nanook of the North,* American images of the Arctic, including those depicting the nature of Western presence there, changed in several key ways. These changes articulated a broader ambivalence about colonialism which stemmed in part from the flight from the Victorian ethos that T.J. Jackson Lears has labeled "antimodernism."[6] For many moderns, non-Westerners and the worlds they seemed to inhabit increasingly provided an escape from—and sometimes even a means of regenerating—a fallen, "overcivilized" Western world (a world that had, in one historian's words, "committed suicide" in the trenches of the Western Front). Although this ambivalence found roots in the late nineteenth century, it increased as the twentieth century wore on. The shock of World War I, of course, augmented the modernist suspicion of progress (a primary rationale for colonial domination) and technology. Reflecting the emergence of Boasian cultural relativism, many observers saw in Native peoples an alternative ethos to that of the industrial capitalist world. Yet this interest manifested a set of key contradictions. Although it was motivated by an ostensible rejection of Western paradigms, the attraction to native culture also embodied colonialist impulses. By 1914, European nations controlled over 85 percent of the territories in the world, and seekers after the pleasures of "otherness" relied on Western political dominance to indulge their fascinations. Through the exertion of colonial power, the West thus made the rest of the world available, in various ways, to its own citizens. Western travelers journeyed to distant lands, collectors amassed exotic objects, prominent artists and writers sought inspiration in the "primitive," scientists researched these new subjects, explorers mapped uncharted territories, and corporations and entrepreneurs transformed colonial resources into vast profits. More contradictions emerged as these European moderns' quest for economic and cultural regeneration sometimes took the form of a renewed enthusiasm for the martial ideal. Thus, antimodernist impulses worked at cross-purposes by simultaneously challenging and rearticulating values and practices integral to the colonial project.

The Arctic, where Western colonialism began in earnest only after World War I, provided an important site on which these contradictory impulses came to bear. As manifestations of burgeoning Western expansion in the region, the famed polar expeditions were only the tip of the proverbial iceberg. Cartographers journeyed north to map the unknown regions, geologists followed in search of minerals and other

[6] See T.J. Jackson Lears, *No Place of Grace: Antimodernism and the Transformation of American Culture, 1880–1920* (Chicago: University of Chicago Press, 1981).

resources, hordes of prospectors descended upon Alaska in the 1890s gold rush, while a lucrative fur trade took off in Alaska and the Canadian Arctic. A few decades later, oil was discovered on Alaska's North Slope. The Arctic had become the new and perhaps the last frontier. These new colonial expeditions simultaneously fulfilled popular desires and, as the twentieth century progressed, tested the Western conscience. Thus, unabashedly boastful displays of colonial might, such as the Eskimo displays in the American Museum of Natural History, were no longer possible after World War I. Torn between the need to articulate colonial power (usually read as racial superiority) and the desire to claim Western innocence, colonial representations of the Arctic grew increasingly fraught in the postwar years.

The works of Peary, Flaherty, and other explorers, as well as critics' responses to them, show this transition and complicate conventional accounts of colonial discourse. Around the turn of the century, representations of the region and its inhabitants (including, most notably, Peary's depictions) were starkly colonial, relying heavily and unselfconsciously on the conventional tropes of discovery, conquest, and appropriation as well as the complementary paradigms of natural history. Later, ambivalence about arctic colonialism showed itself in the changing forms these representations took. While the stunning number of images and artifacts circulating in American society during this period attested to the reality of the conquest, the stories these representations told often both concealed the fact of colonialism and implicitly attempted to naturalize it. Narratives such as Flaherty's *Nanook of the North* (1922) and, later, Gontran de Poncins's *Kabloona* (1941) thus not only provided an exoticized vision of Native life for Western consumption but also documented arctic colonialism in ways that transformed colonial relationships (textually, at least) by masking their motivations and hiding their violence.

As was the case in earlier years, gender frequently became the site where colonial ambivalence was expressed. Around the turn of the century, the zenith of Western expansionism, changing notions of masculinity and rationales for imperialism linked patriarchy and colonial/imperial power.[7] During this period, in Amy Kaplan's words, "imperial expansion overseas offered a new frontier, where the essential Ameri-

---

[7] Several critics have explored the extent to which colonial/imperial history articulates and supports masculinist domination. See, for example, Kaplan, "Romancing the Empire"; Mary Louise Pratt, *Imperial Eyes: Travel Writing and Acculturation* (New York: Routledge, 1992); and Ella Shohat, "Gender and Culture of Empire: Toward a Feminist Ethnography of the Cinema," *Quarterly Review of Film and Video* 13, 1–3 (1991): 45–84. Lisa Bloom's *Gender on Ice: American Ideologies of Polar Expeditions* (Minneapolis: University of Minnesota Press, 1993) explores these issues in the arctic context.

can man could be reconstituted," in good measure through the conquest of Natives.[8] (The Boy Scouts and other fraternal organizations, as
we have seen, drew inspiration from these notions.) After World War I,
a period less frequently analyzed by critics, these relationships grew
more complex as non-Western men—in this case, Eskimos—seemed at
once to embody Western masculinist ideals and to contest (rather than
affirm) the industrial capitalist ethos. These shifting discourses[9] on the
relationship between race and masculinity thus put the colonial relationship into question by idealizing Native subjects. Yet they also reinscribed racial hierarchies. Gender proved important for another reason. World War I marked an important transition for Western women,
who won the vote in 1920 in part because of their wartime presence in
the workplace (often performing conventional male tasks). During the
interwar years, then, going native served a number of interrelated purposes. It articulated widespread ambivalence about colonialism and
modernity by simultaneously reasserting and masking colonial power.
At the same time, it responded to the gender crisis in the West by reaf-
firming and naturalizing patriarchy.

The vexed nature of interwar colonial discourse informed both the
relationships that male travelers constructed with their Eskimo companions and the genres in which they wrote. The language of science,
particularly the emerging discipline of anthropology, characterized an
increasing number of Western stories about colonial encounters from
the turn of the century, including Boas's and Peary's relationships with
the Polar Eskimos they brought to New York. The dispassionate language of science and its claims to value-free knowledge veiled relationships shot through with power and control. More specifically, Boasian anthropology, premised on cultural relativism and aimed at
transforming anthropology into a scientific discipline, claimed to challenge the hierarchies of Victorian notions of social evolution. Yet by
looking at cultures in isolation and with an eye to an "authenticity" located in the historical past, Boas's theoretical framework deflected
questions about the relations between cultures, including the colonial

[8] Kaplan, "Romancing the Empire," 664.
[9] At this point, it should be clear to the reader that I use "discourse" in the Fou-
cauldian sense, since my particular concern is with how Western colonialism
helped to produce a particular kind of knowledge about the Arctic which con-
cretely affected both Natives and non-Natives. It is, however, crucial to bear in
mind that while textual and physical violence are interrelated, they cannot be conflated. While, for example, the display of the Polar Eskimos in the American Museum of Natural History bears marked similarities to the display of Natives in *Nanook of the North* (as will become clearer later in this chapter), the Eskimo
peoples in question obviously experienced these events very differently.

relations enacted by anthropologists, explorers, and collectors. Boas is a figure who spans the historical transition that concerns me here; his work on the Arctic combines representations widely perceived to be of different orders. A collaborator with Peary in staging the Eskimo displays at the American Museum of Natural History in 1897, Boas also profoundly influenced Flaherty, who is generally considered Peary's opposite. Although the "truth" of Flaherty's narratives has always been a matter of some debate,[10] the term "documentary," connoting Boasian scientific objectivity, was first used in relation to Flaherty's work. Audiences have generally viewed his films as portraits of actual life.[11] *Nanook*, moreover, is frequently dubbed the premiere "ethnographic film." I contend, however, that these assertions both manifest the film's (and the explorer's) claims to innocence and betray its complicity in the colonial project. But it is not only in *Nanook*'s form and its claims to apolitical objectivity that Boas's influence can be seen. A Boasian paradigm shapes the narrative as well. Like Boas, Flaherty located "authentic" Eskimo culture in the historical past, a move that anticipates the Natives' disappearance in the present. A double logic thus characterizes Flaherty's work, which both criticizes and reasserts the celebrations of colonialism so explicit in Peary's writing. Genre also proves important in Poncins's later autobiography and Arctic travel narrative, *Kabloona*. Ironically, the intensely personal language of this text in some respects resembles the impersonal language of documentary film. Both deflect historical and political questions about the relationships between the Arctic and the West.

To understand representations of Eskimos during this period, then, is to confront the interrelationships of knowledge and colonial expansion in the age of industrial capitalism. How did scientific knowledge about the Arctic, despite its claims to political objectivity, provide a rationale for colonial expansion? Conversely, how did colonialism and the nature of life in the urban industrial capitalist world shape the knowledge Westerners produced, even the ostensibly value-free language of science and the documentary? How did changing gender roles affect these representations? Finally, how and for what purposes do these texts rewrite the repressed history of Western interventions in the Arctic? Unraveling these tales shows the workings of colonialism and, per-

[10] See Ann Fienup-Riordan's discussion of this issue in *Freeze Frame: Alaska Eskimos in the Movies* (Seattle: University of Washington Press, 1995), esp. 48–53.
[11] According to the conventional wisdom, John Grierson first used the term "documentary" to describe Flaherty's 1926 film, *Moana*. Since then, the appellation has generally been used to describe all of Flaherty's work. On Flaherty's reception, see, for example, Richard Barsam, *The Vision of Robert Flaherty: The Artist as Myth and Filmmaker* (Bloomington: Indiana University Press, 1988).

haps more important, allows us to reread these images in a way that counters rather than supports imperialist domination.

I shall begin by analyzing modern representations of Eskimos and the Arctic, focusing in particular on the transition manifested in the works of Peary and Flaherty. While Peary's writings are unabashedly colonialist, Flaherty's travel account *My Eskimo Friends* and his classic documentary *Nanook of the North* paint different but complementary pictures of Western interventions in the Arctic. These two documents were released in 1922, and both were based on Flaherty's voyages north between 1910 and 1920. While *My Eskimo Friends* foregrounds the process of colonialism, however, *Nanook of the North* disguises its effects. More specifically, it articulates colonial power relations indirectly through a Western-derived discourse on gender. The film presents the Arctic as a fantasy space where Western gender crises, largely the product of changing life in the industrial capitalist world, were magically resolved for 1920s viewers. It thus shows Western men's impulses to go native as a means of reasserting colonial and patriarchal dominance. The desire to go native, however, becomes even clearer in Poncins's 1941 travel narrative, *Kabloona*, which I discuss next. This text masks the author's complicity in the colonial project by showing his transformation into an Eskimo. It thus both articulates and denies its colonialist impulses, even as it both criticizes and affirms other aspects of the industrial capitalist ethos (including patriarchy). I conclude the chapter by returning to the figure of Minik. Like other Natives whom Westerners fail to recognize as historical subjects, Minik's life suggests a rereading of colonial encounters that challenge both the imaginings and practices of the dominant culture.

COLONIALISM, SCIENCE, AND THE QUEST FOR THE NORTH POLE

While the exhibitions of the Polar Eskimos at the American Museum of Natural History in 1897 bore an uncomfortable resemblance to earlier circuslike displays of captured Natives popular through the nineteenth century, both Peary and Boas claimed different motivations.[12] They undertook their pursuits in the name of science (in this case, the nascent

[12] For a discussion of the early days of European-Eskimo contact including Europeans' penchant for taking and displaying captives, see Wendell H. Oswalt, *Eskimos and Explorers* (Novato, Calif.: Chandler & Sharp, 1979); and William C. Sturtevant and David B. Quinn, "This New Prey: Eskimos in Europe in 1567, 1576, and 1577," in *Indians and Europe: An Interdisciplinary Collection of Essays*, ed. Christian F. Feest (Aachen: Rader Verlag, 1987), 61–140.

discipline of anthropology) and dispassionate knowledge. Procuring a live Eskimo specimen would, in Boas's words, "enable [anthropologists] to obtain leisurely certain information which will be of the greatest scientific importance." Other museum officials concurred. "Much valuable information of an ethnological character could be obtained from [these Eskimos]," argued Morris Jessup, president of the American Museum of Natural History, who claimed that "their presence here would be very instructive to scientists interested in the study of the Northern races."[13] While the relationship of this project to colonial enterprises in the Arctic remained unexplored, however, both the knowledge produced by these scientists and the positions they assumed in relation to their subjects were tainted by and complicit in the imperial project. The very presence of the Eskimos—taken from their arctic homes, moved to the colonial center for purposes not their own, and placed on display for the curious—manifested the Western colonial desire for possession and attested to its imperial might. Their location in the American Museum of Natural History was significant as well. There they served as the passive objects of white scientists' studies. Reprising Lewis Henry Morgan's theories of the development of civilization, these scientists placed them—along with animal specimens and other "primitive peoples"—in the realm of "natural" (i.e., prehuman, or at least precivilized) history. They thus rendered them irrevocably primitive, savage, other. Europeans, by contrast, were not subjected to the objectifying and defining gaze of the anthropologist. If the discourses of science and natural history, as Mary Louise Pratt suggests in her seminal work on travel writing, "naturalized" the scientist's position and authority,[14] they also starkly evoked and embodied that authority. Testimony to Western power, the pursuit of "value-free" scientific knowledge simultaneously veiled the uglier face of colonialism, in part by neglecting the political relationships between cultures as an object of study. Exploitation of Native labor and resources as well as the ravages of Western diseases were hidden from Western audiences and replaced by sanitized visions of arctic life "uncontaminated" by European influences.

In the particular case of the Arctic in modern America, the period under scrutiny here, the discourses and practices of science and those of colonization were not just complementary, they were in fact mutually constitutive and interdependent. The American Museum of Natural History and other institutions rewarded Peary handsomely for the variety of specimens he brought back from his voyages, and this money

[13] Cited in Harper, *Give Me My Father's Body,* 33.
[14] See Pratt, *Imperial Eyes,* 28.

helped to finance his numerous exploratory expeditions to the North. In an address to the National Geographic Society (his primary financier) in 1903, the explorer revealed the intersections of these discourses and practices in scientific, nationalistic, and starkly colonialist language. The museum research, he pointed out, complemented his own agenda, and he repeatedly cited the quest for knowledge as a primary justification for his endeavor. Capturing the Pole would "increase our knowledge of the earth." Until "the secret of the Pole has been penetrated and the veil lifted," he proclaimed in the unmistakably sexualized terms conventional in colonial narratives, "no one can say what is there, whether land or water." He augmented his appeal by pointing out that the Pole, "that charmed spot," had long constituted an object of desire for explorers. His sexual metaphors indicate how the pursuit of knowledge and the process of domination intertwined. They also show the link between masculinity and colonial conquest.[15] Proclaiming the North Pole was "the last great geographical prize the world [had] to offer," Peary located these journeys within a long history of Western discovery and conquest. He placed himself in the lineage of such prominent discoverers as Columbus, arguing that the attainment of the Pole, "to show forever that we own the top of the earth," would "complete man's domination of the earth."[16] Concluding his speech, he appealed, in particular, to American nationalism, manifest destiny, and the histories of U.S. conquests of other Native peoples:

> As a matter of prestige [gaining the Pole] is worthwhile.... As a matter of patriotism based upon the obligation of our manifest destiny, it is worth while. The North American world segment is our home, our birthright, our destiny. The boundaries of that segment are the Atlantic and the Pacific, the Isthmus and the Pole.... Believe me, the winning of the North Pole will be one of the great mile-stones of history, like the discovery of the New World by Columbus and the conquest of the Old by Alexander.... Let us attain it, then. It is our privilege and our duty. Let us capture the prize and win the race which the nations of the civilized world have been struggling for for nearly four centuries, the prize which is the last great geographical prize the earth has to offer.... What a splendid feat for this great and wealthy country if, having girdled

[15] See Catherine A. Lutz and Jane L. Collins, *Reading National Geographic* (Chicago: University of Chicago Press, 1993), for a discussion of the gendered nature of colonial discourse in the highly symptomatic case of *National Geographic* magazine.

[16] Robert Peary, "The Value of Arctic Exploration," *National Geographic Magazine* 14, 12 (1903): 429–36.

the earth, we might reach the north and south and plant "Old Glory" on each Pole. How the imagination stirs at the thought![17]

Peary's colonial mindset not only shaped his agenda; it influenced his perceptions of and relationships with "his" Eskimos as well. Although he relied heavily upon them in his quests for the Pole (indeed, his very survival depended upon their wisdom and abilities), he treated them patronizingly and, at times, cruelly. (He soon became notorious for his fits of rage, his blatant manipulativeness, as well as his exploitation of the Eskimos.)[18] Native peoples figured in his accounts as part of the arctic landscape to be dominated and claimed; his delivery of the Polar Eskimos to the American Museum of Natural History in 1897, as well as his collecting of Eskimos corpses and skeletons on other occasions, is perhaps the most compelling evidence of this. In the best-known published account of his travels, *The North Pole: Its Discovery in 1909 under the Auspices of the Peary Arctic Club,* photographs of Eskimos punctuate the narrative along with scenes of rough terrain traversed and animals killed for food or scientific specimens. The very fact of Peary's existence among Eskimo peoples, as well as the relationships he developed with them, established in his mind his dominance over them. Eskimos, he wrote, "are much like children, and should be treated as such." Shouldering the "white man's burden," he "rule[d] them by love and gratitude," censuring them for misconduct while ostensibly looking out for their welfare.[19] He did readily admit that the Natives, with their knowledge of the terrain and their survival skills, were indispensable to his journey. He believed, however, that these "children" could not have made the journey without his supervision:[20] "with their racial inheritance of ice technic and their ability to handle sledges and dogs, [they] were more necessary to me…than any white man could have been. Of course they could not lead, but they could follow and drive dogs better than any white man."[21] Similarly, and more famously, Peary asserted that Matthew Henson, his African-American

[17] Ibid., 436. I have suppressed several paragraph breaks.
[18] See, for example, Peter Matthiessen, "Survival of the Hunter," *New Yorker,* 24 April 1995, 67–77, as well as the account of Matthew Henson, Peary's African-American companion, titled *A Black Explorer at the North Pole* (1912; reprint, Lincoln: University of Nebraska Press, 1989).
[19] Robert Peary, *The North Pole: Its Discovery in 1909 under the Auspices of the Peary Arctic Club* (New York: Frederick A. Stokes Company, 1910), 50–51.
[20] The possibility that they might not consider such a dubious goal worthwhile apparently did not occur to Peary. Judging from his own account as well as that of others, this in fact seems to have been the case.
[21] Peary, *The North Pole,* 272.

companion, was also handicapped by this "racial shortcoming."[22] (Clearly, however, it was not Peary's racial superiority, as he believed, that compelled many Natives to do his bidding. Instead, the reasons were primarily economic. At a certain point, the explorer controlled virtually all trade in the Polar region; in exchange for services he offered rifles and other tools on which Native lives had come to depend.)

The cargo aboard the *Hope*, when it returned from its voyage in 1897, showed the congruence that Peary, like many other Westerners, saw between the Natives and inanimate objects. On board along with the six Polar Eskimos was the Cape York meteorite, the "Iron Mountain" of popular arctic lore. Like the Eskimos themselves, this rarity was both an object of scientific study and a curiosity. Explorers had long sought it, often with tragic results. One ill-fated expedition came to a halt when an overburdened sled bearing a piece of the meteorite disappeared through a break in the ice, dragging the sled dogs into the icy depths of the Arctic Ocean. Undeterred by these stories, Peary persuaded some of his companions to bring him to the famed object. Peary also remained impervious to the Natives' protests. The meteorite had long provided their sole source of metal for tools and other implements, and they feared the loss of it would imperil their chances of survival. To Peary, though, these Eskimos' claims and appeals were meaningless. In an Adamic gesture of naming and colonial appropriation, when he received the meteorite, he immediately carved a *P* on it. Soon thereafter he transported it to New York, where along with the Eskimos it served as an object of display. The Eskimos, too, he viewed as his possessions. At least one Eskimo on the ship, Minik, even bore the colonial insignia. After 1898, Minik lived the remainder of his days in the United States as Minik Peary Wallace (the surname being that of his adopted family).

In the years immediately following the famed polar expeditions, such unveiled colonialist language appeared at least somewhat suspect, if not objectionable, to many Americans. Particularly in the isolationist mood that followed World War I, representations of Eskimos and arctic life began to reflect the public's increasing ambivalence about colonialist enterprises as well as about Eskimo peoples. The work of the explorer and filmmaker Robert Flaherty, best known as the creator of the pathbreaking 1922 documentary *Nanook of the North,* exemplified these changing attitudes. Significantly, in the popular imagination, the figure of Flaherty differs starkly from that of Peary. While Peary's cruelty was by then well known, Flaherty was (and continues to be) considered a

[22] Henson has written an account of the Polar expedition that differs in several key ways from Peary's own account (providing, for instance, a much less glorified portrait of Peary). See *A Black Explorer at the North Pole.*

humane and nonexploitative documentarian of Eskimo life, whose approach was deservedly called "the innocent eye."[23] Unlike Peary, he was reported to have compensated the Natives fairly for their work. Moreover, he generally spoke favorably about them, and by all accounts otherwise treated them decently. Clearly, he carefully nurtured this reputation. The very title of his 1922 travel account, *My Eskimo Friends*, implies that his relations with his companions were equitable and based on mutual respect. These two men from two very different eras thus embody the Janus face of colonialism: one, the callous and at times violent exploiter representing the arrogance of high capitalist America; the other, the benevolent patriarch visiting the Arctic not to conquer or dominate but rather to offer help to the down-trodden.

Flaherty's position, however, was much more complex (and closer to Peary's) than this traditional account suggests. His presence in the Arctic and his accounts of the region and its peoples embodied colonial gestures even as they attempted to efface them. Like Peary, Flaherty relied in *My Eskimo Friends* on the language of discovery, mapping, and conquest. The paradigms of natural history, a discourse which proved fundamental to colonialist enterprises, similarly shaped all of his work. Flaherty shot the footage which became *Nanook of the North* during the same voyages, taken between 1910 and 1920, that he described in the travel account. Yet the two documents tell opposing (but complementary) stories about Western presence in the Arctic. While *My Eskimo Friends* is an explicitly colonial narrative, *Nanook of the North* virtually erases the European presence from the arctic landscape. It thus creates the illusion of Western innocence vis-à-vis the Arctic, a stance that articulates the widespread ambivalence about expansionism characteristic of the post–World War I era. Yet the narrative of *Nanook* evokes the very history it seeks to repress, in large measure through its complicated discourse on gender— one that compelled many Western men to emulate Eskimos (in other words, to go native). The contradictions between the travel narrative and the film, as well as the contradictions within *Nanook* itself, link Flaherty's work to Peary's and to the history of Western colonialism, relationships most commentators on Flaherty's work have ignored.

MY ESKIMO FRIENDS: REWRITING COLONIALISM
IN THE ARCTIC

When Robert J. Flaherty first traveled north in 1910 at the age of twenty-six, a fortuitous event that would eventually bring him fame as a doc-

---

[23] This is the title of Paul Rotha and Basil Wright's biography, *The Innocent Eye: The Life of Robert J. Flaherty* (New York: Harcourt, Brace and World, 1963).

umentarian of arctic life, he was following in the footsteps of his famous father. Robert H. Flaherty was, in the words of his son, the "foremost figure in the iron ore exploration of Canada" during his lifetime, a quest that brought him to the hinterlands of Quebec and Ontario.[24] During the younger Flaherty's lifetime, the Canadian government sponsored new expeditions, this time into the regions surrounding Hudson's Bay. In 1910 officials undertook construction of a railroad in the northern parts of the country. Planners designed the railroad for shipping wheat, iron ore, and other natural resources to the "great markets of the world."[25] Explorers and cartographers played key roles in tapping the resources of the region and bringing the Far North into the world of industrial capital. Vast areas were at the time largely unknown and unplotted, often blank areas on maps. Government-sponsored expeditions such as the one that hired the younger Flaherty were thus voyages of discovery in a dual sense. Mapping the terrain and locating mineral deposits were complementary enterprises that enabled the appropriation of valuable resources.

Flaherty made four trips to the Eastern Arctic between 1910 and 1916 for the purposes of exploration (his later voyages were devoted to work on the film). In *My Eskimo Friends* he describes these journeys. Initially, it was, in part, the lure of the unknown and the prospect of discovery, an appetite fed by his father's adventures, that captivated him and drew him north:

> With [my father's] engineers and prospectors I grew up on explorations whose range, east and west, was more than a thousand miles. Long journeys some of them seemed to be then—through the courses of unmapped lakes and streams, over the height of land and on halfway down the big tumbling rivers whose ends are on Hudson Bay. Hudson Bay was mysterious country. The grizzled old fur traders and the fur brigades of strange Indians, curiously garbed, with hair shoulder-long, whom we sometimes ran into, seemed to be people of another world.[26]

Flaherty's preoccupation with unknown spaces echoes Peary's. For Flaherty, the mysteriousness of the land and the strangeness of the Natives converged, and both contributed to the allure of the Arctic for his readers as well. Landscape descriptions of the unexplored regions dominate good portions of the text, particularly its first half. Two of its

[24] Robert J. Flaherty, *My Eskimo Friends: "Nanook of the North"* (Garden City, N.Y.: Doubleday, Page, 1924), 1.
[25] Ibid., 1.
[26] Ibid., 1–2.

four sections bear names showing his goals of discovery and exploration. These goals become clearest in the first section of the book, "The
Discovery and Exploration of the Belcher Islands," which narrates the
author's "discovery" (although Natives had long inhabited the area) and
mapping of a series of barely known (to non-Natives) islands in Hudson's Bay. Maps of these islands and of other areas are interspersed
throughout the text.

Photographs of Eskimos, some of them still images from what became *Nanook of the North,* also appear in the pages of *My Eskimo
Friends,* illustrating again that both the landscape and its Native inhabitants comprised objects of colonial conquest. If the maps revealed what
was hidden or unknown in the arctic landscape, the photographs (and,
later, the film) accomplished the same goal with its peoples. Their
"mystery," too, tantalized Western audiences. From the beginning,
then, Flaherty's travel account is marked by a discourse of mastery of
the land and its Native inhabitants, both passive objects of his quest for
knowledge. Moreover, the Eskimos, Flaherty implied, readily acquiesced to his dominance, addressing him as "Angarooka," translated as
"white master," thus linking his mastery to race as well as to his role as
explorer/discoverer. They ostensibly treated him royally as well. Occupying the conventional (Tonto-esque) role of Native sidekick, Nanook
in particular devotedly cared for him, carving his bed (aptly, of *"royal*
height and width")* out of snow blocks and anxiously attending to his
other needs.[27] The Eskimos' responses—their immediate recognition of
his mastery—seemed to naturalize the explorer's dominance, thus
transforming an act of conquest into a benign encounter.

Flaherty's acts of mastery reveal themselves in other ways as well,
some of which echo conventional Western accounts of encounters between Natives and Europeans. Naming, a politically charged act of conquest and appropriation, played a significant role in Flaherty's encounters (as it had for Peary before him). Just as the arctic landscape on
his European maps bore (and continues to bear) the names of its Western "discoverers," so too did Flaherty's natives, in his texts at least,
carry the appellations he assigned them. The character Nanook the
Bear, who figures in both *My Eskimo Friends* and the film that bears his
name, was actually named Allakariallak. Flaherty never used his real
(Native) name in either account, though, opting instead for a more
"Eskimo-sounding" alias carrying primitive connotations. This is also the
case with the other Eskimo figures in the travel account and the film.[28]

[27] Ibid., 146 (emphasis mine).
[28] Interestingly, it seems the Eskimos had a bit of fun at Flaherty's expense when it
came to choosing the characters' names. The name of Nanook's screen wife, Nyla,

Flaherty thus literally redefined these Natives for his Western audiences. Flaherty's depictions of the Eskimos also articulated conventional Western perceptions of "primitives." One description narrating the arrival of the explorer's party at a settlement, for example, begins with his driver exclaiming, "'Huskies!' (Eskimos)....Three men, their wives, and a troop of wide-eyed children who looked like bear cubs in their shaggy fur clothing come out to meet us as we galloped down toward them."[29] The Eskimos' location (literally below Flaherty) underscored their place in the racial hierarchy, as did their associations with animals. These associations stuck. Nanook, in both the travel narrative and the film, is Nanook the Bear, and a picture accompanied by this epithet provides the frontispiece of *My Eskimo Friends.* The ways Flaherty defined these Natives for Western audiences carried political implications as well. Because they seemed somehow less than human, their presence on the land was less consequential than the white man's. Thus Flaherty could dub himself a "discoverer" of lands long inhabited by Natives and claim its resources as his own.

If Flaherty's descriptions of Eskimos and their relationships with him support notions of Western superiority, they also suggest that the explorer harbored some doubts about his colonial mission. In another key moment, he described the curious parting of his group and the Eskimos as he and his crew decided to break camp to sail to another "mysterious land": "To the faithful and kindly Eskimos who had served us well, we gave out the last we had—a mirror with a gilt frame, old blankets, clothing, old shoes, precious bits of metal, and an old alarm clock with one hand, knives, old pots and kettles and pans, and most wonderful of all, some oranges.... We said our good-byes regretfully enough. Anxiously they inquired if ever they should see us again."[30] Several things are striking about this passage. First, as Flaherty interpreted this encounter (apparently neglecting the possibility that their interest in his presence was economic rather than personal), the Eskimos welcomed the explorer and his crew warmly and regretted their departure. These responses seemed to legitimate the non-Natives' presence. Furthermore, Flaherty reversed the colonial relationship in this description. While his journey was designed to discover and appropriate arctic resources for Western consumption, here it was he who gave Western goods to the delighted and grateful Natives. Both points conceal or provide a rationale

---

does not actually mean "the smiling one" as Flaherty claimed (based on his informants' translations). Instead, the root *nilaq-* carries vulgar connotations. See Fienup-Riordan, *Freeze Frame,* 49.

[29] Flaherty, *My Eskimo Friends,* 11.

[30] Ibid., 34–35.

for the explorer's presence and his mission in the Arctic. Flaherty's choice of gifts is significant as well, reflecting his perception of the primitiveness of the Natives and their relation (or lack thereof) to modernity. The broken clock, bits of metal, and other outdated items all consigned them to the past, to the trash heap of history.

Ambivalence about colonialism, shown here by the need to justify it and conceal its workings, also emerges in Flaherty's contradictory accounts of Native presence in other regions of the Arctic. While much of the text concerns itself with interactions with the Natives, at other points, their absence is both conspicuous and significant. One such moment comes when Flaherty finally discovers iron ore, the initial object of his quest, on the Belcher Islands (a territory he had "discovered"): "Not only in the red bands of marl and shale, and in the distant masses of yellow which were quartz sites, and in the white-grays which were limestones was the land mass, as I had hoped, an extension of the ore-bearing series of the mainland. Though it was barely exposed, I stumbled over ore itself—rich stuff which lay heavy in my hands!" And a few sentences later: "There was no sight of natives but the boulder rings of their old camp grounds were everywhere."[31] At the very moment he discovered the riches he sought, he evoked and then quickly erased the Native presence (at least a contemporary, permanent one) from the landscape. These Natives' absence legitimated his presence and therefore his claims to the iron ore. But the convergence of these events also shows his doubts about the legitimacy of the "discoverer's" claims, implying that encounters with contemporary Natives at that site would have rendered them suspect.

This ambivalence about the colonial project shows itself as well in contradictions surrounding the presence of wealth in the Arctic. Significantly, after narrating his discovery of iron ore Flaherty cited the correspondence of John Spencer, a nineteenth-century factor of the Hudson's Bay Company, to assert the poverty of the land (thereby contradicting his discovery of its riches) and thus to redefine the objectives of the colonial project. He concluded "The Discovery and Exploration of the Belcher Islands" by quoting sections a letter Spencer wrote in 1849 describing the ventures of Thomas Weigand (a mixed-blood servant of the company):

> Although it so happened that [Weigand] saw but few natives and got but little from them it would be highly ridiculous in endeavouring to make that appear as a sufficient reason for not going again, and that their poverty should for a moment be thought suf-

31 Ibid., 42.

ficient for framing such an idea, an idea in itself as absurd as it is ridiculous, and could only find shelter in a narrow mind, for after our knowledge of these islands, being more or less inhabited, and that those natives are living under no other protective hand than that which nature bestowed upon them, indifferent should we be considered in our endeavour towards bettering mankind, were we to show ourselves indifferent towards them.[32]

Thus did Spencer absurdly redefine the Hudson's Bay Company's mission as helping the impoverished Natives. He then softened his claims about the poverty of the land, asserting that the Company might still legitimately profit from the Eskimo people's benevolence. These impoverished Natives, in other words, would not only benefit from the Europeans' "protection" but would feel such gratitude that they might in fact also "be brought to furnish a valuable portion of trade in Blubber, Foxes, Ivory and whatnot." Flaherty clearly shared the very Western notion wherein whites bring good to natives who then respond by bringing profitable resources in return. That he continued to quote Spencer's correspondence at such length underscores the extent to which Spencer's sentiments reflected his own.

In the final section of *My Eskimo Friends*, Flaherty's project of exploration and discovery dovetailed with the filmic venture that eventually brought him international fame. During his 1913 journey to the Arctic, three years after his first voyage in search of iron ore, Flaherty had brought with him film equipment (which was frequently used by surveyors and cartographers at the time) to begin a new quest. On this particular expedition, it was not iron ore he sought; rather, he was "on the lookout for Eskimos."[33] Flaherty's "hunt for images," as one insightful critic has labeled his project, was not a new venture.[34] From his first voyage to the Arctic as an explorer and prospector in 1910, he had photographed Eskimos hundreds of times.[35] But this time it was different. The earlier photographs of the Eskimos had been a subsidiary part of

[32] John Spencer, cited in ibid., 46.
[33] Flaherty, *My Eskimo Friends*, 119.
[34] See Fatimah Tobing Rony, *The Third Eye: Race, Cinema, and Ethnographic Spectacle* (Durham: Duke University Press, 1996). Rony's argument is in part inspired by Donna Haraway's classic essay "Teddy Bear Patriarchy," in *Primate Visions: Gender, Race, and Nature in the World of Modern Science* (New York: Routledge, 1989), 26–58.
[35] Approximately fifteen hundred photographs taken by Flaherty before the 1922 release of *Nanook of the North* are now housed in American and European archives. See Robert J. Christopher, "Through Canada's Northland: The Arctic Photography of Robert J. Flaherty," in *Imaging the Arctic*, ed. J.C. H. King and Henrietta Lidchi (Seattle: University of Washington Press, 1998), 181–89.

his enterprise of making the arctic world visible, and thus available, to Westerners through maps and other documentary material. During several voyages made between 1913 and 1920, his priorities changed; the Eskimos themselves became the primary object of the explorer's gaze and of his camera as well. It was the mysteries of Eskimo life to which the explorer turned his mapping skills, and in so doing he created *Nanook of the North,* perhaps the best-known "documentary" ever made.

The film quickly became one of his most precious possessions; he took the footage with him everywhere—along with his specimens, maps, and notes—during his travels. The Eskimos found his attachment to the film a great source of humor, laughing wildly at the care they, too, had to lavish on the footage.[36] But despite this excessive care, this new enterprise was initially ill-fated. The footage was destroyed twice, first when a sledge broke through the ice and disappeared along with its precious cargo, and later when Flaherty's discarded cigarette ignited the hard-earned second set of rolls. But the third time was lucky. In 1920, Flaherty completed the footage which he edited and released in 1922 as *Nanook of the North.* Both a box office and a critical success, the film changed forever the way the film-viewing world saw Eskimos and their arctic homeland. Widely acclaimed as the first ethnographic film, it remains a classic even today.

But the quest for cultural knowledge (the filmmaker's stated objective) is a potentially problematic and invasive enterprise which bears stark similarities to other forms of colonial mapping. Lest viewers raise questions, Flaherty provided a ready answer. Just as the Eskimos had welcomed him into their communities, it was they who desired to be seen by the outside world and, because of this, offered themselves up to the camera's gaze. As he told it, they frequently competed with each other to be filmed. In addition, the Natives themselves ostensibly determined the activities Flaherty would film. Nanook (Allakariallak) himself suggested the famed walrus-hunting scene, as well as the failed bear-hunting enterprise (no bears were found) which is absent from the final cut. When Flaherty completed the film, Nanook was reportedly distraught, begging him to remain: "To poor old Nanook the world seemed empty," the explorer claimed. "He hung about my cabin, talking over films we still could make if I would only stay on for another year."[37]

In the conclusion of *My Eskimo Friends,* Flaherty insisted that the Eskimos desired to be seen by the Western world. He had another ration-

[36] Flaherty, *My Eskimo Friends,* 149–50.
[37] Ibid., 169.

ale for his acts of dominance. The film, he believed, could provide some compensation for the devastations of colonialism. In narrating the incursion of Westerners into the Arctic, the film also alludes to its effects. Scenes of death punctuate the narrative, beginning at the beginning of the journey when several Natives suddenly die and the travelers encounter graves of others. Throughout the journey, the threats of starvation and disease, both effects of colonialism, remain constant. The text even concludes with a scene of death—this time, significantly, that of the film's principle figure, Nanook. The last lines read: "Less than two years later [after Flaherty's return home], I received word by the once-a-year mail that comes out of the north that Nanook was dead. Poor old Nanook! Our 'big aggie' [the Natives' term for the film], become 'Nanook of the North,' has gone into most of the odd corners of the world ...and more kablunaks [white people] than there are stones around the shore of Nanook's home have looked upon Nanook, the kindly, the brave, the simple Eskimo."[38] Nanook/Allakariallak likely died at a relatively young age from starvation probably complicated by disease (he was reportedly coughing blood during the filming of *Nanook*), both fates related to the incursions of Westerners (including Flaherty) into the Natives' homeland. These newcomers brought diseases to which Eskimos lacked immunity and drastically reduced animal populations by overhunting and trapping. In conventional form, however, this narrative conceals the dynamics of colonialism, in this case by textually transforming colonial violence into benevolence and even redemption. "Preserving" Nanook on film for non-Native viewers somehow ameliorated the tragedy of his death. Thus, it seems, it was not Native peoples themselves that Flaherty valued, but rather the knowledge he derived from their cultures. Preserving precontact Eskimo life (some vision of it, at least) on film thus denied the tremendous destruction and death wrought by European colonialism. At the same time, the death of the Native made Europeans the legitimate heirs of Eskimo resources and even, as we shall see, Native identity itself.

Flaherty's ambivalence about colonialism in the Arctic and his own role in it, while apparent in *My Eskimo Friends*, reached new heights in *Nanook of the North*. The documentary relates a very different kind of story, one in which the European presence and the effects of colonialism are virtually (although not completely) erased. Anxieties about colonialism, however, emerge in the film in a contradictory and highly gendered discourse that positions the Natives in relation to Europeans in complicated and paradoxical ways. In the film, Eskimos embody particular Western gender and other social ideals that compelled arctic

[38] Ibid., 170.

travelers to go native in the interwar years. These representations, which idealize Natives in some respects, put the colonial enterprise into question. Yet viewers in the 1920s were also reassured about the legitimacy of Western presence in the North. The film "justifies" colonial incursions into the Arctic by evoking racialized and gendered discourses that simultaneously position the Natives as "naturally" subordinate to the sole European in the film (significantly, the fur trader, a quintessential colonial figure). Going native functions in this context, moreover, to conceal Westerners' aspirations to dominance. All of these processes pivoted on and contributed to the changing and contradictory place arctic Natives occupied in the American cultural imagination early in the twentieth century.

IMAGINING ESKIMOS IN MODERN AMERICAN CULTURE

Why was *Nanook of the North* such a stunning popular success? What, exactly, was it about Eskimos that captivated huge Western audiences? The desire Americans expressed for things Eskimo in the interwar years can be understood only by going back to the turn of the century and considering the space these Natives began to occupy in the modern American cultural imagination. While Westerners (*pace* Conrad) have generally projected the basest part of themselves onto Europe's colonized others, they have imagined Eskimos with greater ambivalence, at least since the latter part of the nineteenth century. In part because of Christianity's associations with whiteness and the dominance of whiteness in arctic images (as opposed to the "darkness" of other colonial spaces), Eskimos often seemed to embody better rather than baser versions of Western selves. Many observers have figured the Arctic as a place of cleanliness, purity, virtue, and even redemption. In the twentieth century, Americans' renewed fascination with the region drew upon preexisting and emerging stereotypes to construct Eskimos as the embodiments of Western ideals and the Arctic as a place that could cleanse and even redeem a fallen, "overcivilized" European world. At the same time, however, because of the need to justify colonial enterprises in the North, these images were fraught with contradictions.

Racial indeterminacy also contributed to Westerners' idealization of Eskimos. Unlike Africans or American Indians, Eskimos were not immediately assigned a clear racial space. During the last two centuries, racial classifications of Eskimos and their relations to Europeans have fluctuated widely. Often categorized as racially "other" and thus inferior to Westerners, Eskimos have also been viewed by many as being racially "white," that is, as being of European (frequently Nordic) racial origins. One early observer who saw racial similarities between Eskimos and Europeans was Johann Blumenbach, who is frequently dubbed the founder of physical anthropology. In one of the earliest attempts to formalize categories of humanity according to the emerging concept of race, Blumenbach speculated in 1775 that Eskimos were racially distinct from other Native Americans. They were, he absurdly argued, probably of Finnish origin and should thus be categorized as Europeans.[39] Although Blumenbach's categories were ostensibly based on physical characteristics, he likely drew his perceptions of the Europeanness of Eskimos from Enlightenment notions about the influence of climate on racial and national character. Later commentators frequently echoed Blumenbach's arguments. Early twentieth-century travelers often wrote of the "blonde Eskimos" of the Canadian Arctic, theorizing about their possible European ancestry. More recently, the anthropologist and arctic filmmaker Asen Balikci explained that one reason for the popularity of Arctic documentaries in the 1970s, specifically the Netsilik Eskimo series, was the "whiteness" of the Natives: "We knew that the Bushmen series could not be used in the classroom since the portrayal of black people living in the bush would have reinforced too many stereotypes. The Eskimos however looked very similar to white people, particularly when they removed their coats."[40]

By the early twentieth century, the whiteness of the Arctic and its Natives contributed to a heavily romanticized and idealized vision of the place and its people, and the remoteness of the Eskimos allowed such imagery to flourish. Another key factor was the particular colonial history of the North. While Europeans instigated colonial wars throughout much of North America, and many Indian groups responded in kind with military resistance, Eskimo-European colonial encounters took a different form. The peoples of the Arctic and subarctic regions never engaged in outright warfare with the invaders. There was resistance, certainly—on the part of Alaska Natives conscripted to work in the Russian fur trade, for example—but no armed struggle on a large scale. Far smaller numbers of Europeans in a much more gradual process encroached upon Eskimo lands, and since these places often appeared virtually uninhabitable, few settled there. Colonial goals in the Arctic were also different. Rather than land for settlement, resources such as furs, minerals, and oil caught the attention of European nations and their citizens. Harvesting these riches generally required the Natives' labor (which was frequently forced) rather than their annihilation. As

[39] Ivan Hannaford, *Race: The History of an Idea in the West* (Baltimore: Johns Hopkins University Press, 1996), 207.
[40] Balikci, "Anthropology, Film, and the Arctic Peoples," 7.

was the case with popular representations of African Americans during slavery, many Europeans found comfort in images depicting happy and contented subjects.

For these reasons and others, in contrast to Indians, the fur-wearing, igloo-building inhabitants of the barren Arctic have traditionally been depicted as innocent children of sorts and admired for being peaceful, cheerful, and brave. Although it is difficult to pinpoint the origins of this Eskimo stereotype, it was well established by the turn of the century. The 1905 edition of *Encyclopaedia Britannica* shows how these stereotypes shaped "objective" knowledge; it describes Eskimos as "pleasing," "good-humored," and "apt to break into a 'grin' on very small provocation." They were, the entry continued, "free from many of [the] vicious traits" of other Native peoples, they "never [went] to war with each other" (although they occasionally were drawn into battle with more "vicious" Indians with whom they maintained a "violent enmity"), and were "morbidly anxious not to give offence."[41] Well into the twentieth century, travel accounts painted a similar picture. In *My Life with the Eskimo,* Vilhjalmur Stefansson, writing of his stay with the people of the Mackenzie region in 1907–8, described his companions as "cheerful, self-reliant, and admirable." "In a difficult struggle for existence under hard natural conditions," he continued, "they have acquired the ability to live together in peace and good will."[42] Eskimos, Peter Freuchen observed more than four decades later, had "happy-go-lucky" minds; they "always enjoy[ed] life with an enviable intensity."[43]

In addition, these observers found much to admire in the Eskimos' clever and skillful adaptations to an exceedingly harsh environment as well as the extreme independence and capability for self-determination of the Native peoples of the Arctic. In contrast to modern Westerners, it seemed that Eskimos (the men, at least) were masters of their own destinies. The *Encyclopaedia Britannica* pointed out that Eskimos had "no chiefs or political and military rulers." Rather, men distinguished themselves through their "skill in the chase, strength, shrewdness, or other

[41] *Encyclopaedia Britannica*, 5th ed., s.v. "Eskimos."
[42] Vilhjalmur Stefansson, *My Life with the Eskimo* (New York: Macmillan, 1943), 2–3.
[43] Peter Freuchen, *Book of the Eskimos* (Cleveland: World Publishing, 1961), 210, 194. This stereotype, in large measure, is still with us today. See League of Women Voters, "Children's Impressions of American Indians: A Survey of Suburban Kindergarten and Fifth Grade Children: Conclusion," and Richard Flaste, "American Indians: Still a Stereotype to Many Children," in *American Indian Stereotypes in the World of Children: A Reader and Bibliography,* ed. Arlene B. Hirschfelder (Metuchen, N.J.: Scarecrow, 1982); Ahnna Lake et al., "Le stéréotype des Eskimaux chez les élèves du niveau primaire," in *Etudes/Inuit/Studies* 8, 2 (1984): 141–43.

qualities useful to a wild community."[44] Similarly, the anthropologist Margaret Mead later instructed young readers that Eskimos had "no chiefs of any kind, just stronger men and weaker ones."[45] Given the diversity of Eskimo cultures, the particular character of these fascinations is symptomatic, showing clearly the nature of the West's desires. To these observers, the arctic landscape thus seemed to provide the ideal environment for cultivating many of the characteristics most valued in Western society. Here, in Nature's most intense Darwinian struggle, only the strongest and cleverest survived, and men could determine their own fates and distinguish themselves by their strengths and abilities.[46]

These dual images—the peaceful, happy-go-lucky Eskimo and the brave hunter struggling to survive in a harsh environment—elicited particular enthusiasm in the United States during the 1920s and 1930s in ways that reflected widespread ambivalence about modernity. Eskimos, it seemed, occupied a better world, one that industrial capitalist society had left behind. They represented the happier childhood and lost innocence of white civilization. The stereotype of the cheerful, peaceful Eskimo enjoyed particular popularity in part because it provided a stark counterimage to a Western world ravaged by the violence of the war. Images of independent, skillful male hunters continually engaged in a battle with nature also contrasted favorably with the more mundane lives of American workers in the industrial era. In the age of burgeoning high capitalism, business and industry grew into huge companies which offered workers little independence. The nature of work changed from farming and independent labor to tasks suited to the factory and the office. While middle-class Americans (usually men) found an escape from the confinement of factory and office spaces in the flourishing nature movement, Eskimos, it seemed, lived their entire lives outdoors. In Western fantasies, they lived unfettered by social conventions, a notion

---

[44] *Encyclopaedia Britannica*, 5th ed., s.v. "Eskimos."

[45] Margaret Mead, *People and Places* (Cleveland: World Publishing, 1959), 103.

[46] These representations were selective, focusing on the lifeways of a small minority of Eskimo people. Although they constitute a minority (about one-fifth) of Eskimo peoples worldwide, the Central Eskimos of Canada—and later, the Polar Eskimos, with whom they share many characteristics—have captured the world's attention to the exclusion of other groups. These were the igloo-dwelling nomadic hunters of seals, polar bears, and walruses who, according to the myth, struggled continually to survive in a brutal environment. Meanwhile, other more numerous groups have gone almost completely unnoticed by Westerners. By far the largest single group of Eskimos are Alaskan Yupiit, yet traditional Yup'ik life (led for the most part in relatively large societies in a land with no snow igloos or walruses or polar bears) has been infrequently represented in popular culture, and is even unrecognizable as "Eskimo" to most observers.

particularly appealing to a population living in an era of increasing governmental regulations.

These images, in other words, provided a fantasy of freedom from the violence, constraint, and tedium of modern American life. Such idealization of the "savage," David Spurr observes, typifies Western representations of others during periods of imperialist expansion and, in particular, articulates the nostalgic impulses of industrial capitalist society: "primitivism is symbolically the precise reverse of American capitalism and therefore constitutes an object to be admired in the abstract—the dream of its own opposite that lives at the very heart of the capitalist imagination." And yet, Spurr contends, the distance between the European self and its others is not always as vast as it sometimes seems, and herein lies another sense in which Eskimo images became significant in the colonial context: "this idealization always takes place *in relation* to Western culture itself: far from being a gesture which turns its back on the West in order to accept some alternative mode of being, it conceives an idea of the Other that is readily incorporated into the fabric of Western values."[47] Such was the case with Eskimo images in the early twentieth century. If Eskimo life appeared to provide an alternative to the practices of an industrial and capitalist world, it also seemed to replicate many of its core values. Eskimos were, according to these images, clean, honest, democratic, ingenious and extremely hard working. As Balikci notes, "the sum of these virtues is very similar to those found at the core of the American Protestant ethic."[48] What arctic narratives promised, then, was not an escape from industrial capitalist society, but rather the life it promised but failed in reality to deliver: a utopian space of absolute freedom, contentment, social equality, and unalienated labor. Representing Eskimos in this way—as apparently different from but fundamentally the same as Westerners—not only eliminated the challenges that Native differences (and, indeed, the Natives' presence) posed to European hegemony, it had other important effects as well. Rendering these Natives as embodying Western ideals also questioned the justice of Western colonialism in the region even as these representations rearticulated European racial dominance. When located inside this Eurocentric framework, Natives could only occupy a subordinate position, in part because they functioned primarily as means for Westerners' self-realization.

*

[47] David Spurr, *The Rhetoric of Empire: Colonial Discourse in Journalism, Travel Writing, and Imperial Administration* (Durham: Duke University Press, 1993), 128.
[48] Balikci, "Anthropology, Film, and the Arctic Peoples," 7.

Clearly, as I have already implied, these images have highly gendered overtones which resonated with controversies over changing men's and women's roles in early twentieth-century Western society. Since the early nineteenth century, manhood had been embodied by independence and self-sufficiency in the workplace. The ideal man was the "self-made man,"[49] defined by "success in the market, individual achievement, mobility, wealth ... [and] economic autonomy," and during at least part of the century opportunities for white, middle-class men were plentiful.[50] All of this changed, however, around the turn of the century. An economic downturn (brought about in part by the slowing of Western expansion) and the completion of the transition to industrial capitalism changed traditional men's roles and left fewer opportunities for independence and initiative. A more diversified work environment, too, played an important role as women entered the workplace, frequently performing "male" tasks, in significant numbers. Nonwhite immigrants also comprised larger parts of the labor force around and after the turn of the century. As a result, male gender ideals began to change. The notion of "masculinity" replaced "manhood" as the ideal state of manliness. Whereas manhood denoted "an inner quality, the capacity for autonomy and responsibility," masculinity "referred to a set of behavioral traits and attitudes that were contrasted now with a new opposite, femininity": "One could replace the inner experience of manhood ... and transform it into a set of physical characteristics obtainable by persistent effort in the gymnasium. The ideal of the Self-Made Man gradually assumed increasingly physical connotations so that by the 1870s the idea of 'inner strength' was replaced by a doctrine of physicality and the body."[51] Whereas previously men had established their manliness through their work, the nature of the modern workplace for middle-class men now seemed antithetical to truly masculine occupations requiring physical strength, aggressiveness, and endurance. Significantly, these were arenas in which the vast majority of women could not compete with their male counterparts. As a result, sports and professional athletics attained new heights of popularity during this period.[52] Meanwhile, as opportunities for middle-class men in the workplace narrowed, opportunities for leisure grew.[53] Thus, strenuous travel provided one means for middle-class men to buoy their masculinity.

[49] Michael Kimmel, *Manhood in America: A Cultural History* (New York: Free Press, 1996), 18. See also Bederman, *Manliness and Civilization*, esp. chap. 1.
[50] Kimmel, *Manhood in America*, 23.
[51] Ibid., 120.
[52] See Higham, "Reorientation of American Culture."
[53] Bederman, *Manliness and Civilization*, 13.

The Arctic, in the popular imagination, proved an ideal wilderness destination. It was already a highly gendered place, thus a perfect site for inculcating men with masculine virtues. It was, after all, one of the harshest environments on earth and (as Peary had declared) one of the few remaining colonial prizes. Moreover, life in that region unquestionably required strength, cunning, and endurance in its inhabitants. Theodore Roosevelt, perhaps the best-known advocate of the "strenuous life," ardently supported Robert Peary's "manly" quest for the North Pole and even wrote an introduction to Peary's account of his voyages. But Peary was not the only visitor to capitalize on the fascination of the male Arctic. Perhaps the best-known writer of the period to pen masculinist texts set in the Far North is Jack London. For London, life in the Arctic was the antithesis of civilized existence. While civilization softened and weakened modern men, the Arctic cultivated toughness and cunning.

In *The Call of the Wild,* written in 1903, London tells the story of the pampered dog Buck, who was stolen from his sunny California ranch and sold to prospectors in the North. Forced to toil as a sled dog in the Alaskan wilderness, Buck struggled but soon adjusted to the changes in his environment. While most Southland dogs perished from the harshness of their new lives, Buck proved to be the (Darwinian) exception and eventually flourished in the Arctic. Constant toil soon transformed him into a creature "in perfect condition, without an ounce of superfluous flesh"; "the one hundred and fifty pounds that he weighed," the author wrote with admiration, "were so many pounds of grit and virility."[54] In *The Call of the Wild,* this transformation was figured as a devolution, an atavistic journey from civilization "into the primitive." The primordial life of the Northland awakened in Buck the "strain of the primitive," the instincts of his "wild fathers." Not only did he become hard and virile, he also discovered bloodlust, the "joy of the kill" unknown to life on the California ranch. Eventually freed altogether from the constraints of human society, Buck became a true creature of the wild. He joined a pack of wolves (the quintessential symbol of wildness) and became the fiercest hunter among them, instilling terror in both the animals and the people in the region.

It was not only the physical challenge of arctic life that toughened Buck but also the fact of existence outside the constraints of civilized society. He was removed from "the heart of civilization," from the world of civilized law (symbolized by his residence in Judge Miller's house) to a natural world of "primitive law," the "law of club and fang" where the rule was "master or be mastered." Here, in a land where only the

[54] Jack London, *The Call of the Wild* (New York: Bantam Books, 1981), 83.

strongest survived, Buck devolved into a creature "overspilling with vigor and virility," master of his fellow creatures as well as of his own destiny. London's arctic world provided freedom and opportunities for self-determination for its human inhabitants as well. His novels teem with miners and prospectors, drawn to Alaska by a fierce independence and the possibility of striking it rich during the gold rush. These men, too, found in the Arctic a counterpoint to the constraints and enervating influences of civilized society. Like Flaherty's narratives, London's "last frontier" was, then, figured both as a place of unlimited economic possibility (the fantasy of capitalism) and as industrial capitalism's opposite, an escape from the realities of life in the modern world.

Both the changing notions of masculinity and a vision of the Arctic influenced by London compelled male travelers to journey north in the interwar years. But the interwar years proved different from the turn of the century. In the earlier period, the arctic environment provided opportunities for developing masculinity. Later, however, it was not only the place that seemed important. Eskimo men began to serve as models for Western men to emulate rather than simply as objects of colonial domination, in part because Eskimo society provided a fantasy of unquestioned male dominance. These visions drove later travelers not only to go north but to go native as well.

OF ICE AND MEN: GENDERING CONQUEST
IN *NANOOK OF THE NORTH*

When he made *Nanook of the North*, Flaherty certainly must have borne in mind the nature of the Western world's fascination with Eskimos and the Arctic. The complicated late-nineteenth- and early-twentieth-century images I have been describing shaped both the film and the audiences' responses to it. Like most representations of Eskimo life, *Nanook* takes place in the extreme regions of the Canadian North. Its cast of characters consists of a nuclear family headed by Nanook the Bear (introduced as "a great hunter" and "chief" of the "little kingdom" of Ungava), his wife Nyla ("the smiling one"), their children (a son, Allegoo, and a baby called Rainbow), and Cunayoo (probably Nanook's second wife). From time to time, other characters join them, most often other men in the numerous hunting scenes. In its opening sequences, the intertitles capture the images characterizing these Eskimos in the popular imagination: "The sterility of the soil and the rigor of the climate no other race could survive; yet here, utterly dependent upon animal life, which is their sole source of food, live the most cheerful people in the world—the fearless, lovable, happy-go-lucky Eskimo." It is, in

FIGURE 11. Still from Robert Flaherty's film *Nanook of the North* (1922) showing Nanook hunting seals, courtesy of the Museum of Modern Art Film Stills Archive.

fact, the precariousness of these Natives' existence, their constant struggle to survive in this harshest of environments, that drives the narrative. The camera repeatedly spans the frozen landscape, and in the first minutes of the film, viewers learn that "the desert interior, if deer hunting fails, is the country of death." Flaherty repeatedly pits the harshness of the land against Nanook's strength and skill in scenes which show him staving off certain death by hunting seal and walrus and, in the end, "almost perishing from the icy blasts" of a "threatening drifter." Shortly after the release of the film in 1922, reports of Nanook's death reinforced Flaherty's depiction of the perils of arctic life.

The film, in other words, depicts Eskimo life in terms that responded to Western fascination. While Eskimos seemed to embody key Western values (such as a European family structure and codes of masculinity), their strenuous lives also differed from those of Westerners in important ways. These differences Flaherty explained in part by locating the narrative in the past, before the introduction of the European clothing and technology, which had by that time become commonplace in arctic communities. In so doing, he adopted the dominant racial discourse of the day which located non-Westerners in the historical past. In Johannes Fabian's terms, images such as those produced by Flaherty drew upon the "episteme of natural history" and the framework of evolution which identified cultural difference as temporal distance.[55] In *Nanook,* as we shall see, the natural history paradigm, rather than colonial violence, explained the Eskimos' fate. This framing, moreover, points to one of the most important contradictions in the film. While Eskimo life was sited outside the time frame and the ethos of modern industrial capitalism, it was also subjected to its progressivist logic. Thus, this conceptual framework further negates the differences between Eskimos and Europeans by placing the Natives within a "universal" historical discourse, one that foreshadows their disappearance.

There were other reasons for placing Nanook's story in the past. By turning back the hands of time, Flaherty erased most (but not all) evidence of colonialism, thus creating the illusion of Western innocence. While the opening credits indicate that Revillon Frères, the French fur-trading company, sponsored the film (the film was, in fact, initially designed as a feature-length advertisement for the company, which in the 1910s and 1920s was engaged in fierce competition with the Hudson's Bay Company) and that Flaherty obtained the footage during his travels as an explorer, viewers find little explicit evidence of Western colonial presence and its effects in the story the film tells. Flaherty explained the reasons for these absences quite explicitly by evoking the narrative of evolution and its correlate, the myth of the vanishing race. He was not interested, as he frequently stated, in the "decay" of the Eskimos after white contact; rather, he wanted to capture their "primitive majesty" before whites destroyed their character and, eventually, the people

[55] See Johannes Fabian, *Time and the Other: How Anthropology Makes Its Object* (New York: Columbia University Press, 1983).

themselves.[56] The film accounts for this destruction in similarly obfuscating ways by rewriting this history into a more palatable story of Eskimo struggles against nature shaped by the "episteme of natural history" described by Fabian. Moreover, these struggles culminate in the Natives' death, thereby attributing the effects of European colonialism to "natural" rather than political processes.

One of the methods Flaherty used to recast this history in *Nanook of the North* was to articulate it through a European-derived discourse on gender. By focusing on the life of a single male character whose family depends upon his success as a hunter and his ability to meet the challenges of his arctic environment, the film enacts masculinist fantasies familiar in mainstream American culture. Nanook repeatedly staves off starvation by hunting large and dangerous animals like walruses and ogruks (large seals). During a single year, the intertitles instruct, Nanook slew seven of the most masculine of all arctic animals, polar bears. These, "in hand to hand encounters he killed with nothing more formidable than his harpoon." By contrast, Nanook's wife Nyla, "the smiling one," inhabits the film world quietly and gently. In this way, she, too, performs conventional Western gender roles. She appears only infrequently and then often in the background, behind her husband, usually preoccupied with the care of their children. Her space is the domestic sphere. The camera almost always finds her indoors attending to household chores. While Nanook's life celebrates the self-sufficient male individual, the archetypal warrior against nature, Nyla's merely echoes the Victorian "angel of the house," just another element in Nanook's otherwise fierce world. In the character of Nanook—strong, independent, unfettered by social conventions, and dominant over women and nature—1920s viewers found a compelling model of modern Western ideals of manhood and family life. Nyla's character, on the other hand, responded to contemporary debates in the West, such women's suffrage, the role of women in the workplace, and the stability of the nuclear family. Performance of conventional Western gender roles by "primitive" Eskimos "naturalized" male dominance and female submission and domesticity for Western audiences.

The narrative of the film is gendered in a subtler way. Not only can viewers identify with the fantasy enacted by Nanook, but the very act of spectatorship also performs a masculinist dream of colonial mastery. Recalling Peary's travel narratives, in the opening sequences of *Nanook* the camera pans the vast and forbidding (yet hauntingly beautiful and, thus, desirable) arctic landscape. Flaherty interposes these early scenes with shots of maps of the region described as "mysterious Barren lands

[56] Quoted in Claude Massot, dir., *Nanook Revisited* (Ima Productions, 1990).

... illimitable spaces which top the world." These scenes create an illusion of possession and (for the spectator, vicarious) mastery of the landscape. Along with the landscape, Eskimos provide another focal point of the camera's gaze. In its opening scene, the camera fixes on the face of Nanook who, in an unconventional gesture repeated several times in the film, looks directly at the camera and, through it, meets the eyes of the viewer. There are different (in fact, contradictory) ways of reading this gesture, and I shall suggest alternative possibilities below. But here it seems to promise the spectator a primary (though vicarious) encounter with the landscape and the Natives. Moreover, Nanook's good-humored expression in these encounters with the camera's eye assures viewers that this meeting will be pleasant, not confrontational. It seems to welcome the non-Native spectator's gaze and, by implication, the Western presence in the Arctic.

The discourse of gender in the film, then, works in contradictory ways, alternately identifying the Native and the white male spectator as the embodiment of masculine ideals. Laura Mulvey's "Visual Pleasure and Narrative Cinema," her path-breaking analysis of the gendered nature of looking at popular films, is instructive in unpacking these contradictions. Reprising Freud, Mulvey defines scopophilia, the act of "taking other people as objects, subjecting them to a controlling and curious gaze," as a fundamental element of film spectatorship.[57] Specifically, she contends that the patriarchal unconscious shapes popular film in such a way that its images play on and replicate conventions of sexual difference, gender roles, and unequal power relations. Women in popular films thus serve as erotic objects both for the character of the hero and for the male spectator who, by identifying with the hero and participating in his power, vicariously possesses the female star. In this way, the spectator constitutes himself as a patriarchal subject. Although Mulvey does not take race into account in her analysis, particular aspects of her argument illuminate spectatorship in *Nanook of the North* and, one could argue, the genre of ethnographic film. The film enacts patriarchal and colonialist fantasies that converge in complex ways. Most obviously, the work mimics the conventions of Hollywood cinema, as described by Mulvey, by sexualizing the female characters (particularly Nyla, a beautiful woman whose gestures frequently imitate those of a starlet). In two rather striking and intimate scenes, the film shows the women bare-breasted as they prepare for or emerge from bed. The nudity is purely gratuitous (and unconventional at the time *Nanook* was

---

[57] Laura Mulvey, "Visual Pleasure and Narrative Cinema," in *Film Theory and Criticism: Introductory Readings,* ed. Gerald Mast and Marshall Cohen, 3d ed. (New York: Oxford University Press, 1985), 806–7.

released), and its presence is particularly significant given that both women were by all accounts Flaherty's common-law wives with whom he bore children. In these scenes, the male spectator thus reenacts the explorer's possession of Native women's bodies, and these relationships articulate the sexualized nature of colonial conquest (also exemplified by Peary's accounts).

Less obvious but equally significant is the gendering of the male character of Nanook in relation to the viewer, and here is where the film's most resonant contradictions emerge. This process is evident at several points, but it is most striking in a somewhat anomalous but pivotal scene early in the film depicting the Eskimos' arrival at the white man's trading post. This is the only encounter between whites and Eskimos in *Nanook of the North,* and significantly, the masculinist image of Nanook disintegrates in this scene. While at the beginning of the film Nanook the brave hunter constitutes a clear counterimage to that of the smiling, feminine Nyla, upon his only encounter with a white man in the film, Nanook is transformed into the "smiling one" (i.e., the childish, happy-go-lucky Eskimo, the other aspect of the stereotype). He is, in a word, *feminized* in relation to the trader, the sole representative of the European world in the film. At the trading post, we watch Nanook cheerfully bartering for beads and candy and, like a young child, showing off his puppies. The trader's manner also suggests the childishness of his guest. He "entertains" Nanook and "attempts to explain" to him the workings of the gramophone, described patronizingly as "how the white man cans his voice." Nanook's wonderment at this example of European technology—the quintessential marker of Western progress—further suggests its superiority. Moreover, his peculiar reaction in this scene (directed by Flaherty) evokes childishness in a particularly resonant way. Reminiscent of the responses of children presented with new objects, he actually *bites* the record.

It is not only the image of Nanook that is key here; the working of the camera is pivotal as well. We see Nanook, for example, smiling broadly at the trader as well as at the camera and, through it, at his Western audiences. While the camera focuses on the faces and bodies of the Natives, the white trader (the only non-Native in the film) escapes the camera's gaze. Audiences never see his entire face or body; only fleeting and partial glimpses of him appear on the screen. Like the spectator, he sees but remains unseen, thus articulating colonial power relations. Not only does the figure of Nanook provide the focus of this scene, he also looks alternately (while laughing, an unconventional gesture usually read as a mark of childishness) at the trader and, through the camera, at the spectator. His very posture also marks him as inferior. To 1920s audiences, frontal photography would have signaled the lack of

FIGURE 12. Still from Robert Flaherty's film *Nanook of the North* (1922) showing Nanook listening to the gramophone, courtesy of the Museum of Modern Art Film Stills Archive.

sophistication and even the subjugation of its subjects, as one critic has shown, in part because of its similarity to "photographic documents like prison records and social surveys in which this code of social inferiority framed the meaning of representations of the objects of supervision and reform."[58] As I have suggested, in *Nanook of the North* the trader occupies the position of power in this encounter, and through a series of exchanged looks as well as the workings of the camera, the spectator identifies with the trader, the colonial figure who dominates the indomitable Eskimo. In the film, then, the figure of Nanook both embodies Western masculine ideals and, at the same time, serves as the object of a masculinist fantasy of domination. Rendering the male Eskimo in this way—as an ideal Western-style male subject who capitulates to the white male—makes him a worthy object of conquest and thus further ennobles the dominating Westerner.

[58] John Tagg, *The Burden of Representation: Photographies and Histories* (Amherst: University of Massachusetts Press, 1988), 36–37.

The film, then, performs a series of apparently contradictory but related maneuvers. By locating in Eskimo life the lost virtues of white civilization, the film first constructs Natives in a way that questions the colonialist project. Then, in a circular move, by evoking reconstituted Western gender hierarchies (which the film "naturalizes" by siting them in a "primitive" society), *Nanook of the North* reinscribes these colonialist racial hierarchies by feminizing the Eskimos in relation to Europeans. The gaze, then, serves a somewhat different function here from what it does in Mulvey's analysis. On one hand, the spectator is gendered male both by his surrogate relationship to the trader and his vicarious domination of the Natives (travel and colonial conquest, after all, are masculine occupations).[59] However, the conquest he enacts is accomplished in the name of both patriarchy and racial superiority, thus claiming colonial mastery on behalf of all white Westerners. Just as Hollywood cinema constructs a masculine subject distinct from female objects, ethnographic film (or this one, at least) creates a white, colonial subject rendered superior to the Native objects it dominates.

The discourse of race is, in fact, present from the beginning in the narrative of death that shapes Nanook's story. Death, embodied in the constant threat of starvation, threatens the Natives throughout the film. At the outset, Flaherty describes the land as "the country of death" where the hungry Eskimos in the film live continually on the thin edge of starvation. The film thus veils the effects of colonialism by making nature (rather than the colonizer) the threat. An absence of food is not the only danger, however. Death is also associated—but only implicitly—with the Western presence in the trading post scene, which strikingly contrasts the Western and the Eskimo worlds and points to the superiority (in material terms) of the Europeans. The post signifies wealth: layers of lavish white furs adorn its outer wall, and the trader's home is a place of bounty (food, warmth, clothing) in other respects as well. By contrast, Nanook's meager household possessions, as we later see them, consist only of a pot, a lamp, and a few skins. In addition, the visit provides the Eskimos' only respite from the ever-present threat of starvation, which is momentarily quelled by a fit of overindulgence as the trader "banquets" Nanook's children on biscuits and lard. His son, Allegoo, eats to excess, so that the trader has to administer him with a dose of castor oil to alleviate his suffering. The trader's generosity thus reverses the colonial relation-

<hr>

[59] Western women also traveled to colonized regions during this period, but the Arctic remained a largely male domain. For discussions of the relations of gender and colonial conquest, see Pratt, *Imperial Eyes,* and Caren Kaplan, *Questions of Travel: Postmodern Discourses of Displacement* (Durham: Duke University Press, 1996).

ship by highlighting his benevolence and generosity; it is not he but the Natives who benefit materially from this encounter.

Yet representing the relationship between the Eskimo and European worlds in this way also implied that the Native world would inevitably disintegrate upon continued contact with Westerners. The encounter with technology (the gramophone), capitalism (the riches of furs and other excesses), and "progress" embodied by the trader, the film implies, spells death for the Natives. Yet their demise results from their innate inferiority, their inability to adapt to progress, rather than from Western domination. In *Nanook,* viewers not only see the Eskimos' inadequacy when confronted by superior European technology but also witness the corruption of the Eskimos' innocence, signified by the Eskimo child (or the Eskimo-as-child) becoming sick from the trader's gifts, an inauguration into the world of capitalist consumption. The implications of the Eskimos' entry into the technological world of capitalism become clear in the final sequence of the film, a metaphorical death scene. Fearing the strength of the oncoming storm, Nanook and his family build an igloo and go to sleep. Outside, their master dog howls mournfully as snow buries the igloo, a symbolic grave. In this scene, Flaherty, like other filmmakers and writers of his generation, foretold the "inevitable" disappearance of the Eskimos in the face of encroaching white civilization. In the evolutionary framework he evoked, the primitive, however tragically, must disappear upon the arrival of the more advanced (read superior) Western world.

The death of the primitive, staged over and over, enables the birth of the Western subject as spectator/conqueror. Although Flaherty tried to purge the dynamics of colonialism from *Nanook of the North,* his project bears marked similarities to Peary's and the exhibition of the Polar Eskimos at the American Museum of Natural History. Both the museum and the filmic display articulate colonial relations by rendering the other as a spectacle for audiences who themselves remain unseen and unscrutinized. In addition, both foreground the way the "primitive" and (ostensibly) technologically unsophisticated Eskimos constitute the childhood of Western "civilization," and both narrate the death of the Natives. In a society that conflated modernity and progress (whatever its professed ambivalence toward both), this formulation seemed to confirm Western superiority and to naturalize colonial dominance. Through its narrative and its documentary genre, though, Flaherty's film renders Western intervention in the Arctic doubly invisible. In reality, however, the "documentary" value of Flaherty's work does not lie in its accuracy in portraying Eskimo culture. Rather, the contradictions in the film reveal much about the colonial relationship between the West and the Arctic—in particular, the need of modern colonial culture at once to claim its innocence and to enact its dominance.

Flaherty's story did not die with the symbolic death at the end of the film. Indeed, it lived and grew over the years, culminating some years later in Gontran de Poncins's immensely popular 1941 travel narrative, *Kabloona.*[60] While *Nanook of the North* both enacts and conceals Western colonial domination by making Eskimos embody Western ideals, *Kabloona* goes even further. In this travel account/autobiography, Poncins narrates a self-transformation accomplished by actually going native, by inhabiting the experiences and occupying the physical space of Eskimo peoples themselves. In doing so, he makes even clearer the extent to which going native fundamentally confirms (rather than criticizes) Western ideals and white racial dominance.

KABLOONA AND THE (ANTI)COLONIAL SUBJECT

Like Robert Flaherty, Gontran de Poncins led a life characterized by both privilege and displacement. The child of an aristocratic French family, he did not find it easy to inhabit the worlds he encountered. As a young man, he studied painting at the École des Beaux-Arts, where he quickly grew bored. He then went into business. He soon tired of this occupation as well and decided to travel to the far reaches of the world as a journalist. This choice was, perhaps, overdetermined. A descendent of Michel de Montaigne, he shared not only his famous ancestor's name (he was christened Jean-Pierre Gontran de Montaigne de Poncins) but apparently some of his fascinations as well. Curiosity drew him to exotic areas throughout the world—Tahiti, New Caledonia, and, eventually (in 1938), the Canadian Arctic. What he discovered there, he believed, was a nobler way of life and, perhaps, a means of saving a fallen Western world. Initially, the lure of the Arctic for Poncins stemmed from a general disillusionment with civilization. At the beginning of his popular arctic travel narrative, *Kabloona*, published in 1941, he explained his motives for traveling north:

[60] The inclusion of this text in a discussion of North American travel literature and film requires a word of explanation. Although Poncins was French, the text was first published in the United States in English in 1941; the French edition followed six years later. In many ways, the book was primarily an American phenomenon. Upon his return from the Arctic, Poncins submitted well over a thousand pages of notes in French and English to an editor at Time-Life Books. The editor shaped the text into its published form, and Time-Life successfully marketed it to large American audiences. The French edition of *Kabloona* is a translation of the English Time-Life edition.

I had not been possessed instantly by a conscious and urgent need to go into the Arctic and live with a primitive people. These things operate slowly....You find yourself feeling that something is obscurely yet radically wrong with your life....Your world becomes progressively more stuffy, less tolerable...your friends seem to you more and more to be talking nonsense, leading a meaningless existence, content with a frivolity and a mediocrity to which you find yourself superior....The thing is at work in you.[61]

Later, his editor described his journey as "a quest for peace, for serenity, for a community of men" lost in the civilized world.[62] This quest led him to the land of the Eskimos.

Poncins's search, in other words, was for an experience missing in the modern West, an experience he located in "primitive" societies. In *The Culture of Consumption*, T. J. Jackson Lears argues that for historical reasons this goal was a common one during the early part of the century. Emerging during the nineteenth century, consumer culture had reached full bloom by the 1920s (only a few years before Poncins embarked on his journey to the North). Some consumers, however, sought more than the material goods that advertisers promised would transform their lives. As the nature of the workplace grew increasingly monotonous and unfulfilling, experience itself became commodified. "Feelings of unreality," Lears contends, "stemmed from urbanization and technological development; from the rise of an increasingly interdependent market economy; and from the secularization of liberal Protestantism among its educated and affluent devotees."[63] Increasingly, members of the middle class sought "real life," and real life, it seemed, was elsewhere. Similarly, Poncins's journey north was in part a quest for an authentic experience lost in the modern West. His presence in the Arctic was an acquisitive one in a more literal sense as well. Throughout his voyage he sought Eskimo artifacts and other objects, frequently trading items of little economic value such as tobacco for objects of great rarity.

Yet while Poncins's narrative bears several key marks of the industrial capitalist world, the story he told takes the form of a flight from this world and its values. The account describes his arrival in Canada from

[61] Gontran de Poncins, *Kabloona* (New York: Time-Life Books, 1980), 3–4.
[62] Lewis Galantière, introduction to *Kabloona*, by Gontran de Poncins (New York: Time-Life Books, 1980), xxii.
[63] T. J. Jackson Lears, "From Salvation to Self-Realization: Advertising and the Therapeutic Roots of the Consumer Culture, 1880–1930," in *The Culture of Consumption: Critical Essays in American History, 1880–1930,* ed. Richard Wightman Fox and T. J. Jackson Lears (New York: Pantheon Books, 1983), 6. See also Lears, *No Place of Grace.*

France, then his arduous journey from King William Land to Pelly Bay in the Far North. Each mile traveled took him further from civilization, until he eventually arrived at the place where the Eskimos endured "the hardest physical existence lived by man anywhere on earth."[64] Poncins, like Flaherty and others of his generation, envisioned the Arctic and Eskimo life in gendered terms, as an arena where "men of [his] soft world" (292) could regenerate their failing masculinity by enduring physical hardships. In *Kabloona,* as in *Nanook of the North,* Eskimo women also occupied subservient roles. They thus provided a stark—and apparently welcome—contrast to the "shrill intervention of women in affairs in our civilized communities" (258). But for Poncins, it was a more general discontent with civilization that motivated his flight from France. In the introduction to *Kabloona*, Poncins's collaborator Lewis Galantière writes,

> To put it simply, [Poncins] didn't like "progress."...In rebellion against all the family stood for, he went to Italy, learned the rayon trade as a factory workman, and before he was 30 years old was sales director of its British branch. And then one day he threw it all over, his bones rejected the fat they were accumulating. Poncins went forth on a quest for peace, for serenity, for a community of men—somewhere, anywhere—whose roots were in something eternal, something that was not self-centered, savagely competitive and destructive of happiness.[65]

The Arctic, in Poncins's mind, seemed to be everything the capitalist industrial West was not. While the West was dominated by ever changing technology, life in the Arctic was ruled by an indomitable and less ephemeral nature. The fast pace of the modern world slowed there. Nature and human whimsy, rather than the clock, governed daily affairs. In other ways, too, Eskimos seemed to enjoy freedoms practically unimagined by "civilized" people. Their lives even appeared more meaningful. While mundane tasks governed "frivolous" Western lives, the need for survival motivated virtually all of the Eskimos' activities. These Natives were spiritually nobler as well. Unlike their acquisitive, "savagely competitive," and individualistic Western counterparts, Eskimos practiced gracious hospitality and self-sacrificing communalism.[66]

---

[64] Poncins, *Kabloona,* xxvii. Hereafter cited by page number in the text.
[65] Galantière, introduction to *Kabloona,* xxii. I have suppressed a paragraph break.
[66] In the literature of the period, Eskimo life frequently provided a fantasy of life in pre- or anticapitalist society. See, for example, Fridtjof Nansen's introduction to

It was particularly these latter attributes with all their spiritual connotations that drew Poncins, along with the related absence of the individualism so highly prized in the Western world. For him, it was the renunciation of material possessions that most starkly differentiated the Eskimo world from the white one. At the beginning of the narrative, it is in fact the inability to spend money that marks Poncins's departure from the "white man's world" and his entry into the true Arctic. With the sole exception of the trading post, described as a "storehouse of wealth" and the "sum of the white man's civilization" (98), life in the remotest parts of the Central Canadian Arctic was spartan, devoid of material wealth. The farther north he traveled, the truer this became. There, in the remotest northern regions, he encountered his "true" Eskimo people who lived this stark, ascetic life. Lest his ideals be marred by comparisons with less perfect, "poor specimens," he carefully distinguished these Eskimos from their more southern relatives, whose homes lay too close to the contaminating Western world and whose base and hopeless poverty was utterly different from the pristine simplicity of the inhabitants of the Far North: "Looking at [the Eskimos] as they loaded their sleds, seeing how each was helped by the rest, how all labored in common with no hint of selfishness as they ran from igloo to igloo...it came to me that here was indeed the communal life, the Biblical clan which hitherto I had imagined only against a background of sand and date palm...they formed a common being" (78–79). For its author, this scene held explicitly Christian overtones. The West, tainted by selfishness and material greed, was a fallen world. The Arctic, by contrast, was a space of (white) purity and even redemption.

When he reached the Far North, Poncins very literally encountered a redeemed white man who lived, suitably, in one of the remotest regions of the Arctic hinterland. In Pelly Bay, the homeland of "uncontaminated Eskimos" and a world "filled with light," he met Father Henry who, in his quest to save Eskimo souls, had renounced all the accouterments of civilization and adopted Native ways. This "true" arctic life also quickly transformed Poncins. Preferring the Eskimos' selfless communalism to European rapacity, he, too, renounced materialism and shed the selfishness that had characterized his youth. Significantly, Christianity and "Eskimoness," in Poncins's mind, were thus elided: "*We Eskimos*—so to say—were a community. It was not precisely that everything here was owned in common, for it was not; it was better than that. It was, if I may say so, *Christian*. Each member of the community was concerned to see that all the others were provided for" (263, emphases mine). When, near

Diamond Jenness, *People of the Twilight* (Chicago: University of Chicago Press, 1959), and Peter Freuchen's novel *Eskimo* (New York: Horace Liveright, 1931).

the end of the narrative, he declared, "I had become an Eskimo," it was, ironically, because he had taken to heart these Christian virtues (273). His description of his transformation also carried heavily Biblical overtones: "I had lost all I owned, but had found great riches. Like a religious, I possessed the veritable treasures, those which could not be taken from me. I had lost the world, but I had found myself, had exchanged the glitter for gold. Within me had lain potentialities for moral serenity, and I had not known it. Storm and danger had been my salvation" (320).

These Biblical references notwithstanding, Poncins's flight from the values of the industrial capitalist West also included distancing himself from its colonial practices. Thus, although both the church and the trading post (colonial institutions that controlled many aspects of life in the Canadian Arctic) made his redemptive voyage possible, he denied the presence of either in his transformation. His fate, he claimed, depended completely upon the Eskimos. Of course, in one sense, this was true. Since he was a *kablunak* (a rather inept white man), his skills fell short of the demands of arctic life, and he did depend upon the Natives for survival. Nevertheless, he also had access to money and trade goods, both by then critical to Native life in the North. This explains in part the Eskimos' service to him. But he even somewhat disingenuously disclaimed his economic privilege as well, contending that the Eskimos exploited him, not he them. They repeatedly invaded the privacy of his igloo, treating it like "conquered territory," and appropriated all of his personal possessions, including his food. In a reversal of the colonial gaze, they scrutinized and mimicked both his appearance and gestures. According to Poncins, these shrewd Natives similarly exploited the trader, capitalizing on his generosity to obtain more trade goods than the furs they offered were worth. The colonial politics and power present in Peary's and Flaherty's narratives were turned upside down in other ways as well. While both earlier explorers had exercised their dominance by giving names to their subjects, it was the Eskimos who dubbed Poncins "Kabloona." Acceding to this reversal (necessary for his transformation into an "Eskimo"), Poncins never used his given name in the text (although, a couple of times, he used his nickname, "Mike").

Nevertheless, despite Poncins's overt critique of the values and practices of the modern West, his narrative replicates the values of bourgeois capitalism and colonialism. Thus, the radical difference of the Arctic was not really a difference at all. It was, instead, recuperated into a space complementary rather than challenging to the modern Western world. Poncins's journey, then, was not an escape from European values and institutions, but rather a search for them in another, non-Western place. The journey narrated in *Kabloona* begins at the trading post (a symbol of the vices of materialistic civilization) and ends at the church in Pelly Bay (a counterspace characterized by Father Henry's renunciation of all material possessions). Eskimo values he defined in Christian rather than Native terms, thereby negating their identity and any fundamental challenge they might pose to Western practices. Eskimo peoples, too, he related to Europeans; they were, he contended, living embodiments of our Stone Age ancestors. Similarly, the arctic landscape he marked as colonial space by using European names and making analogies to European places. Like Flaherty, Poncins had traveled north only to find a mirror image of the West he had fled, for only in appearance was this community essentially different from the society he left; actually the two were complementary.

For all of its romanticization of Eskimo life, then, ultimately *Kabloona* did not challenge the racial hierarchies of the West. Symptomatically, although Poncins's Eskimos were nobler and purer than their European counterparts, they were at the same time baser as well. With striking ambivalence, Poncins assigned them both the virtues of civilization and its repressed vices. The following Conradian scene, significantly located in a filthy subterranean space characterized by darkness rather than light, reveals the latter tendency. Here, Eskimos provide a marked contrast to the Christianized vision of arctic life Poncins created elsewhere:

> I emerged into the igloo. But was this an igloo? This witch's cave black on one side with the smoke of the lamp and sweating out on the other the damp exudation caused by the warmth of the lamp and human bodies! Within, nothing was white save an occasional line that marked the fitting of block to block; and the odor was inconceivable....I was too newly come from the Outside to see in the igloo anything but filth...as if these Eskimos had worn their party clothes to the Post and were here revealing their true selves, the maculate bodies they covered with skin and fur to hide the truth from the White. And to heighten the horror of the scene, one of these Eskimos would fling himself from time to time into the porch...to drive out the dogs; and a howling would resound as of murder committed in a subterranean chamber. (60)

No longer angelic, these Eskimos represented the other repressed elements of industrial capitalist society: the carnal and the animalistic. These formulations are two sides of the same coin. Embodying both the extreme vices and virtues of Western civilization, these Natives were not real, historical subjects. Marked as Europe's "primitive" (less evolved) ancestors, they had no place in the modern world. Poncins made this point clear in one particular scene at the trading post, a scene that strikingly mirrors Nanook's encounter with technology in the trading post scene in Flaherty's film. Fascinated by the "toys of civilization," the Eskimo tried in childish fashion to play with them, but all of the objects—the stove, the watch, even the cigarette holder—refused to work for him. Poncins drew the obvious conclusion: "'We are not for you,' these things seemed to say....What was he, an Eskimo, doing, playing at being a white man?" (191). While Poncins found purification and redemption in the Eskimo world, the Eskimo, by contrast, found no place in the white world. Having accomplished his own redemption by going native, Poncins thus redrew these racial boundaries in a way that confirmed white superiority.

At the conclusion of the narrative, Poncins returned to France to a world entering another bloody war. In the end, he realized that he belonged to Europe and not to the Arctic, and he returned home a renewed and purified man: "I had lost the world, but I had found myself." The fantasy of arctic experience—the loss of selfhood, the renunciation of possessions, the spiritual values—ultimately proved not to be a challenge to the world Outside. Rather, they comprised a site of purification from its filth, a space of renewal and redemption, as well as an opportunity for regenerating the self (capitalism's privileged element). And this ritual of renewal, to return to Lears, is an essential part of the ethos of the culture of consumption. In addition, the lesson of Poncins's experience—that consumption (in this case, of culture) brings about personal transformation—embodies the logic of capitalism. The Arctic and Eskimo life, in Poncins's story, thus consolidated and completed Western identity and power; they did not disrupt it. In other words, while his narrative, like Flaherty's stories, claimed to position Eskimo life in the Arctic as an alternative to the industrial capitalist world, in *Kabloona* this last "frontier" functioned in much the same way Frederick Jackson Turner's frontier had. The Arctic provided a site for enacting a racialized vision of progress that naturalized white dominance, while going native ultimately confirmed Western values and colonial practices.

TALKING BACK: THE LAUGH OF NANOOK

In the years between the world wars, Flaherty and his contemporaries told captivating and romanticized tales of arctic travel and life, tales that veiled the violence of these colonial encounters and catered to the demands of Western audiences. Many Eskimos, however, told and continue to tell different stories. In *Nanook Revisited,* a 1988 documentary exploring Flaherty's relationships with "his" Eskimos, some contemporary Inuit people give their own accounts of the explorer's expeditions, suggesting alternative (anticolonial) ways of interpreting particular scenes in the film. One commentator, viewing *Nanook of the North,* explains that Flaherty (like the famed photographer Edward Curtis before him) staged much of the "documentary" to suit the demands of the "Southern [white] imagination" by dressing the Eskimos in polar bear skins and scripting a number of key scenes. "People didn't wear polar bear skin pants around here," he observes. "I think that the southern image of Inuk was somebody running around in polar bear skin pants. Robert [Flaherty] doctored this particular scene so that the image would fit the imagination." Watching the pivotal trading post scene, considering perhaps the actors' contrived ignorance of Western technology (by then, long a staple of arctic life), he continues, "I'm not so crazy about this scene." Charles Nayoumealuk, whose father knew Allakari-allak (Nanook), concludes "[*Nanook of the North*] was a film for white people."[67] Thus, while Flaherty's "documentary" promised viewers truth and objectivity, it instead delivered a product shaped by Western—rather than Eskimo—realities and desires. In most cases, however, stories such as Flaherty's were the only ones Western audiences heard, or perhaps wanted to hear.

Yet many Eskimos (like the Inuit in *Nanook Revisited*) have challenged these conventional accounts. These include Minik, the child captured by Peary in 1897. Early in the twentieth century (before Flaherty's visit), he provided a counternarrative of colonialism, an account very different from those offered by arctic explorers, filmmakers, anthropologists, and museum officials. He was outspoken in his criticism of these figures, and he expressed his views in letters he wrote to friends and in reports of interviews with the press. It was, perhaps, his tragic position that enabled him to articulate these critiques. Torn from his arctic home at a young age and forced to live the remainder of his days as a colonial subject, he quickly learned to navigate both the Western and Eskimo worlds and to comprehend the relations between them. Indeed, his very survival depended upon his ability to do so. As an adult, Minik looked upon the white world and remembered the fate of his companions; what he saw both saddened and outraged him. What others greeted as the benign pursuit of scientific knowledge, for example, he viewed as

---

[67] These men were interviewed in Claude Massot's documentary *Nanook Revisited.* Apparently, however, the these critiques were lost on the filmmaker, whose primary goal seems to have been to celebrate Flaherty and the presence of other white men in the Arctic. Moreover, the documentary incorporates many of the problems inherent in earlier works, for example, by presenting contemporary Inuit life as a degenerate version of the pristine existence portrayed in *Nanook of the North.*

cruelty and greed. He described how the Natives would hide their possessions when ships landed in his arctic village. "We knew what white men do," he explained, "so our men hid all the furs and ivory to keep them from being stolen."[68] Minik served as a witness to the events colonial culture persistently denied. Colonialism depends, to some degree, on its ability to silence its subjects and to conceal its workings. Peary, for instance, studiously neglected in his voluminous writings any mention of the hapless Polar Eskimos whose fates he so profoundly affected. Similarly, after the deaths of Minik's companions, Boas claimed there was "nothing particularly deserving severe criticism" about the way the museum handled the affair.[69] For years afterwards, other institution officials even absurdly denied that the museum possessed the Eskimos' corpses. Minik testified to the factuality of events that Flaherty and others had purged from their accounts and attempted to exclude from historical memory.

Minik's life and his sharp criticisms of Peary, Boas, and officials of the American Museum of Natural History also discredited romantic tales of colonial encounters in the Arctic and challenged stereotypes of Native peoples. He accomplished what many observers believed Eskimos could not: he inhabited the modern world with agility and some degree of success, and it was perhaps in part for this reason that the white world lost interest in him. The tragedy of his life was not evidence of his "primitiveness" or of some innate inability to adapt to the contemporary world. Rather, it showed the devastating consequences of the Western colonial desire for all things Native. Minik saw this clearly. As an adult, he resisted all attempts by anthropologists and others to "collect" him. He was no one's "Eskimo friend," and he spent much of his life trying to escape the Western world and return home to the Arctic. This was not easily accomplished, however. An embarrassed Peary had long since washed his hands of Minik's plight, and since virtually no other ships sailed to the more distant arctic regions, there was little chance of returning home without Peary's help. A suicide attempt finally drew the attention and sympathy of a New York actress who helped make other arrangements for Minik's return.

Minik's life and words as well as the deaths of his companions thus questioned the entire expansionist enterprise, the notion of Western superiority, and the nature of conventional colonial narratives. Science and exploration were the causes of his own suffering as well as the bitter fate of his companions. Nor did colonial greed and perverse curiosity die with these Natives. After the death of Minik's father, museum

[68] Harper, *Give Me My Father's Body,* 19.
[69] Ibid., 94.

officials staged a fake funeral and burial of his body to placate the grieving boy, then surreptitiously placed his bones on display. Getting back his father's bones was Minik's other lifelong struggle, one which he never accomplished.[70] Indeed, part of his desire to return home was the very realistic fear that the museum would display his own body after his death. Shockingly, acquaintances of Minik had in fact suggested that he donate his brain to the museum. When he recoiled in horror, they were surprised that he failed to grasp the "scientific point of view."[71] In a press interview granted the day before his departure from the United States, he charged: "You're a race of scientific criminals. I know I'll never get my father's bones out of the American Museum of Natural History. I am glad enough to get away before they grab my brains and stuff them in a jar!"[72] Although Westerners labeled them savages, he contended that his own people were free of the more insidious vices of civilization. He wrote to a friend:

> You can't know the sad feelings I have, Dob. No one can know unless they have been taken from their home and had their father die and put on exhibition, and left to starve in a strange land where the men insult you when you ask for your own dear father's body to bury or to be sent home. These are the civilized men who steal, and murder, and torture, and pray and say "Science." My poor people don't know that the meteorite that they used till Peary took it fell off a star. But they know that the hungry must be fed, and cold men warmed, and helpless people cared for, and they do it. Wouldn't it be sad if they forgot those things and got civilized and changed kindness for science?[73]

Deploying, perhaps, the West's images of noble Natives against itself, Minik's critique not only challenged the benevolent and paternalistic posturing of colonial agents but also questioned core Western values and showed the violence of imperialism, as evidenced in Native lives lost not to a "natural" process of entropy but to Western greed and a will to power.

Ultimately, twenty years after the deaths of his father and their companions, Minik met the same fate. Once back in the Arctic, he quickly learned that life in New York had rendered him unfit for an arduous arctic existence. He then returned to the United States. The location

---

[70] The American Museum of Natural History resisted returning the bones until 1993, when media attention and public pressure made retaining them too controversial. See Harper, *Give Me My Father's Body*, 238.

[71] Ibid., 142.

[72] Idem.

[73] Ibid., 132.

between cultures that positioned him as an apt critic of Western colonialism also made him a stranger in his own home. "I had to learn the language again....I lived as they lived...," he said of his sojourn in the North, "but I found I couldn't settle down and marry. You see, I'd been educated."[74] His return to the United States, however, predictably failed to bring him peace, and he soon began planning for another trip north. But this journey was not to be. After combating several bouts of pneumonia throughout his short life, he finally succumbed to another Western disease to which he lacked sufficient immunity and died in the influenza epidemic of 1918. His final home in life as well as in death was, appropriately, a literal no-man's-land, a territory in northwest New Hampshire whose boundaries had been disputed by the United States and Canada until the mid-nineteenth century. Meaningful, too, was the date of his death, 29 October 1918, only a few days before the end of World War I, Europe's bloodiest war. In the years following the war, arctic colonialism, of which Minik's life was one tragic example, began to be rewritten in a more palatable style for Western audiences. His story shows the terrible consequences of Western incursions into the Arctic, consequences the most familiar arctic narratives conceal. It also suggests the terrible irony of the name of the ship that carried him to the United States in 1897. While the images and practices I have been describing provided "hope" and regeneration for the Western world, they spelled suffering and death for the Natives.

Contrary to the predictions of these explorers and scientists, however, modern arctic Natives have entered the Western world in less tragic ways. If the twentieth century has been the period of high colonialism in the Arctic, it has also seen a stunning amount of resistance to these incursions and, more recently, consolidations of Native political power. Many important events in Eskimo/Inuit history followed by several decades the early-twentieth-century predictions of the Natives' inevitable demise. In 1971 Congress passed the Alaska Native Claims Settlement Act, the largest land settlement in U.S. history. Despite some major shortcomings, particularly with regard to sovereignty rights, ANCSA has enabled Alaska Natives, including Eskimos, to exert considerable power in state politics. Later, the Inuit Circumpolar Conference of 1977 created a pan-Eskimo/Inuit coalition to address issues germane to Native populations of all the arctic regions. In Canada, the 1991 Nunavut settlement (in which Inuit people gained control of 770,000 square miles of the Northwest Territories) marked a substantial victory in the battle of Native Canadians for political and economic rights. Currently, a number of Eskimo/Inuit writers and filmmakers are creating

[74] Ibid., 213.

works which contest conventional images of Eskimo peoples and narratives of arctic colonialism.[75] Far from disappearing, contemporary Eskimo and Inuit peoples are becoming increasingly visible and powerful in world affairs.

In the spirit of these contemporary Natives' voices of resistance, Allakariallak (Nanook) shall have the final words here. There is, I briefly observed above, another way of reading the pivotal scene in which the character of Nanook encounters the trader at the fur trading post. As I have noted, his laugh, directed alternately at the trader and, through the camera, at the viewer, is usually read as a marker of his childishness and his deference to white authority. In *Nanook Revisited,* Charles Nayoumealuk reports that "each time a scene was shot, as soon as the camera was starting to shoot, he [Allakariallak playing Nanook] would burst out laughing. He couldn't help it. Flaherty would tell him, 'be serious.' He couldn't do it. He laughed each time." Perhaps, he suggests, Allakariallak was actually laughing at Flaherty—at his peculiar requests and his odd scripting of the scene—and, through Flaherty, at the expectations of non-Native viewers. While the final chapter of arctic colonialism remains to be written, perhaps the last word—and the last laugh—will be his.

*

In the years following World War II, Americans for the most part lost interest in Native peoples, to some extent because no crisis such as that marking the period following World War I sent Westerners to Native America in search of an alternative ethos. Instead, complacency and prosperity characterized middle-class European-American life throughout the 1950s. Native peoples, however, were not so fortunate. Termination and relocation, the government's latest assimilationist policies, placed Native Americans' rights and capacity for self-government under siege yet again. Perhaps predictably, these devastating dilemmas

---

[75] Joseph Senungetuk, an Inupiat Eskimo from Alaska, for example, writes about misrepresentations of Eskimo peoples in *Give or Take a Century: An Eskimo Chronicle* (San Francisco: Indian Historian Press, 1971). More recently, Canadian Inuit filmmaker Zacharias Kunuk has documented local Inuit life in a number of experimental films including *Nunaqpa* (Igloolik Isuma Productions, 1991) and *Qaggiq* (Igloolik Isuma Productions, 1989). In addition, organizations such as the Eskimo Channel in Alaska and the Inuit Broadcasting Corporation (IBC) in Canada are challenging stereotypical representations of Inuit/Eskimo life and producing media which breaks many of the conventions (see David Poisey's and William Hansen's remarkable film on the IBC, *Starting Fire with Gunpowder* [Tamarack Productions, 1991]).

proved to be of little interest to the broader American society. It was not until these Americans confronted another crisis of their own, this one brought about in part by the war in Vietnam, that they renewed their fascination with Native America. This time, Indians, once irredeemably savage and suitable only as a testing ground for white manliness, underwent another transformation in ways that brought them closer to the position Eskimos now occupied in the cultural imagination. Like the peaceful, happy-go-lucky Eskimos of the interwar years, Indians in the 1960s and 1970s seemed to embody an alternative to a corrupt and violent Western world. What this "new" Indian offered, however, was not only the Eskimo's innocence but also a spiritual, environmentally conscious alternative to the hyperrational and industrialized European-American world. During the 1960s and 1970s and in the subsequent New Age movement, Indians thus served as another kind of tourist destination, this one offering a renewed connection to the earth and the hope of spiritual regeneration.

CHAPTER THREE

The Making of an Indian:
"Forrest" Carter's Literary Inventions

IN 1976, FORREST CARTER published *The Education of Little Tree,* a book that quickly ranked among the most widely circulated, critically acclaimed, and, ultimately, controversial texts on Native America. Recognizing the long-standing appeal of Native American autobiographies, its publishers originally marketed the book as a true story, as the author's remembrances of his 1930s boyhood in the Tennessee hill country where he was raised by his Cherokee grandparents. Audiences responded with immediate enthusiasm, and book sales skyrocketed. The success of *The Education of Little Tree* is easy to explain. A nostalgic tale of a bygone era populated by earth-loving and peaceful Indians, *The Education of Little Tree* offered a vision of Native life that counterposed the fractious world of America in the 1970s. The text in fact explicitly addresses a number of concerns central to the nation's political climate since the watershed 1960s. Racial violence, the history of U.S. colonialism, the domination of corporate monopolies, and the power of a hopelessly corrupt government—each of these subjects finds a place in *The Education of Little Tree.* The book thus responded to the preoccupations of audiences reeling in the aftermath of the Vietnam war (which ended in the year the novel was published), the civil rights era, and the Watergate scandal. Moreover, *The Education of Little Tree* is a poignant story charmingly told. As a result of its widespread appeal, though aimed primarily at a youth market, the book soon jumped its target audience and garnered readers of all ages. While some found it simply a "good read," others looked to *The Education of Little Tree* for "a fresh perspective for a mechanistic and materialistic modern world."[1] Others had different political agendas. Carter has been called the "guru of new-age environmentalists."[2] Those searching for "a human document of universal meaning" found *The Education of Little Tree* similarly appealing.[3] Nor

[1] Rennard Strickland, "Sharing Little Tree," foreword to *The Education of Little Tree,* by Forrest Carter (Albuquerque: University of New Mexico Press, 1991), vi.
[2] Dan T. Carter, quoted in Felicia R. Lee, "Best Seller Is a Fake, Professor Asserts," *New York Times,* 4 October 1991, A11.
[3] Strickland, "Sharing Little Tree," v.

did its popularity soon fade. The book reached the top of the *New York Times* bestseller list in 1991. That fall, fifteen years after its original publication, it had sold nearly half a million copies, and its sales continue to hold steady. It has also won numerous awards and considerable critical acclaim. Indeed, academic audiences provide a good part of the book's vast readership, as it is now included in the Native American canon used in primary and secondary schools as well as in universities.[4] Critical to the book's reception is its claim to authenticity. Readers, according to one critic, have found *The Education of Little Tree* to be "as accurate as it [is] mystical and romantic," a true depiction of Cherokee beliefs and ways of life.[5]

At the height of the popularity of the book in the autumn of 1991 (twelve years after the author's death), controversy arose regarding the authorship of the text. Questions about the authenticity of its story soon followed. The controversy arose in academia. While researching a biography of the former Alabama governor George Wallace, historian Dan Carter uncovered evidence that *The Education of Little Tree* was not, in fact, written by a Cherokee named Forrest Carter. Shockingly, both the text and its author were the inventions of Dan Carter's distant cousin, Asa (Ace) Earl Carter, whom he describes as "a Ku Klux Klan terrorist, right-wing radio announcer, home-grown American fascist and anti-Semite, rabble-rousing demagogue and secret author of the famous 1963 speech by Gov. George Wallace of Alabama: 'Segregation now… Segregation tomorrow…Segregation forever.'"[6] As Professor Carter explained to the *New York Times,* Asa Carter had spent most of his life engaged in such activities as writing and distributing racist and antisemitic pamphlets, assaulting Nat King Cole during a 1956 concert, and shooting two fellow Klansmen in 1957 in the course of a financial dispute. In the mid-1950s, Carter had even founded his own klavern, the Original Ku Klux Klan of the Confederacy in Birmingham.[7] The group

---

[4] Sherman Alexie satirizes the tendency of instructors to teach palatable visions of Native America by using texts like *Black Elk Speaks, Lame Deer: Seeker of Visions,* and *The Education of Little Tree* (all written or cowritten by white men). See Alexie, "Introduction to Native American Literature," in *Indian Killer* (New York: Atlantic Monthly Press, 1996).

[5] Strickland, "Sharing Little Tree," vi.

[6] Dan T. Carter, "The Transformation of a Klansman," *New York Times,* 4 October 1991, A31. See also Carter, "Southern History, American Fiction: The Secret Life of Southwestern Novelist Forrest Carter," in *Rewriting the South: History and Fiction* (Francke Verlag: Tübingen, Germany, 1993), ed. Lothar Hönnighausen and Valeria Gennaro Lerda, 286–304. My brief discussion of Carter's life is largely based on the latter essay.

[7] Interestingly, the name Carter chose for his klavern suggested ties to the first Klan and reflected another one of his invented pasts. Before he identified as an

was implicated in a string of terrorist bombings that shattered black churches, homes, and synagogues. Its members organized mobs protesting Autherine Lucy's admission to the University of Alabama in 1956. The following year, they reportedly abducted and castrated a young black man. The real Carter, it seemed, had lived a life far different from the idyllic and gentle existence described in *The Education of Little Tree*.

Predictably, neither the book's devoted audience nor the University of New Mexico Press (no doubt eyeing its profits) accepted Dan Carter's exposure of his disreputable kinsman. So Professor Carter offered proof: there was, he said, no evidence of the existence of "Forrest Carter" prior to the 1970s. Furthermore, "Forrest" and Asa Carter were the same age, shared the same address and looked identical in photographs. In short, Carter concluded, "Forrest" Carter was "simply the last fantasy of a man who reinvented himself again and again in the 30 years that preceded his death in 1979."[8] When confronted with these facts, Carter's widow, his former literary agent, and his editor ultimately admitted the fraud,[9] and the book was reclassified as "fiction." Yet its popularity did not suffer. It remained on the bestseller list (under its new category) for several weeks during the following year, and it continues to sell to this day. In 1997, Paramount Pictures capitalized on the popularity of *The Education of Little Tree* by releasing a film version to enthusiastic audiences.

The controversy over the authorship and authenticity of the book raises a number of complex questions. The first concern the author's motives. Why would the "home-grown fascist," "rabble-rousing demagogue," violent white supremacist described by Dan Carter construct the gentle, romantic portrait of Indian life presented in *The Education of Little Tree?* The apparent disparity between the politics of Asa and Forrest Carter has given many people pause. When initially confronted with Dan Carter's allegations, the author's literary agent replied: "Anyone who wrote *Little Tree* could not have worked for George Wallace."[10] But he did. So what are we to make of Carter's "transformation"

Indian, Carter had claimed he inherited his white supremacist ideals from generations of ancestors who had been Klan members and sympathizers. His great-grandfather, as he told the tale, served as a grand dragon of the Original Knights of the Ku Klux Klan during Reconstruction. Others suffered at the hands of regulators who seized their land for taxes. But these stories, too, were fictions. Reality was much more mundane. While Confederate veterans populated the family tree, the Carters were relatively ordinary Alabama farmers. See Carter, "Southern History, American Fiction."

[8] Lee, "Best Seller Is a Fake," A11.

[9] Carter, "Southern History, American Fiction," 286.

[10] Eleanor Friede, quoted by Lee, "Best Seller Is a Fake," A11. Analyses of *The Education of Little Tree* which discuss the relationship between the text and the author

from Klansman to Cherokee? Why did he choose to remake himself as an Indian? And finally, how does the book retain its popularity and its veneer of authenticity despite the revelation that it was written by a white supremacist?

Ironically, the idyllic portrait Carter paints in *The Education of Little Tree* in many respects actually complements the author's earlier Klan politics. Reading this book together with Carter's earlier novel *Gone to Texas* reveals that his fiction articulates a white supremacist vision despite the Indian sympathies it claims. By going native, specifically by eliding the characters of the Confederate outlaw (historically, the originary figure of the Ku Klux Klan) and the Indian in these works, Carter attempts both to vindicate the South from its violent racial history and to redeem an explicitly white supremacist perspective fallen into disrepute.[11] In these two texts, going native thus serves to regenerate white society and to naturalize its power. Given these goals, Carter's choice to reinvent himself as an Indian seems unsurprising. In the popular culture of the 1960s and 1970s, Natives represented a challenge to the status quo. They thus won the sympathy and interest of people representing the entire political spectrum, ranging from the far right (a striking example is President Richard Nixon) to the left (most obviously, members of the counterculture who embraced Indian practices and beliefs).[12] As a result, Indianness proved an effective symbol for very different—and often opposed—causes.

One critical reason Carter's work proved compelling was that his fictions resonated with questions about race, American history, and the nature of progress—specifically, the value of technological advance-

---

include Henry Louis Gates, Jr., "'Authenticity,' or the Lesson of Little Tree," *New York Times Book Review*, 24 November 1991, 1 ff.; and Lawrence Clayton, "Forrest/Asa Carter and Politics," *Western American Literature* 21, 1 (1986): 19–26. To date, no sustained textual analyses of Carter's works have been published.

[11] In forging a relationship between white Southerners and Indians, Carter drew on the historical ambivalence of white supremacist organizations toward Natives. During the 1930s, for instance, some Ku Klux Klan–associated groups claimed alliances with Native peoples because their leaders "correctly reasoned that you couldn't get a more native American than the Indian," while others contended that Natives were "a type of true Aryan" (see Wyn Craig Wade, *The Fiery Cross: The Ku Klux Klan in America* [New York: Simon and Schuster, 1987], 269–70.) It is important to note, however, that these groups more often targeted Native peoples than embraced them.

[12] Remarkably, despite his political conservatism, Richard Nixon still ranks among the politicians most sympathetic to Native causes. His administration supported such controversial measures as the return of Blue Lake to the Taos people. On the preoccupations of "Hippie Indians," see, for example "Happy Hippie Hunting Ground," *Life*, 1 December 1967, 66–71. Philip Deloria analyzes this phenomenon in *Playing Indian*.

ment and its relationship to white civilization—that obsessed many Americans during the 1960s and 1970s. These preoccupations stemmed in large measure from two events that became deeply intertwined in the public consciousness: the civil rights movements and the Vietnam war. Civil rights challenged not only a handful of rabid white supremacists in the South but also the structures underlying the broader American society. African Americans were not the only ones who forced European Americans to question their own power and privilege. Native Americans along with other minorities demanded social changes to remedy their systemic marginalization and oppression.[13] If minority activism raised questions about racial oppression in the present, Vietnam forced Americans to rethink their faith in civilization and to consider other racial conquests in their collective past. From the beginning, the war had been linked in the popular imagination with the nineteenth-century conquest of Native America. Early on, commentators dubbed Vietnam "Indian country," and initially this analogy rallied support for the war effort. It seemed to demonstrate that "'progress' can and must be defended by 'savage war'" and that "resistance to that model is equivalent to an attempt to reverse the course of history."[14] As the years wore on, however, and Americans for the first time witnessed the horrors of war on nightly television broadcasts, public sentiment began to change. In particular, *Life* magazine's photographs of the My Lai massacre in 1969 created doubts about the justice of the war and, by implication, the defensibility of the earlier conquest of Native America.[15] "Machismo, national identity and mythic history," as one observer has noted, numbered among the casualties of America's defeat in Vietnam.[16] This troubling history further challenged America's racial hierarchies including the legitimacy of white ownership of Native land.

[13] For an account of Native activism during this period, see Paul Chaat Smith and Robert Allen Warrior, *Like a Hurricane: The Indian Movement from Alcatraz to Wounded Knee* (New York: New Press, 1996).

[14] Slotkin, *Gunfighter Nation*, 493. See also Patricia Nelson Limerick, "The Adventures of the Frontier in the Twentieth Century," in *The Frontier in American Culture: An Exhibition at the Newberry Library, August 26, 1994–January 7, 1995*, ed. James R. Grossman (Berkeley: University of California Press, 1994).

[15] Ralph Nelson's Western film *Soldier Blue* (Avco-Embassy, 1970), for example, depicted the 1864 massacre of Black Kettle's Cheyenne at Sand Creek, an event that has become an emblem of the conquest of Native America, in a way that reflected on My Lai. One particularly powerful Native account of the massacre is Simon Ortiz's book of poetry, *From Sand Creek* (Oak Park, N.Y.: Thunder's Mouth, 1981).

[16] Alan Fair, "The Beast in the Jungle: Mailer, Eastlake and the Narrating of Vietnam," in *Tell Me Lies about Vietnam: Cultural Battles for the Meaning of the War*, eds. Alf Louvre and Jeffrey Walsh (Philadelphia: Open University Press, 1988), 71.

Meanwhile, the emerging environmentalist movement struck another kind of blow. While nineteenth-century Americans had confidently embraced an idea of progress embodied in industrial technology, their late 1960s descendants suspected that progress thus defined actually threatened human survival.[17]

The role of Native America in these crises was complex. As both the original victims of European Americans and as contemporary activists, Natives challenged self-justifying accounts of American history as well as the social structures that assured white privilege. At the same time, many saw Indians as offering solutions to white America's problems. Indians, the "archetypal victims of White America's bigotry and imperialism," now became "important symbols of rebellion," in part because they seemed to represent "those virtues [Americans] once claimed as [their] own" as well as political resistance to the capitalist/imperialist ethic.[18] Progress, as Elémire Zolla famously claimed in 1969 in *The Writer and the Shaman,* was "the chief culprit, the actual agent of the slaughter" in the genocide of the Indians.[19] As European-American society now confronted the same demon and apparently faced its own annihilation, Indians seemed capable of rescuing modern society from itself:

> Gradually, as society becomes more humanized, it will be obliged to adopt certain features of Indian sociality. The Indian tribes will emerge as the only force capable of facing the social problem.... [O]nly the Indians—or at any rate those faithful to the tradition, who resist the threat of being transformed into the interchangeable parts of the production process, transformed from actors in sublime rites into the spectators of movie or television screens, from explorers of the divine into superstitious believers in progress—they alone in America have kept intact a living idea of spiritual needs. The deadening environment of concrete, asphalt, and steel has not yet atrophied their senses, nor has Enlightenment barbarism destroyed their religious strength.[20]

[17] See Roderick Nash, *Wilderness and the American Mind* (New Haven: Yale University Press, 1982). Other seminal treatises discussing the destructiveness of industrial technology include Theodore Roszak, *The Making of a Counter Culture: Reflections on the Technocratic Society and Its Youthful Opposition* (Garden City, N.Y.: Doubleday, 1969), and Herbert Marcuse, *An Essay on Liberation* (Boston: Beacon, 1969).

[18] Slotkin, *Gunfighter Nation,* 590.

[19] Elémire Zolla, *The Writer and the Shaman: A Morphology of the American Indian,* trans. Raymond Rosenthal (New York: Harcourt Brace Jovanovich, 1973), 3.

[20] Ibid., 280. Here, Zolla echoes sentiments expressed by Stan Steiner in his influential work *The New Indians* (New York: Harper & Row, 1968), 155.

Too often, however, self-criticism turned to self-vindication. Identifying Natives as victims of progress raised uncomfortable questions about white America's accountability. Naming an abstract and disembodied notion of progress as "the actual agent of slaughter" enabled European America to dissociate itself from the racial violence in its own past as well as from racism in the present. Conquest, it seemed, was an agentless enterprise. Moreover, defining white Americans as the contemporary victims of progress identified them with its earlier victims, the Indians. More and more often, in fact, European Americans imitated Indians, donning faux Native clothing, forming Indian-inspired communes, and claiming Native history as part of their own. Symptomatically, a 1971 issue of *Life* magazine titled "*Our* Indian History" instructed readers that "the United States may yet learn [from the Indian] some lessons about restoring the balance between man and his surroundings."[21] Going native, then, ironically undermined challenges to the power and authority of white America. At the same time, Indianness even seemed to provide a means to regenerate white society. Yet missing from this renewed fascination with Native America were Native peoples themselves, who continued to confront crushing problems of their own, frequently at the hands of those who so eagerly sought their wisdom. Too often, these Native peoples' lives clashed with the more comfortable images of earth-embracing Indian spirituality found in popular culture.

It was from this complex cultural landscape that Forrest Carter emerged in the 1970s and found an eager audience among the disaffected. He took as his themes the American obsessions with race, progress, and the white nation's past, and he used going native to "resolve" these problems. In *Gone to Texas*, a novel that begins the ideological work completed in *The Education of Little Tree*, Carter quite predictably turned his mind to the nineteenth century: the period of the Indian wars, heated conflicts over slavery, and the birth of industrial technology. *Gone to Texas* elides the characters of the outlaw and the Indian, two important figures in these historical events, as it rewrites the history of America's origins. Carter, like many of his contemporaries, thus both challenged and reinscribed the notion of progress and the racial hierarchies at the core of American social structures. *The Education of Little Tree*, the text that shows Carter himself going native, picks up where *Gone to Texas* leaves off. Its narrative reflects on white America's violent history as well as on racial conflicts during the civil rights era. By addressing these issues, Carter spoke to mainstream audiences as well as to his own cohort of "fascist demagogues." It is, perhaps, not in fact

---

[21] *Life*, 2 July 1971, 38 (my emphasis).

accidental or even ironic that a Klansman should author works on race and progress that proved wildly popular during that turbulent era. Although Carter's fans found it unbelievable that a violent white supremacist could pen the gentle tale of Little Tree, it is indicative of postwar American history that the political left and the far right—both ultimately concerned with maintaining white dominance—could converge in Asa/Forrest Carter and his work.

INDIANS, OUTLAWS, AND OTHERS: FORREST CARTER'S WEST

To understand the complex racial and political dynamics at play in Forrest Carter's work, we must begin at the beginning, when Asa Carter became "Forrest" and the boundaries between the Confederate outlaw and the Indian grew blurred. "Forrest" Carter actually emerged in 1973 with the publication of his first novel, *The Rebel Outlaw: Josey Wales* (later retitled *Gone to Texas*). Initially, the author used Bedford Forrest Carter as his nom de plume, filing this name on the requisite copyright forms. The reference was startlingly obvious to any student of Southern history. A former slave owner and one of the Confederacy's most aggressive generals, Nathan Bedford Forrest attained notoriety in the postbellum years as a key leader of the South's invisible army, the Ku Klux Klan. An insurance salesman and railroad entrepreneur, Grand Wizard Forrest traveled for several years throughout the southern states recruiting new members. His efforts proved massively successful. The rapid growth of the Klan in the late 1860s, in fact, owed much to his efforts.[22] His political work thus complemented Asa Carter's later activities. When Carter changed the name of his first novel to *Gone to Texas* upon its reissue in 1975, he dropped "Bedford" and was thereafter known only as "Forrest." Dropping "Bedford" and "rebel" suggests an effort to hide the allusion to Reconstruction, a move paralleled in the narrative. At the same time, "Forrest," as we shall see, is a name that carries a double valence key to the tensions complicating Carter's work. The story soon found a wide and enthusiastic audience. Shortly after its reissue, Clint Eastwood acquired the movie rights, retitled the film *The Outlaw Josey Wales* (1976), and cast himself in the leading role. Now a classic, the film helped revive the defunct Western; it was the first of its genre to make a profit at the box office in years.[23] Such was the success of *Gone to Texas* that Carter

[22] Wade, *Fiery Cross,* provides a useful discussion of the origins and rise of the Klan as well as Nathan Bedford Forrest's role in its growth.
[23] Lawrence Clayton, afterword to *Josey Wales: Two Westerns by Forrest Carter*, by Carter (Albuquerque: University of New Mexico Press, 1989), 414.

published a sequel, *The Vengeance Trail of Josey Wales* in 1976, the same year *The Education of Little Tree* appeared. In a final novel, Carter further pursued the Indian preoccupations that provided the focus of his "autobiography." *Watch for Me on the Mountain* (1978) dramatized the life of the famed Apache leader Geronimo in ways that bore marked similarities to the lives of Carter's earlier Western heroes.

Tensions between fact and fiction, history and narrative, prove central to all of Carter's novels. In *Gone to Texas,* Carter retells a familiar history about the origins of the white nation in racial conquest during the period following the Civil War by narrating the story of Josey Wales, a former Confederate soldier turned outlaw. Because it shows its protagonist confronting savagery and eventually establishing a settlement in Texas, the text resembles countless other Western narratives of the beginnings of American civilization in the conquest of savagery, a paradigm Frederick Jackson Turner helped to popularize in his influential 1893 frontier thesis speech.[24] In *Gone to Texas*, however, Carter responded to the social anxieties of his era by complicating these familiar conventions. Although the novel adopts the antithesis between savagery and civilization central to the Western genre, at times it reverses the value of these terms. No longer figured simply as the "savage" (read inferior) counterparts of "civilized" (superior) whites, some Native characters in the narrative serve instead as exemplary figures for whites to emulate, in part because they still occupy a place outside modern society. It is in fact European Americans in the story who most often exhibit "savage" qualities. This reversal articulates a widespread ambivalence about modernity and the value of civilization (though not about white dominance) typical of the counterculture era. The text refigures conventional stories of America's origins in other ways as well, primarily by identifying both Indians and poor Southern whites as victims of Northern whites, agents of modernity. Of all Carter's novels, *Gone to Texas* shows most clearly the convergence of the figures of the Southern outlaw and the Indian in its author's imagination. It also reveals the contradictions surrounding progress—which must be both rejected and reaffirmed to regenerate whiteness—germane to his work.

[24] Although it seems startlingly obvious that racial violence is fundamental in the Western, critics often overlook or underemphasize its importance. Jane Tompkins's erasure of Native peoples and the racial dynamics of the genre in *West of Everything: The Inner Life of Westerns* (New York: Oxford University Press, 1992) is unfortunately symptomatic. Tompkins's work, like a number of other notable studies, emphasizes gender instead. The voluminous work of Richard Slotkin on the frontier in American culture, especially *Gunfighter Nation,* which includes lengthy discussions of Westerns, constitutes one important exception to what remains a blind spot in scholarship on the genre.

Gone to Texas thus provides the necessary starting point for an analysis of *The Education of Little Tree*. At the end of both texts, however, Carter rearticulates conventional visions of the nation's history in a fantasy of white society's new beginnings (ironically, predicated on the disappearance of Native America). Despite Carter's indictments of progress as it is embodied in modern industrial life, then, this fantasy closely resembles the model of civilization both novels claim to criticize. This vision necessitates misrepresenting the historical relationships between Native peoples and Southern whites. The discrepancies between historical fact and narrative vision are clearest in *Gone to Texas*. They show the ideological work that this novel undertakes, just as they clarify the importance of *The Education of Little Tree*.

The particular histories Carter drew upon in *Gone to Texas* are significant in other ways. They evoke a number of key racial and economic conflicts that ravaged the South in the nineteenth century, conflicts the novel attempts to "resolve" to the benefit of white Southerners by rewriting this complex history. For the temporal frame of the novel, significantly, Carter chose the Reconstruction era, the period in which blacks first attained some degree of political power in the South and in which Confederate outlaws violently fought these changes in part by forming the so-called invisible army, the Ku Klux Klan.[25] This historical context is critical, in part because it constitutes the origins of the civil rights conflicts that preoccupied Carter during and after the 1950s. As the terrorist arm of the Southern democrats, the Klan aimed to keep the region, in the words of one historian, "a white man's country." The 1865 Louisiana Democratic party platform, like much other political rhetoric of the period, clearly articulated this goal: "That we hold this to be a Government of white people, made and to be perpetuated for the exclusive benefit of the white race; and...that people of African descent cannot be considered as citizens of the United States, and that there can, in no event, nor under any circumstances, be any equality between the white and other races."[26] Opposition to Reconstruction, as is well-known, proved largely successful in the end. Abandoned by their Northern allies in 1876, blacks quickly lost political ground. White Southerners implemented segregationist policies and commenced a reign of terror (carried out in good measure by the Klan) aimed to subdue black aspirations to political and social equality. Some eighty years later, in

[25] This historical context and these conflicts recall another important cultural artifact: D. W. Griffith's notorious 1915 film, *The Birth of a Nation*. Griffith's work almost certainly influenced Carter, who reportedly screened the film during at least one gathering of his klavern.

[26] Cited in Allen W. Trelease, *White Terror: The Ku Klux Klan Conspiracy and Southern Reconstruction* (New York: Harper and Row, 1971), xv.

naming his own klavern "The Original Ku Klux Klan of the Confederacy," Carter aimed to resolve the racial turmoil of his own era in a similar way. The civil rights period, however, ended somewhat differently. If activists fell short of achieving racial amity and equality, they succeeded in overturning legal segregation and opening the door for increased black political power. Soon, even Carter's staunch ally George Wallace succumbed to the tide of antisegregationist public opinion. Increasingly isolated politically, Carter turned instead to the world of fiction to articulate his racist agenda.

In a sense, Carter found in literature a means of remedying—textually, at least—his failure in fighting for school segregation and other forms of white supremacy. By rearticulating the conflicts of the 1950s and 1960s in the historical context of the postbellum South, an era which saw white supremacy reaffirmed, Carter fantasized a similar resolution to the challenges posed by contemporary civil rights activists. His novels provide such visions of white social regeneration and the reestablishment of white political power, although these visions are less explicit and are thus more widely acceptable than his Klan activism was. Central to most of his work (but especially *Gone to Texas*) are the dilemmas that confronted postbellum Southerners: interracial conflicts and the sweeping changes resulting from the transition to industrial capitalism. Predictably, in *Gone to Texas,* race and progress intertwine. The cross-racial alliance Carter forged in his fiction between the Confederate outlaw who goes native and the Indian depends on their mutual resistance to progressivist politics embodied in Northern industrialism. In the narrative, government soldiers (the instruments of Northern progressivism) target both agrarian Southerners and earth-embracing Indians, who become allied politically because of their shared values as well as their shared fates. In addition, both ostensibly share a fundamentally "primitive" nature, a quality that renders them distinct from, and in some ways superior to, their more civilized and thus corrupt Northern counterparts. But despite this criticism of progress and civilization, Carter relies in the end on progressivist logic to assert the racial superiority of the white outlaw, a fact that draws the outlaw and the Indians in his narrative to their markedly different fates.

Gone to Texas opens with a violent and tragic loss, one that resonates with the historical context of the story. On a spring morning in 1858, the text begins, a young mountain farmer named Josey Wales glances up from his plowing to discover smoke rising from his cabin, located some distance away. Sounds of gunfire quickly follow, and the terrified man rushes to the aid of his family. Arriving at the smoldering cabin, Wales finds the charred remains of his wife and baby boy, clinging to each other even in death. As the narrative unfolds, this loss takes on monumental proportions in terms of postbellum racial and economic conflicts. The historical setting of this opening scene is the bloody Missouri-Kansas border war, a dispute that began around 1855. The antagonisms that gave rise to the war stemmed from the economic changes sweeping most of the nation in the mid-nineteenth century as well as the related debates over slavery. Geographically, Missouri numbered among the states comprising the border between the North and South, a location that placed it at the nexus of social change and political conflict. Like most Western stories, the novel thus sites itself in disputed territory, a frontier of sorts on which battles over land were waged. These battles were ideological as well. While neighboring Kansas entered the Union as a free state, slavery was legal in Missouri. In economic (though not human) terms, however, its importance was only marginal, and this led to divided loyalties within Missouri during the Civil War. From the mid-1850s to the postbellum years, violence took hold of the entire border region. Both slaveholders and poor farmers, popularly dubbed "white trash" or "pukes," drew the contempt of Kansans to the North as well as Missourians who had become part of the rapidly industrializing economy of the state. The hostilities were mutual, prompting raids across the Kansas-Missouri border as well as a civil war of sorts within Missouri itself. During these years, in the words of one historian, Missouri "plunged into the worst guerrilla war in American history," a period of utter "cultural chaos."[27] It is to this conflict that Josey Wales's family falls victim in *Gone to Texas* as Kansas "Redleg" raids cross over into Missouri, igniting the border regions. These deaths, moreover, symbolize in the novel the losses of Southern innocence, of the agrarian-based economy, and of the stubborn independence of mountain folk. Ultimately, these sacrifices comprise the book's most fundamental tragedy.

Although race constituted a central part of this historical controversy, Carter attempted (not always successfully) to exclude any explicit mention of it from the novel, instead reframing the conflict as a battle for Southern values and a quest to avenge slain loved ones. Indeed, vengeance proves Josey Wales's primary motive in *Gone to Texas*. The mountain man's creed "Where the soil's thin, the blood's thick" compels such revenge.[28] Thus the fictional Wales, inspired by countless historical figures, joins one of the bands of guerrilla outlaws that terrorize the border. Banks and railroads, symbols of Northern industrialism, provide frequent targets, as do "traitors" to Southern ideals. In the

---

[27] Michael Fellman, *Inside War: The Guerrilla Conflict in Missouri during the American Civil War* (New York: Oxford University Press, 1989), xvi.
[28] Forrest Carter, *Gone to Texas*, in *Josey Wales*, by Carter, 5.

terms of the novel, the goals that compel the outlaws' violence are both noble and necessary for self-preservation. Union armies arrest and murder women (a grievous affront to Southern chivalry), shamelessly burn homes, and ravage the countryside in an effort to depopulate the border regions.[29] Not only does the text thus ignore the maintenance of white supremacy as a motivation for outlaw violence, it casts white Southerners simply as the victims of Union aggression, thus overlooking the widespread racial violence in which the xenophobic border populations actively engaged. The novel's most effective way of suppressing racial conflicts is to invert them. While the violence of the Ku Klux Klan often involved the burning of houses and the wielding of fiery crosses, in *Gone to Texas* it is a white family who perishes by fire.

Despite its "nobility," Wales's desire to avenge his wife and child seems hopeless. Recognizing defeat as the war nears its end, other members of the guerrilla band accept the Union's offers of amnesty. Betrayal, however, is not for Wales. "The fierce mountain clan code," Carter writes, "would have deemed it a sin for him to take up life. His loyalty was there, in the grave with his wife and baby. His obligation was to the feud."[30] All of Wales's companions abandon him save one, a boy of eighteen named Jamie Burns. With Jamie's refusal of amnesty begins another partnership destined to end tragically. The character's surname links him with the deaths of Wales's wife and child, thus associating him with the Southern values embodied by these characters and foreshadowing his own violent death. Wales's relationship with Jamie also suggests a familial bond. The outlaw often tenderly cares for and defends the boy as if he were his own child, cradling his head in his arms and tousling his hair, especially later in the story after he becomes wounded. The novel also describes him as a childlike character, even as "a little boy," given to naïve remarks and charming grins (41). His name is a diminutive form, too. But Jamie proves important for other reasons as well. With him, the text introduces a key element: the issue of race that the narrative usually attempts to hold at bay. While Carter rarely gave

[29] In recasting the frame of the border war and attempting to purge race from its terms, *Gone to Texas* functions much like other works of outlaw fiction published since the latter part of the nineteenth century. These works, in the words of one historian, created "the legend of the noble guerrilla," justifying—even ennobling—the violent activities of former Confederate soldiers and sympathizers. Authors of this myth "created a subspecies of the argument that theirs was the noblest of lost causes. They had been men of honor defending womankind, home, and neighborhood against the barbarous invader. They had only responded to attacks." Fellman, *Inside War,* 247. See also Slotkin, "Mythologies of Resistance," in *Gunfighter Nation.*

[30] Carter, *Gone to Texas,* 10–11. Hereafter cited by page number in the text.

physical descriptions of his characters, in this case he made an exception, pointing out Jamie's eyes of gray (the color of Confederate uniforms) and the "blond hair that spilled to his shoulders" (10). These characteristics mark him as white. Through them the text thus redefines what is at stake (but hidden) in the outlaw's quest for vengeance. While the novel generally conceals the role of race in its conflicts in order to ennoble the outlaw, by racializing Jamie's character the narrative implicitly recasts the outlaw's defense of "kin" as a defense of whiteness. This, in fact, proves to be the novel's most fundamental goal, although it relates in contradictory ways to the text's critique of progressivism.

Jamie dies shortly after the breakup of the guerrilla band, and this painful event starkly symbolizes the victimhood of the South (figured here as an innocent child) at the hands of Yankees and Carpetbaggers. In Lexington, the outlaw and his young companion rob a bank, a "Carpet-bag bank, Yank Army payroll" and thus a "legitimate" guerrilla target. Gunfire erupts during their getaway, and Jamie is shot through the lung. His prolonged death is described in excruciating detail to elicit the reader's sympathy. Despite Wales's valiant attempts to save him, the boy soon begins coughing blood, and as gangrene sets in, he gradually succumbs to fevers and delirium. He eventually dies, significantly as the partners find themselves surrounded by Union soldiers seeking to capture them (thus clarifying who is to blame for the tragedy). Saddened by yet another personal loss, Wales nonetheless continues the course he and Jamie began in their flight from the Union soldiers. He heads to the Indian Nations in Oklahoma.

When Wales finally reaches the Nations, the narrative reveals part of the complicated logic that creates the peculiar elision of Confederate outlaw and Indian in *Gone to Texas*. Initially, Wales heads to the Nations in an effort to save Jamie—"He trusted the Cherokee, and he trusted his medicine" (20)—but in the end, as we shall see, it is actually Wales's own salvation (and, by extension, the salvation of Southern values including, ironically, racial whiteness) that is as stake. In Carter's rendering, the outlaw's trust in the Cherokee stems from both political alliances and philosophical convergences:

> The mountain man did not have the "land hunger" of the flatlander who had instigated the government's action [the forced removal of the Cherokees from their lands in the late 1830s]. He preferred the mountains to remain wild...free, unfettered by law and the irritating hypocrisy of organized society. His kinship, therefore, was closer to the Cherokee than to his racial brothers of the flatlands who strained mightily at placing the yoke of society upon their necks.... [The Cherokees'] code was the loyalty of the moun-

tain man with all his clannishness....When the War between the States had burst over the nation, the Cherokee naturally sided with the Confederacy against the hated government that had deprived him of his mountain home. (58–59)

Yet despite these contrived similarities, by specifying "clannishness" as one of the qualities shared by Indian and outlaw, the novel again evokes the defense of race, here in an unmistakable allusion to *the* Klan.

In *Gone to Texas*, then, not only do Southern mountain folk and Cherokees share a love for the land and a disdain for civilization, they also share a common history as victims of Northern progressives. But here, too, significant contradictions emerge in the relationship between the narrative and the historical events that provide its frame. These contradictions aim to conceal violence inflicted on the Indians by the same "noble" white Southerners the text identifies as their allies. The "government's action" referenced in this passage is the Cherokee removal of 1838.[31] Pursuant to Andrew Jackson's policy of removing eastern tribes to lands West of the Mississippi River, an action designed to free lands for white settlement, government soldiers cruelly rounded up seventeen thousand Cherokees with no prior notice and forced them at gunpoint to walk from their homelands (roughly, the region where North Carolina, Tennessee, Georgia, and Alabama converge) to Indian Territory (present-day Oklahoma). Detachments departed during the fall, and for most the journey took between five and six months. Harsh weather, disease, malnutrition, and accidents took their toll, particularly on the very old and very young. In part because of the stunningly high number of casualties, probably one-third of the Cherokee Nation, the event has been named the "Trail of Tears." It has also come to represent the violent displacement of countless other Natives peoples from their lands and the conquest of Native America more generally.

Gone to Texas explains the Cherokee removal as the work of Northern soldiers, an account that likens the removal to the situation of some white Missourians during the border wars waged years later. In reality, however, the dynamics leading up to this event were much more complicated. Removal aimed to clear Indian land to make way for white settlement, a process white Southerners had begun before government policy

[31] The events leading to the Cherokee removal are more complex than most accounts of them, including the one in the novel, suggest. See Theda Perdue, "The Conflict Within: Cherokees and Removal," in *Cherokee Removal: Before and After,* ed. William L. Anderson (Athens: University of Georgia Press, 1991), 55–74, and idem, *Slavery and the Evolution of Cherokee Society 1540–1866* (Knoxville: University of Tennessee Press, 1979).

mandated it. Years before, white Georgians had begun appropriating Indian land and property at will, frequently physically assaulting tribal members. The Cherokees found no redress in court since Indians could not legally testify against whites. Some state agencies, in fact, even actively encouraged and participated in the dispossession of the tribe. Considering white Southerners' roles in this terrible history raises the question of the legitimacy of their claims to the land, claims that, in the novel, form the essence of their collective agrarian-based identity. The narrative answers this question by eliding two historical events that occurred nearly two decades apart (the Cherokee removal and the Missouri-Kansas border war) and suggesting that both Cherokees and white mountain men recognized their "kinship" through the experience of removal as well as shared values. In rewriting these events in this way, the text not only deracializes the dynamics leading to the Cherokee removal, thus avoiding the question of white Southerners' culpability, but also (temporarily) deracializes the Indians in forging their "kinship" relations with white Southerners.

To create the illusion of Southern innocence, the novel distorts the complicated relationships between European Americans (from both the North and the South) and the Cherokees in other ways. While it is true that the Cherokee Nation allied itself for a time with the Confederacy during the Civil War, this decision was highly controversial among tribal members. Nor did the alliance stem from an abstract sense of kinship with and loyalty to white Southerners. To some, an alliance with the South seemed natural. The Cherokees had long held African slaves, and wealthier tribal members even practiced Southern-style plantation slavery. The tribe's exclusion of blacks from political life also mirrored policies of Southern states.[32] European-style slavery, though, proved controversial among the tribe's members, garnering support mostly from nontraditionals and the minority economic elite who benefited from the institution. Debates about slavery later figured into the decision about which side, if any, the tribe should support during the Civil War. For most Cherokees, an alliance with the Confederacy seemed unthinkable. Not only did the majority oppose slavery on ideological grounds, they also remembered their suffering at the hands of white Southerners before and during removal. There were other reasons for opposing a Southern alliance. The protection of treaty rights required at least neutrality if not an

[32] The 1827 Cherokee Constitution not only legislated that blacks could not hold public office, it also attempted to exclude free blacks from residence within the Nation. Perdue's *Slavery and the Evolution of Cherokee Society* provides an important account of these policies and of the development of European-style slavery among the Cherokees during the period of colonization.

active alliance with the Union, the guarantor of the treaties. Initially, when the war broke out, neutrality was in fact the official Cherokee position. Later, in 1863, General Stand Watie brought the tribe into alliance with the Confederacy against the wishes of the majority through a complex series of political maneuvers. In 1865, as the war neared its end, the Cherokee Nation renounced its alliance with the South and announced its support for the Union. These debates worsened long-standing factionalism within the tribe, giving rise to violent internal conflicts.

If *Gone to Texas* refigures the complex historical relationship between Confederates and Cherokees, so too does it misrepresent the tribe's stance toward modernization and industrialization, another basis for the alliance between Indians and mountain men in the novel. One of the supreme ironies of the removal is that the Cherokees, perhaps to a greater extent than any other Native nation, had acculturated in an effort to diminish white hostilities and, ultimately, to preserve their land base. They established schools, learned English, developed a Cherokee alphabet, converted to Christianity, adopted a judicial system and constitution, and abolished many traditional practices. They conformed economically as well. Farming, ranching, weaving, and even the plantation system had become staples of Cherokee society by the early nineteenth century.[33] These distinctions earned them the status of a "civilized tribe" but did not shield them from white aggression. Despite their adoption of European structures, the Cherokees along with other tribes in the region faced dispossession and removal.

Regardless of these historical complications, *Gone to Texas* forges an alliance between Indians and white mountain folk based on the experience of removal, opposition to progress, and support for the Confederacy. This imagined common history draws Wales to the Indian Nations after Jamie's death. Wales soon finds it the basis for a more personal bond as well. Shortly after his arrival in the Nations, he meets Lone Watie, a man whose past mirrors Wales's own. Like Wales's family, Watie's family, too, had perished at the hands of government soldiers, in his case twenty years earlier on the Trail of Tears. Like Wales, he had cast his allegiances with the Confederates during the war. (Carter even named Watie's cousin Stand Watie, after the only Indian general of the Confederacy.) Like Wales, Lone had also shunned the Union's offer of amnesty after the South's defeat. Wales and Watie share the same philosophy as well. Echoing again the creed of the Ku Klux Klan, both

---

[33] See William L. Anderson, introduction to *Cherokee Removal,* ed. Anderson, vii–xvi; William G. McLoughlin, *Cherokee Renascence in the New Republic* (Princeton: Princeton University Press, 1986).

name "clannishness" and blood loyalty as their personal creeds. Wales thus immediately recognizes that "Lone Watie merited his trust. He was of his kind." The two men soon establish a partnership based on "a common cause, a common suffrage" (59, 64).

Yet while the narrative thus "resolves" nineteenth-century conflicts between Cherokees and white Southerners, it nonetheless manifests a profound anxiety about the legitimacy of the white mountain folks' claims to the land they occupy, an anxiety that stems from their culpability in the conquest. Wales's flight to the Nations responds to this anxiety by revising Southerners' role in this history. His arrival recalls the original arrival of whites on Indian land. But in order to vindicate white Southerners of their role in the conquest and dispossession of Natives, the text rewrites another historical event, this time the Cherokee removal. Predictably, though, in this retelling, Wales (representing white Southerners) is himself a victim of the removal rather than a beneficiary of it, a formulation that echoes the parallels the novel draws earlier between victims of the border wars and the Cherokee removal. In *Gone to Texas,* for both Wales and Watie, even the Nations provide no safe haven from the Union soldiers on their trail. In search of a new life, in an event that recalls the removal, they flee Indian territory and head for Texas, mythical haven of the outlaw. On their journey West, the two men acquire a peculiar menagerie of followers, all displaced and homeless like themselves. Little Moonlight, an outcast Cheyenne woman, Wales saves from rape by two white bootleggers at an army trading post. She follows in their trail, along with a "mangy red-bone hound" with "nowheres to go neither." Another tragedy adds more members to the odd quartet. Comancheros—Anglo, Mexican, and "breed" Indians who trade with Comanches—attack a wagon train, killing the men in the party. Here, Wales finds another opportunity to demonstrate his chivalry by rescuing the women, Laura Lee and Grandma Sarah, from inevitable rape and murder. Their peculiar alliance deflects questions about how race influences the situation of the white members of the group and that of these particular Indians. Moreover, none of them can claim any historical relationship to Texas. In the novel, then, this site of new beginnings initially seems free of the troubling racial histories that render the mountain men's claims to the land questionable in earlier scenes.

These new beginnings at the narrative's end rely upon the racially inflected, progressivist vision the novel claims to reject. As we have seen, Wales's implicit goal from the beginning of the story is the defense of whiteness, and in the novel's closing scenes the fantasy of white racial regeneration is finally realized. Both historically and symbolically, Texas provides the ideal site for staging such a fantasy. Texas, of course, was acquired by the United States in an imperial war against Mexico, and for many this victory seemed to demonstrate white superiority. In the following decades, Texas remained remote from the American establishment. Through the late 1860s, vigilantism served as the primary mode of social control. Here, guerrilla bands held sway, and the Klan found a stronghold; both groups kept nonwhites in check through violent terrorist campaigns.[34] For these reasons, during the postbellum years, Southern nationalism reemerged and flourished in Texas. Equally important, though, is the mythological significance of the state, including its identity in the American cultural imagination as the quintessence of the West. Texas in the novel thus provides an "opportunity for renewal, for self-transformation, for release from constraints associated with an urbanized East,"[35] and it thus constitutes the ideal location for a renewal of white society.

These processes of renewal and self-transformation comprise the closing scenes of the novel. Arriving in Texas at a ranch inherited by Grandma Sarah and Laura Lee, the group finds an Edenic setting, the perfect scenario for the novel's fantasy of social regeneration. Soon, however, the group confronts another "Indian problem" as the Comanches—natives of Texas—challenge these outsiders' claims to the land. Wales acknowledges the validity of this objection, announcing "This is their [Comanche] land...not our'n" (142), and here anxieties about white occupation of Indian land become explicit for the first time. In the scenes that follow, the narrative again resolves the problem posed by the Indians' presence, this time by evoking the linked discourses of race and progress.

Anticipating the Comanche threat, Wales rides off to meet the infamous Comanche chief Ten Bears, and this encounter literalizes the "kinship" between the Indian and the outlaw. The chief's own story, it turns out, resembles Wales's. The Yankee "bluecoats" have treacherously murdered his sons, compelling the father to seek revenge. Ten Bears targets Wales's group as his next set of victims, but the outlaw approaches him first. The speech Wales delivers during this encounter is one of the most striking passages in the novel:

> What ye and me cares about has been butchered...raped. It's been done by them lyin', double-tongued snakes thet run guv'mints. Guv'mints lie...promise...back-stab...eat in yore lodge and rape

[34] See James Marten, *Texas Divided: Loyalty and Dissent in the Lone Star State 1856–1874* (Lexington: University of Kentucky Press, 1990).
[35] Lee Clark Mitchell, *Westerns: Making the Man in Fiction and Film* (Chicago: University of Chicago Press, 1996), 5.

yore women and kill when ye sleep on their promises. Guv'mints don't live together...men live together. From guv'mints ye cain't git a fair word...ner a fair fight. I come to give ye either one...'er to git either one from ye....

... I'm sayin' men can live without butcherin' one 'nother and takin' more'n what's needin' fer livin'...share and share alike. (177–78)

In this passage, the novel again collapses the distinct histories of Indians and Confederates into a narrative of common victimization at the hands of the Northern establishment. Wales's words have the desired effect. Ten Bears understands that the "vicious hatred of Josey Wales matched his own...hatred for those who had killed what each of them loved" (177). In a stereotypical scene, the two men then slash their palms and clasp hands, becoming "blood brothers." Thus, the novel once again overturns the challenges Natives pose to white possession of the land, this time by literalizing the kinship bond between outlaw and Indian. Now gone native, a "blood relative" of the Comanches, Wales attains the right to live undisturbed on Indian land.

The novel effaces the racial boundaries between Indian and white outlaw in other ways. Carter's descriptions primitivize both characters, and their primitiveness makes them superior to "civilized" Northerners. Ten Bears, for instance, is "the greatest horseman of the Plains and each of his warriors [is] equal to 100 of the bluecoats" (158). It is, in part, their impunity, their dauntlessness, and their propensity to violence that renders these Indians such efficient soldiers. In *Gone to Texas,* we often see them traveling, "glutted with loot and scalps from raids," fearlessly slaughtering enemy and innocent alike. Wales, too, shares some (but, significantly, not all) of these qualities. The novel often describes him in animallike terms, particularly in his most violent moments—for example, "he rolled his body with the quickness of a cat....Josey fanned the [gun's] hammer" (23). At other times, it explicitly depicts him as a "savage": "Josey Wales had two pistols in his hands ...and the earsplitting .44's bounced and ricocheted all around them.... Laura Lee heard a sound that began low and rose in pitch and volume until it climaxed in a bloodcurdling crescendo of broken screams that brought pimples to her skin. The sound came from the throat of Josey Wales...the Rebel yell of exultation in battle and blood...and death. The sound of the scream was as primitive as the man" (134). The terminology also points to the similarities between the two men. If Ten Bears is the "greatest" of "war chiefs," Wales is himself a "guerrilla chieftain" and a "mighty warrior." Even Wales's physical appearance evokes savage Indianness: the scar that crosses his cheek, at first glance, resembles "war paint."

But if the novel at times elides the figures of the white outlaw and the Indian, it also carefully redraws these racial boundaries. The qualities that ennoble the outlaw's violence—the fact that self-defense and chivalry motivate his actions—differentiate him from the Indian. The Comanches, by contrast, attack both viciously and randomly, targeting enemy and innocent alike, sometimes driven purely by bloodlust. Women also number among their victims. In stark contrast to Wales's tenderness toward his wife, Grandma Sarah, and especially Laura Lee, Ten Bears treats his own wives cruelly: he "woke in his tepee at dawn and kicked the naked, voluptuous young squaw from beneath his blankets" (173). Moreover, unlike the outlaw who kills quickly and (by implication) humanely, the Comanches seem to revel in their cruelty, often indulging in torture. They also engage in abominable practices like cannibalism.

Ultimately, Wales is the figure on whom racial contradictions come to bear. Although he is the most "Indian" of the white characters in the novel (the blood of Ten Bears literally runs in his veins), he is also the character who guards the same racial boundaries he crosses. At the novel's beginning, as we have seen, he is literally the protector of whiteness embodied in the character of Jamie. Wales performs this role in other ways as well. Symptomatic of Americans' collective fears, much of the text's anxiety about race centers on the prospect of miscegenation. On several occasions, Wales rescues women from interracial rape. Laura Lee confronts the dim fate of rape by Comanches before the outlaw rescues her. Little Moonlight, too, Wales saves from two white bootleggers at the trading post. Significantly, rape is the only form that interracial sex takes in the story, and as a form of violence it carries with it the threat of death. This kind of crossing of racial boundaries, also involving an exchange of bodily fluids, thus provides a stark contrast to the blood bonding between men. While the latter provides a means of white rebirth without the danger of racial contamination, miscegenation suggests only death.[36]

The novel redraws boundaries between the races in other ways as well. The same primitive traits that render the outlaw an efficient warrior and locate him outside the corrupt Eastern establishment make the Indians unfit for life in the contemporary world. The two groups thus meet different ends. For Wales, the encounter with Ten Bears marks what the text labels his "rebirth." His claim to Indian

---

[36] Carter's sequel to *Gone to Texas*, titled *The Vengeance Trail of Josey Wales*, explores this theme more explicitly.

land is secured in a way that assures his innocence. Soon after, local town folk falsely report Wales's death to authorities, thus releasing him from the relentless pursuit of the government soldiers who have plagued him since the end of the war. Local Texas Rangers willingly look the other way. "There's about five thousand wanted men this year in Texas," one Ranger reports, "Cain't git 'em all...ner would want to....What's good back east where them politicians is at...might not be good fer Texas. Texas is a-goin' to git straightened out...it'll take good men" (202).[37] And Wales does indeed dedicate himself to the task of rebuilding Texas. Importantly, though, Wales's Texas, embodied by life on the ranch, soon begins to look much like the eastern establishment it initially sought to reject. The outlaw settles down on the ranch and marries Laura Lee in a "proper" church ceremony. Soon, they have a child, a "blue-eyed and blond"—that is, emphatically white—boy named Jamie. Significantly, while Jamie Burns (Wales's companion at the beginning of the novel) had eyes of gray, the color of the Confederacy, the baby's eyes are blue, the color of the Union symbolizing progressivism. *Gone to Texas* thus concludes by realizing the outlaw's aims defined at the story's outset: the defense of Southern agrarianism and racial whiteness. It does so, however, by embracing the same notions of progress and civilization it criticizes in the beginning.

While this new society is founded only by the permission of the "brutal, savage Ten Bears" (181), its continuity also depends upon his death, and here the novel's reliance on progressivist logic becomes most explicit. The final page narrates both the birth of Wales's baby and the disappearance of the Comanche, who euphemistically "came no more." These two events—the birth of a child marked racially white, named Jamie, and thus linked metonymically to the Southern society lost at the text's beginning, and the death of the Indians—are interdependent. The Indians' disappearance (apparently a natural phenomenon rather than the work of human agents) thus secures white society's possession of Indian land in a manner that renders these new occupants innocent of conquest. In this way, the narrative enacts one final Indian removal, one that obviously repeats the Cherokee removal. Lone Watie and Little Moonlight, the Indian residents of the ranch, perform another kind of disappearance by adopting the ways of white society. By suggesting that Indians must vanish to make way for white civilization, the novel further supports the logic of progressivism. In *Gone to Texas*, then, going native serves only as a vehicle for white regeneration and ulti-

[37] Most of the ellipses are Carter's.

mately poses no threat to white racial purity or to the privileges of white society.

LEARNING FROM THE INDIANS:
THE EDUCATION OF LITTLE TREE

If *Gone to Texas* imagines a history in which the Confederate outlaw gone native naturalizes white Southerners' claims to the land and thus enables the political / social regeneration of white society in the Reconstruction era, *The Education of Little Tree* repeats and extends this project in several ways. Structured as a set of lessons on Native life (or, more precisely, Carter's stereotypical vision of it), the book provides an instruction manual of sorts on how to go native. It thus marks another transition in the relationship of the dominant European-American culture to Native America. In the latter part of the twentieth century, Natives cultures as well as Native land constitute the objects of white America's hegemonic desire, which I discuss in the following chapter. In telling its own story, *The Education of Little Tree* not only articulates these aspects of white dominance over Native America but, like other forms of going native, also reflects on other power struggles within the broader American culture. More specifically, the text explicitly applies its vision of white racial dominance to the situations of African Americans during both the Reconstruction and the civil rights eras. Significantly, Carter originally published *The Education of Little Tree* in 1976, exactly one hundred years after the end of Reconstruction. The book, in a sense, undertakes its own reconstruction effort by reconfiguring postbellum history and contemporary racial conflicts in a way that naturalizes white supremacy. To perform this ideological work, *The Education of Little Tree* relies upon and repeats the rewriting of American history, particularly white Southerners' occupation of Native land, that Carter undertook in *Gone to Texas*. The book thus tells a similar story about the conquest of Native America, specifically the removal of the Cherokees, only to resolve questions about the conquest by eliding the identities of Native and Southern whites and then by narrating the disappearance of the Natives.

The first chapter of *The Education of Little Tree* defines America's repressed history of conquest, specifically the appropriation of Native land, as one of the novel's central themes. The story begins, just as *Gone to Texas* did, with a tragic loss of family. Set in the Depression era, the story begins when the five-year-old protagonist loses his mother only a year after his father's death. Heartbroken and bereft, the orphaned child goes to stay with his Cherokee grandparents in Tennessee hill country and thus begins a new life in the woods with these loving and indulgent caretakers. The loss of his parents and his relocation to the mountains (a place that signifies premodernity in the text) initiates the boy's discovery of his "true" (Native) identity. He immediately dons moccasins, acquires the name "Little Tree" (a diminutive form of "Forrest"), and begins his lessons which for the most part entail learning the ways of nature. Utilizing a common colonial trope, the text elides "nature" and "Indianness" and opposes them to modernity. Indians, the boy soon understands, "gave themselves...to nature, not trying to subdue it, or pervert it, but to live with it...so that they could not think as the white man."[38] Soon Little Tree, in true "Native" fashion, is navigating mountain trails, catching his own game, and even—absurdly—conversing with trees. As the child's new name suggests, "nature" even takes the place of his family as "Father mountain makes him welcome with his song," the spring branch declares "Little Tree is our brother," and "Mon-o-lah, the earth mother...bounce[s] [him] on her breast" (5, 7). Not only does the narrative thus define Natives as part of the natural, premodern world, it also links Little Tree's loss of his parents to a broader and more fundamental loss: Native peoples' loss of land during the conquest.

A later chapter, this one narrating the Cherokee removal, defines white America's appropriation of Native lands as one of *The Education of Little Tree*'s central themes even more explicitly. Here, the child's grandparents relate the devastations of removal in a way that echoes the retelling of this event in *Gone to Texas*. Compelled by greed and corruption, Northern whites cruelly rounded up the Cherokees, forcing them to leave their cherished homelands on pain of death. Thousands perished, and the survivors endured the heartbreak of family members' deaths as well. Again, the text associates loss of family with loss of land as this section reflects back on and further clarifies the implications of the deaths of Little Tree's parents. By poignantly relating this story and by defining Natives, quite literally, as children of nature, the narrative raises an important problem: the legitimacy of white Southerners' claims to the lands previously occupied by the Cherokees and, by extension, white ownership of any Native lands. Like *Gone to Texas*, though, *The Education of Little Tree* immediately attempts to resolve this problem to the benefit of white Southerners by distorting historical facts. Those Cherokee who fled to the mountains during the removal, as the novel tells the story, found fast friends among the mountain folk. "The people of Granpa's [Scottish] Pa were mountain bred," Carter

[38] Carter, *The Education of Little Tree* (Albuquerque: University of New Mexico Press, 1986), 123. Hereafter cited by page number in the text.

wrote; "they did not lust for land, or profit, but loved the freedom of the mountains, as did the Cherokee" (43). The novel thus explains this peculiar alliance in the same way that *Gone to Texas* did. It imagines a "kinship" between the outlaw and the Natives: both Confederates and Indians ostensibly share both common values and a common enemy in the "guvmint" that dispossesses and otherwise persecutes them (39, 44). *The Education of Little Tree,* in fact, explicitly repeats the earlier novel's elision of the figures of the outlaw and the Indian, as the boy's Cherokee grandfather in the story is named Wales after the figure of the outlaw gone native in *Gone to Texas.* (Remarkably, the transformation from the outlaw Wales in *Gone to Texas* to the Cherokee grandfather in *The Education of Little Tree* thus parallels Carter's own transformation from Asa to "Forrest." The name "Forrest" also signifies this convergence by evoking at once the historical figure of Nathan Bedford Forrest and the "nature" ethos embodied by the Indian characters.) In *The Education of Little Tree,* as in the earlier novel, these similarities between mountain folk and Indians ultimately render the former the proper heirs of Indian land and, in this particular case, the proper heirs even of Native cultures and identities as well.

In order for white mountain folk legitimately to inherit these Native things, *The Education of Little Tree* must narrate the disappearance of the Natives in its story, much as the earlier novel did. Indeed, the text both foreshadows and explains this disappearance very early in its second chapter, titled "The Way," when Little Tree learns his first and most important lesson. Embarking with his grandfather on their first hunting expedition together, Little Tree witnesses a hawk dive from the sky overhead and kill a quail. Granpa explains the event to the distressed child with a lesson in social Darwinism: "Don't feel sad, Little Tree. It is The Way. Tal-con caught the slow and so the slow will raise no children who are also slow.... Tal-con lives by The Way. He helps the quail" (9). Echoing Lewis Henry Morgan's nineteenth-century arguments about social evolution, this drama reflects on *The Education of Little Tree*'s narrative by implying that the stronger (white) race will inevitably prevail over the weaker ones. Furthermore, it naturalizes the disappearance of Natives and the subjugation of African Americans as "the Way" of nature, as part of the "natural" course of progress. The consequences for the Natives in the story become clearest near the novel's end, when Little Tree enters the white world.

The implications of this lesson for the relations between Southern whites and Indians become explicit in another story. This one is significantly located halfway through *The Education of Little Tree,* showing its special importance in the novel. This particular vignette solidifies the relationships between mountain folk and Indians, again by citing their shared traits. At the same time, it reinvokes a progressivist, social evolutionary logic ("the Way") that spells death for Natives and legitimates whites' power over African Americans. While the Depression era constitutes the time frame of Little Tree's early life, this one chapter is a flashback to an earlier time, to Granpa Wales's childhood in the postbellum years. This earlier time frame is significant because of the racial dynamics it invokes, specifically the Indian removals and Reconstruction. The vignette repeats these events, and its time frame links these histories to the socioeconomic changes stemming from the transition to industrialism that swept the South during this period.

The story begins in 1867. Wandering in the mountains, Little Tree's grandfather Wales (then a boy himself) discovers that a previously abandoned homestead has become occupied by a peculiar group—a white woman who "looked frailed and wore-out," her "two young'uns who looked worse..., was dirty and had stringy hair and legs like canes," a "stooped over" old black man who lives in the barn, and a one-legged white man in a "ragged gray [Confederate] uniform" (115). That the farm had been abandoned remains unexplained, but given the particular history the text narrates, the clear implication is that this land was previously owned by other Southern whites who had been driven out by Northerners during the war. Its occupation by this newer, pitiful cast of characters, then, reiterates one of Carter's primary themes: that Southern whites have been victimized by Northerners in a way that repeats the Indian removals. The story reinforces this parallel as the group soon establishes an intimate relationship with this land that the text defines at the outset as being quintessentially Native. As Granpa looks on, the woman and two men embark upon a Sisyphean endeavor: the woman and one-legged man strap leather harnesses on themselves and try to plow a field while the black man guides the plow. The enterprise seems hopeless, and this fact, along with their pitiful condition, further attempts to elicit the reader's sympathy.

Although the farm is sited in the Cherokees' territory, the story leaves aside the question of these Natives' claims to it. Furthermore, the remainder of the narrative actually renders this question irrelevant by representing the homesteaders as the victims rather than as the agents of displacement, much like the Natives. Both their condition and the futility of their endeavor point to the fate of agrarianism (a way of life that suggests Southern nationalism) in the modern industrializing world. Just as progress dictates the disappearance of the Natives, so too does it doom the agrarian lifestyle of Southern whites. At this point, however, the plot takes a surprising turn. When the homesteaders' efforts to farm seem entirely hopeless, a Union soldier takes pity on them. He gives them a mule, donates a sack of seed corn, brings them several baby apple trees, and helps them plow the field. Soon, the apple trees and the corn sprout up, and the group begins planning for the harvest. Granpa keeps track of their progress from his hiding place in the woods and helps out from time to time by leaving gifts of fish. Before long, though, the group's dreams are shattered. The Regulators (symbolizing here Northerners' perfidy) arrive and declare that they intend to seize the land for nonpayment of taxes. Violence erupts. The one-legged man points his musket at the Regulators, who immediately shoot him. They kill the black man, too, for threatening them with his hoe. Even the Union sergeant is killed when he tries to intervene. A rich man then takes over the land and establishes a sharecropping system. The group, in other words, undergoes the same process of removal that the Cherokees had. Also significant is the fact that the story repeats a familiar progressivist narrative: Indians—who "vanish" without explanation and apparently without white violence—are replaced on the land by farmers, whose lifestyle then gives way to more complex economic systems that prefigure the development of industry. Though tragic, this series of events appears natural and inevitable.

This vignette is remarkable for other reasons as well. Its progressivist vision harks back to Little Tree's lesson about "the Way," and both carry clear racial implications that affirm the power of white Southerners (now distanced from the conquest of Natives). Not only does the story imply that Natives will "naturally" succumb as society progresses, it implies that they accept this fate without question. While these settlers (representing the next stage of progress) have encroached upon Indian land, Granpa welcomes them, even leaving gifts to help them survive. Granpa literally knows his place, remaining hidden (vanished?) in the woods throughout the story. But even more surprising are the actions of the black character, whose story recalls the history of slavery. Predictably, the black man does not reside in the house with the whites. Rather, he lives in the barn. This arrangement mirrors that of the plantation South, where blacks were lodged in slave quarters. The black man's choice to live in the barn suggests the familiar though absurd mythology that blacks preferred enslavement to freedom. Even more strikingly, the character dies with a hoe in his hand, ironically defending an agrarian system that institutionalized slavery. This suggests again that he embraces his subservient position. This story, then, naturalizes and legitimates white power over Natives and African Americans by indicating both that this is the proper order of things and that these oppressed peoples cheerfully accept, even desire, this domination.

If the story of the farm in the clearing romanticizes and legitimates the enslavement of African Americans in the past, other passages in the novel similarly reflect on the struggles of blacks during the contemporary civil rights era. Indeed, the novel evokes this as one of its central concerns in its opening chapter, which repeats and rewrites a key civil rights moment. This occurs when Little Tree and his grandparents board a bus headed for their mountain home. The question of race immediately comes to the fore when the driver and passengers begin to ridicule them. "How!" the driver mimics, and the passengers erupt in laughter. Next, a woman shouts a war whoop, eliciting a similar reaction among her fellow passengers. Little Tree and his grandparents then walk "to the back of the bus," clearly a racialized space recalling the conflict over bus segregation and the subsequent bus boycott in the mid-1950s. In the novel, though, the back of the bus is not an undesirable place signifying its occupants' oppression. Rather, it is a comfortable place where Little Tree finds a sense of love and belonging. "I sat in the middle between Granma and Granpa," Carter wrote, "and Granma reached across and patted Granpa on the hand, and he held her hand across my lap. It felt good, and so I slept" (3). Significantly, though, while the text thus romanticizes segregation, it also implicitly acknowledges this as a distortion of the truth. Little Tree, for instance, responds to the passengers' racist ridicule with a decisive and obvious misreading: "I felt better about it, knowing they was friendly" (2). At the same time, he observes another onlooker, a sick woman with "unnatural black all around her eyes" (3), suggesting that the text itself sees blackness unnaturally.

Despite the self-consciousness of its misreadings of this historical event, the novel romanticizes racial segregation in a later passage as well. This one reflects and rewrites the battle over school segregation (a battle in which Grand Wizard Carter actively and violently engaged). Near the end of the story, social workers compel Little Tree to leave the mountains, citing his grandparents' unfitness to raise him. They place him in an orphanage/boarding school. This school is an all-white school, and this fact suggests an important historical context: the 1950s battles over the integration of black students into Southern schools. As was the case in these historical events, race in the novel raises the question of the child's fitness to attend the all-white school. "We have no Indians here, half-breed or otherwise," the headmaster informs Little Tree upon his arrival (185). Shunned by the other children, Little Tree grows utterly miserable. His only friend is Wilburn, a boy with a club foot who is also a misfit by virtue of an inherited deformity—and here, too, *The Education of Little Tree* restates the connection between outlaw and Indian drawn in *Gone to Texas*, as Wilburn vows that when he grows up he will take to "robbing...banks and such" (193). Finally, Little Tree's unsuitability for the school becomes clear during a class lecture in an event that again reveals his closeness to nature. In this scene, the teacher holds up a picture of several deer in a spring and asks the children what they are doing. When Little Tree correctly replies that they are mating, the teacher sends him to the headmaster, who whips the child until blood flows down his legs. This incident, which shows him to be irredeemably "savage," secures his release from the white school and enables his joyful homecoming back in the mountains. Ultimately, in the novel's terms, removal from the all-white school is in the child's best interests, an outcome implying that school segregation in Carter's own era was best for African-American children as well.

By associating Natives and African Americans in these passages, Carter suggests that both groups properly occupy the same subservient position and both will share the same fate as casualties of "the Way" of nature that dictates that only the fittest (in this case, whites) survive. Indeed, in the boarding school, Little Tree's fate—and, by implication, the fate of all Natives—becomes explicit. If the school story invokes 1950s battles over school segregation, it also suggests the history of Native boarding schools, those institutions designed to "kill the Indian and save the man" through assimilation. Importantly, Little Tree must leave the mountains (signifying premodernity) to attend the school located in the flatland (signifying modernity). Just as Native children beginning in the nineteenth century were forced to attend boarding schools to "civilize" them, so too is Little Tree forced by government agents (in this case, social workers) to enter the modern world. Here, Little Tree confronts his fate. During a holiday celebration, a Christmas tree—a young male pine, literally a "little tree" taken from its home in the woods—is erected in the school, where it dies a slow death. The death of the tree suggests that the Native characters, all of whom bear names derived from nature (Bonnie Bee, Willow John, Wales, Little Tree), will similarly perish. In fact, the text concludes by narrating their deaths. Willow John, a character who is "misplaced somehow—touching this fringe of the white man's civilization" (150), dies first, and Little Tree's grandparents pass away shortly thereafter. Their deaths occur during a "hard freeze winter," and the text's description again implies that their passing is both natural and inevitable: "Granpa said hard winters were necessary occasional. It was nature's way of cleaning things up and making things grow better. The ice broke off the weak limbs of the trees [linked figuratively to the Indians], so only the strong ones come through" (206). Predictably, the "strong one" who remains after this last removal is Pine Billy, the sole white man among the mountain dwellers. In the concluding scene, Little Tree, orphaned again, leaves the mountains. He then confronts once more the Indians' loss of land as he heads (like Josey Wales before him) to the Indian Nations, only to discover that "there was no Nation" (215)—in other words, that those Natives, too, have disappeared. By narrating the Natives' disappearance, then, *The*

Education of Little Tree, like *Gone to Texas,* envisions a world in which white authority and white possession of the land remain unchallenged.

Yet these deaths do not mark the disappearance of everything Native from the narrative. Rather, in this later novel, white regeneration depends upon going native in another way, this time by incorporating Native practices. While the narrative of progress differentiates Natives from whites and dictates that they will "vanish," it also shows that once they have disappeared, whites must adopt their ways to remedy modernity's problems. *The Education of Little Tree,* like *Gone to Texas,* foregrounds the contrast between the preindustrial agrarian world and modern society, and this contrast becomes most obvious in the relationship between Indians and the encroaching industrial white society. Symptomatically, the novel periodically evokes the discontent of the Depression era as bemused mountain folks ponder "folks...jumping out of winders in the big cities," "rumors of wars," and other urban violence (145). The city dwellers who wander into the mountains, too, appear hopelessly corrupt, greedy, and violent. The Cherokees' mountain home, by contrast, seems idyllic. Here, Natives commune happily with each other and with nature while remaining free from the drudgery of modern life. Granpa's trade (distilling whiskey), for instance, is described as a pleasurable ritual that contrasts with other forms of labor. Little Tree observes: "Granpa had never held a job in public works. 'Public works,' to mountain folks, meant *any* kind of job that paid for hire. Granpa couldn't tolerate regular hire. He said all it done was used up time without satisfaction" (64). Indeed, this is the case with other characters in the novel, from the demoralized sharecroppers to the city folk who throw themselves from windows in utter despair. Although mountain life seems idyllic, this contrast is in part what renders it unviable in the world. At the novel's end, even Little Tree recognizes that the premodern world must succumb to progress, so he buries Granpa's still and hires himself out as a farm laborer.

Yet even as the narrative shows that Native peoples must disappear, it nonetheless preserves what it deems most valuable about them: their culture (or, rather, a stereotypical vision of it), which provides a means of improving the white world. Little Tree's lessons thus become lessons for the text's readers on how to go native. Just as Little Tree quickly learns that the Cherokees' customs are superior to those of the white world, so too is the reader encouraged to understand this point. The Cherokees refuse to exploit the land, and they live by nature's rules. As Granpa Wales instructs the boy: "Take only what ye need. When ye take the deer, do not take the best. Take the smaller and the slower and then the deer will grow stronger and always give you meat. Pa-koh, the panther, knows and so must ye" (9). Others, by contrast, "store and fat themselves with more than their share," start "wars over it," and "make long talks, trying to hold more than their share" (10). The book, in other words, takes the form of an instruction manual of sorts, conveying these lessons and others (among them, the cycles of nature, tips on how to live in the woods, and the importance of being honest and thrifty) to an audience it implicitly acknowledges as non-Native by virtue of being in need of these instructions. In this way, *The Education of Little Tree* resembles turn-of-the-century Boy Scout manuals, which similarly passed on Indian lore, figured as white civilization's past, for the entertainment and betterment of white readers. In addition, it recalls Flaherty's *Nanook of the North*, which in the 1920s preserved on film what the filmmaker deemed valuable in Native life while overlooking the fate of the Natives themselves. There is, however, a key difference between *The Education of Little Tree* and these predecessor narratives. While in the earlier part of the century these texts responded to fears that white civilization would degenerate, they nonetheless conveyed confidence in its superiority. During the period in which Carter wrote, by contrast, many believed that white society must turn to Natives to reinvigorate its own values and practices. By going native, just as Asa Carter had become Forrest, they hoped to ameliorate modernity's ills and thus, ironically, to preserve the power and privileges of whiteness.

Interestingly, though, *The Education of Little Tree* betrays evidence of the historical distortions it employs to accomplish this end. It manifests this awareness most obviously through a repeatedly expressed anxiety about the nature of signification, about the gap between words and things. Words, Granpa insists over and over again, distort the meanings of things; "damn fool word-using," he complains, "gits folks all twisted up" (79). Words, for example, enabled the government to dispossess the Cherokee when they signed the treaties. First the soldiers said "the paper meant that the new white settlers would know where they could settle and where they would not take the land of the Cherokee. And after they had signed it, more government soldiers came with guns and long knives fixed on their guns. The soldiers said the paper had changed its words" (40). Words, too, allowed others to distort the history of the events that followed the signing of the treaties: "They called it the Trail of Tears for it sounds romantic and speaks of the sorrow of those who stood by the Trail. [But a] death march is not romantic....It would not be a beautiful song. And so they call it the Trail of Tears" (42). In reflecting on the discrepancies between words and things, fiction and history, and the power of narrative to distort the truth and thus to dispossess the powerless, Carter could have been referring to his own fictional enterprise.

In Carter's fictions, then, as in the popular culture of his era, Indian-ness serves as an important symbol through which to articulate a range of racial conflicts and historical contradictions. Identified with white Southerners (thus deracialized), Indians vindicate these South-erners of a violent racial history and naturalize their possession of the land and even Native culture; identified at other times with African Americans (thus racialized), Indians serve to reinscribe other racial hierarchies, past and present. Both narratives, moreover, accomplish white racial regeneration through the possession of Native things. Rendered placeless and timeless, divested of history, community, and claims to the land, the imagined Indians in these texts also become dissociated from a concrete Native presence. In this way, Carter's fictions foreshadow the changing roles Native America began to play in the years following the turbulent counterculture and civil rights era, in the so-called New Age. Moving from a project of refiguring history in *Gone to Texas* to a project of personal transformation in *The Education of Little Tree*, Carter's work shows the extent to which mainstream Americans began to imagine Indianness as a set of individual qualities rather than as a community-based and historically determined iden-tity. Symptomatically, whereas Asa Carter had to claim a false identity in order to "become" a Cherokee called "Forrest," in the succeeding years Indianness became so dissociated from Native people that such claims grew unnecessary. By separating Native peoples from their land, history, and culture, *The Education of Little Tree* anticipates this change.

But it was not until 1997, when *The Education of Little Tree* was re-leased as a film, that this change became startlingly obvious. In the film version, Granpa Wales—still the repository of Indian knowledge—is now racially white.[39] Early on, he explains: "I was born white...but when I met your Granma...we was married, and I begun to see the world through Cherokee eyes." He becomes, in the words of another character, a "white Injun." Importantly, the film neglects any mention of the Indian Nations or any other communities of Native people bound to a particular place. Its narrative thus concludes not with Little Tree heading for the Nations (although this proves a false hope in the book). Rather, he heads to the woods with Willow John, the one who has "the magic," to learn "all there was to know about being an Indian." Count-less New Agers, as we shall see in the next chapter, follow Little Tree's

---

[39] Richard Friedenberg, dir., *The Education of Little Tree* (Paramount Pictures, 1997).

path by journeying into the woods in search of Native wisdom. In the New Age, in other words, Indianness has been transformed in American popular culture into an abstraction, into pure knowledge, into an essence divested of the histories and the presence of Native people. Indianness, it seems, can now be fully possessed by white society.

CHAPTER FOUR

Rites of Conquest:
Indian Captivities in the New Age

TWICE EACH YEAR, the New Life Expo tours major cities throughout the United States, providing one of the primary venues for the latest New Age trends. It draws tens of thousands of aficionados to its exhibition booths, healthful eateries, and workshops. A descendant of the nineteenth-century expositions we toured in Chapter 1, the New Life Expo also features more sensational spectacles, including sellers of crystals and other spiritual paraphernalia, promoters of various therapies for mind and body, and vendors of literature purveying alternative truths. Like its predecessor expositions, this Expo also features a variety of things Native American. Medicine wheels, feathers, dream catchers, and other Indian-inspired spiritual aids attest to the New Age movement's fascination with the Native world. These items, however, reflect an interest in Native America that differs from that which drew nineteenth-century fairgoers to Indian exhibits (although they retain the same binary frame). Where earlier expositions explicitly celebrated the white viewers' superiority to the Natives on display, thus naturalizing the military conquest of Native America, these New Life Expos suggest that the relationship between Native America and European America has changed during the last century. Rather than displaying Natives as the West's inferior others, New Agers claim that colonized peoples, including Natives, are in many respects fundamentally superior to their Western counterparts. Compelled by the conviction that modern Western societies confront terrible crises (including environmental destruction, spiritual bankruptcy, and rampant health problems), the movement goes native in its quest for solutions. By repositioning Natives thus, New Ageism apparently counters the colonial paradigms celebrated in nineteenth-century expositions and offers a new model of relations between European Americans and Native Americas.

A workshop at one New Life Expo held in New York City in the late 1990s provides a particularly apt example of the movement's collective desire to go native. This session, "Plains Indian Spirituality," proved one of the exposition's most popular events. Dozens of eager seekers of Indian wisdom flocked to hear the speaker, an earnest young European-

American man, instruct them in "traditional" Native ways. His tale was familiar.[1] During a visit to the Comanche reservation some years ago, he told his listeners, he had been adopted by an elderly medicine man, ostensibly the last medicine man of his tribe, who then taught him an ancient Indian wisdom that was "dying out." Since then, this young man had committed himself to sharing these important teachings with the non-Indian world. What were these teachings? Curiously, this "Indian" knowledge resonated with New Age concerns. Native spirituality, he explained, affected physical healing. He instructed his eager listeners that the essence of Plains spirituality is about "going out into nature and praying" and learning that "we are all related." The Medicine Wheel, a site in Montana sacred to several tribes, provided "a mirror of oneself" with practical applications: "you can find your path in life by looking at it." His listeners were enthusiastic, if a bit lazy. "Do Plains Indians have any techniques we can easily learn?" one asked. The event concluded with several listeners signing up for costly guided tours of Indian country, which the speaker promised would allow participants "to live in the Indian world" (albeit only for a few days).

Such New Age fascinations with Native America reveal a series of disturbing problems. In New Age practices, "Native" traditions generally reflect a heavily European ethos. In this particular case, the fixation on self-discovery and self-healing articulate the very Western ideologies of bourgeois individualism. At the same time, the teacher's selling of "Indian" knowledge and experiences manifests a profoundly capitalist mindset. In these ways as well, the workshop typifies broader New Age practices. Because it distorts Native traditions and turns them into consumer goods, the New Age represents another, newer phase in European America's colonization of Native America. This is true despite the movement's claims to have freed itself from this troubling history. In fact, New Agers' desire to go native reproduces, even as it extends, the history of colonization, shown in this case by the compulsion to own Native cultures and even Native identities. Moreover, this latest phase of colonization attempts to ensure that Native America no longer offers a fundamental critique of Western values and practices.

In this regard, the New Life Expo's displays and this particular workshop are far from unique. Other New Age events manifest the movement's desire to go native even more strikingly, and they exhibit similar

---

[1] The story, in fact, is all too familiar. With characteristic wit, scholar Vine Deloria, Jr., describes the wise old Indian man who instructs a white apprentice in ancient Native lore as a prevalent Western fantasy; see "Foreword: American Fantasy," in *The Pretend Indians: Images of Native Americans in the Movies,* ed. Gretchen M. Bataille and Charles L. P. Silet (Ames: Iowa State University Press, 1980), xi–xiii.

problems. Across the country, for instance, New Age groups have formed "tribes." A few of these tribes, including Vincent LaDuke's "Medicine Bear Tribe" and Ed McGaa's "Rainbow Tribe," are even led by Native peoples themselves. Meanwhile, other seekers of Native wisdom flock to traditional sacred sites, often despite protests of local tribes.[2] Yet these Native fascinations, though important, comprise only part of a panoply of disparate beliefs and practices characterizing the movement. These include UFOlogy, channeling, meditation, homeopathy, and alternative therapies and religions.[3] Together, these practices are enormously popular. In the United States alone, tens of millions of people report engaging in some form of New Age practices, including transcendental mediation, yoga, and mysticism.[4] By the mid-1990s, sales of New Age paraphernalia had reached one billion dollars annually, while the publishing industry brought in an equal amount from New Age literature. Ironically, given its vast profitability, the single element that unites the various strands of New Age thought is the perception that the modern capitalist world with its overemphasis on material accumulation and individual competitiveness has gone awry in spiritual, racial, economic, and ecological terms. The movement, in the words of one commentator, thus ostensibly "marks a radical break with the modern condition" by offering (for sale!) "a set of values, which apparently rupture or transcend what modernity has to offer."

Such discontents have characterized modernity since its tumultuous beginnings. What makes the New Age movement's reactions unique are both the particular nature of its preoccupations and the notion that personal growth and "inner spirituality serv[e] as *the* key[s] to moving

---

[2] Sun Bear (né Vincent LaDuke) has written numerous books. Eagle Man (né Ed McGaa) describes his organization in *Rainbow Tribe: Ordinary People Journeying on the Red Road* (San Francisco: HarperCollins, 1992). On New Age pilgrimages to Bear Butte and Native responses to these incursions, see "New Age Rites at Sacred Place Draw Indian Protests," *New York Times*, 27 June 1994, A14. Director Susan Smith has documented, however uncritically, some women's participation in "Indian" sweat lodges; see Smith, dir., *Sweating Indian Style* (Women Make Movies, 1994). On the debates surrounding New Age appropriations of Native spirituality, see Christopher Shaw, "A Theft of Spirit?" *New Age Journal*, July/August 1995, 84–92.

[3] In its preoccupations and orientations, the New Age isn't really new. Rather, it has roots in the counterculture as well as other "alternative reality" traditions. See Robert Ellwood and Harry B. Partin, *Religious and Spiritual Groups in Modern America* (Englewood Cliffs, N.J.: Prentice Hall, 1998); and J. Gordon Melton, "A History of the New Age Movement," in *Not Necessarily the New Age: Critical Essays*, ed. Robert Basil (Buffalo: Prometheus Books, 1988), 35–53.

[4] Paul Heelas, *The New Age Movement: The Celebration of the Self and the Sacralization of Modernity* (Oxford: Blackwell, 1996), 109.

from all that is wrong with life to all that is right."[5] Individual self-transformation rather than political action, in fact, provides the New Age's primary preoccupation. Indeed, the quest for an alternative spirituality to accomplish personal growth motivates the movement's widespread desire to go native, and thus to escape modernity's ills, although again this particular concern with personal growth finds no place in Native traditions.[6] For many, then, Indianness (or, more precisely, European America's latest Indian imaginings) provides a (profitable) counterpoint to the destructiveness and spiritual bankruptcy of modern technological culture. In his influential and best-selling 1991 book, *In the Absence of the Sacred: The Failure of Technology and the Survival of the Indian Nations*, Jerry Mander provided a case in point by drawing on a series of popular stereotypes to contrast Native and Western life. To keep it simple, he offered a quick guide in the form of a table of "inherent differences" between "technological peoples" (mainstream Americans) and "Native peoples." Here, he characterized American society as hierarchical, destructive of the natural world, materialistic, patriarchal, and increasingly dominated by greed-driven corporate monopolies. By contrast, Indian societies were defined as close to nature, nonhierarchical, profoundly spiritual, generous, and matrilineal.[7] Not only are unacculturated Native peoples inherently different from mainstream Americans, Mander argued, but they may provide the key to the regeneration of the technology-driven West because they have historically been its victims.

In the New Age, then, we have in some ways come full circle from the beginning of our story. In the late nineteenth century, world's fairs and other cultural events typically celebrated technology, materialism, and a masculinist vision of imperial conquest, including the conquest of Native America. The New Age, by contrast, seems intent on replacing

[5] Ibid., 3, 16. Andrew Ross has suggested that this particular orientation stems from the dearth of leftist political movements in the 1980s. See Ross, "New Age—A Kinder, Gentler Science?" in *Strange Weather: Culture, Science and Technology in the Age of Limits* (London: Verso, 1991).

[6] According to one survey, at least one-fourth of New Age spiritual seekers engage in what they believe to be Native American practices. See Michael York, *The Emerging Network: A Sociology of the New Age and Neo-Pagan Movements* (Lanham, Md.: Rowman & Littlefield, 1995), 165.

[7] Jerry Mander, *In the Absence of the Sacred: The Failure of Technology and the Survival of the Indian Nations* (San Francisco: Sierra Club Books, 1991), 215–19. Typically, Mander failed to see the tremendous diversity of Native peoples, whom he presented simply as a monolithic group. He even explicitly claimed that "all American Indian cultures are alike." Also typical was his failure to consider how different cultures have changed over time. These errors, along with his more specific discussions of "Indian" traits, show a remarkable ignorance about Native America.

these values with Native-inspired alternatives. On closer examination, though, the situation appears more complex. Although the New Age movement claims to have parted ways with modernity, it actually replicates its fundamental values and practices. Specifically, the hyperindividualism of the movement, its emphasis on personal growth, and its profound materialism show the influence of the industrial capitalist ethos.[8] The movement's relationship with Native America is similarly complicated, and it further affirms these particularly Western values. Here, the New Age seems to work at cross-purposes, torn between its need for alternative cultural models and its unwillingness to challenge European America's political and cultural dominance. While the New Age valorizes a distorted (Westernized) vision of Indianness, for example, it pays little heed to the historical presence or contemporary dilemmas of Native Americans. In Sherman Alexie's words, the New Age "blindly pursues Native solutions to European problems but completely neglects to provide European solutions to Native problems."[9] Moreover, middle-class whites dominate the movement, and their relationship to Native America remains one of possession aimed at regenerating white society. In other words, the movement's practices belie its claims to have wrested itself from America's colonial history.

An exemplary case is one of the movement's emblematic texts, Lynn Andrews's *Medicine Woman*. A striking instance of going native, Andrews's "autobiography" shows the extent to which this particular fascination with Native America both articulates and extends the history of conquest. This relationship becomes clear in its narrative as well as in its form. *Medicine Woman* utilizes the conventions of that most starkly colonial of genres, the captivity narrative. Since the beginning of the conquest, captivity narratives have provided opportunities for the dominant culture to tell self-justifying stories of its colonial encounters with Native others in the wilderness.[10] In so doing, they remain deeply

[8] See Ross, "New Age—A Kinder, Gentler Science?" 21.

[9] Sherman Alexie, "White Men Can't Drum," *New York Times Magazine*, 4 October 1992, 30. Alexie's novel *Reservation Blues* (New York: Warner Books, 1995) also criticizes New Age appropriations of Native culture. Other critiques of the New Age include Wendy Rose, "The Great Pretenders: Further Reflections on White Shamanism," in M. Annette Jaimes, ed., *The State of Native America: Genocide, Colonization, and Resistance* (Boston: South End Press, 1992), 403–22; Andrea Smith, "For All Those Who Were Indian in a Former Life," *Cultural Studies Quarterly*, winter 1994, 70–71; and Laurie Anne Whitt, "Cultural Imperialism and the Marketing of Native America," *American Indian Culture and Research Journal* 19, 3 (1995): 1–32. See also Terry Macy and Daniel Hart's film, *White Shamans and Plastic Medicine Men* (Native Voices, 1995).

[10] This is not to suggest, however, that captivity narrative conventions have remain unchanged, or that these narratives have always functioned in exactly the

implicated in the process of conquest, and this fact explains in part their popularity over time. Captivity narrative conventions continue to shape high and popular literature alike as captivity remains a dominant paradigm for representing white/Indian encounters. Films, especially Westerns, frequently rely on the genre's conventions as well. Indeed, many of the instances of going native analyzed in this book retell captivity stories; these include *Dances with Wolves,* the rituals of fraternal organizations, Gontran de Poncins's sojourn into the Arctic, and the victims of the Comanches and Comancheros in *Gone to Texas.*

Andrews's best-selling *Medicine Woman* employs captivity narrative conventions in particularly striking ways by rewriting the classic of the genre, Mary Rowlandson's seventeenth-century narrative, *The Sovereignty and Goodness of GOD, Together With the Faithfulness of His Promises Displayed; Being a Narrative of the Captivity and Restauration of Mrs. Mary Rowlandson.* Both narratives describe captivity in the wilderness at the hands of "diabolical" Indians. Both experiences, too, result in spiritual regeneration for their protagonists. Finally, both texts have the conquest of Natives and the appropriation of Native things as their primary motivations. The fact that Rowlandson, who wrote her narrative during King Philip's War, is a clear literary ancestor of Andrews, who is certainly the queen of New Age performances of Indianness, underscores the extent to which going native in the New Age remains implicated in white America's conquest of Native America. A reading of these two narratives highlights how white America perpetuates its violent racial history, albeit in veiled forms, as the twentieth century draws to a close. From the colonial period to our own era, in other words, the flawed terms of American identity (displayed so starkly in late-nineteenth-century expositions) have been continually reasserted and reenacted in rites of conquest of Native America. At the same time, however, the juxtaposing of these texts shows how European America's relationship with Native America has changed over time. Today, Native cultures and identities comprise objects of desire rather than objects of revulsion. In this section I will first read *Medicine Woman* next to Rowlandson's narrative. Then, I will explore a third "eye," that of Leslie Marmon Silko, whose novel *Gardens in the Dunes* refigures the conventions of the captivity narrative once again, this time criticizing these fascinations. This Native novel deconstructs the paradigms underlying

---

same way. For a discussion of how the cultural functions of captivity narratives changed between the seventeenth and the nineteenth centuries, see Roy Harvey Pearce, "The Significances of the Captivity Narrative," *American Literature* 19, 1 (1947): 1–20.

various forms of going native and, in so doing, challenges European America's hegemonic aspirations.

In February 1676, as King Philip's War raged in colonial New England, a small group of Narragansett Indians attacked the Puritan settlement of Lancaster, Massachusetts. The war itself, known to Indians as Metacomet's rebellion, spanned the years 1675–78. The Indians' military campaigns aimed to expel the colonists from their lands.[11] The invasion of the east coast of North America was only a few decades old, but already these Europeans had reduced the Native population of the region to a small fraction of its former number, prompting a degree of military resistance unprecedented in Native North America.[12] King Philip's War brought together a loose confederation of Northeast tribes (among them the Narragansetts) who joined forces, struck English settlements, and eventually brought the colonies to the brink of defeat. The Narragansetts' attack on Lancaster proved its most pivotal moment. Its importance derives not so much from the nature of the attack itself. Rather, it prompted a series of events that changed how European Americans saw themselves, their "errand into the wilderness," and their relationship with Native America. During the attack, the Narragansetts took a number of captives, among them Mary White Rowlandson, wife of the local minister. Throughout the colonial period, such captives commonly served both sides as pawns in political and trade negotiations. Rowlandson's captivity, though, proved exceptional. Her narrative of the eleven weeks she spent with the Narragansetts, published in 1682, quickly found its audience. Soon it became one of the best-known and most influential works in American literature.

The Soveraignty and Goodness of GOD draws much of its popularity from the story it tells. The first version was widely circulated; more than thirty editions appeared, and it was reprinted steadily well into the nineteenth century.[13] More recently, in this century, academics have canonized the narrative, ranking it one of the most important texts in

---

[11] Had they been successful, the Narragansetts and their allies, rather than the Puebloans, would bear the distinction of winning the first organized military campaign against the invaders. They were not, so the honor goes to the Pueblo resistance of 1680, which expelled the Spanish (if only for a few years) from what is now the U.S. Southwest.

[12] See Stannard, *American Holocaust*, esp. 107–17.

[13] Julia Stern, "To Represent Afflicted Time: Mourning as Historiography," *American Literary History* 5, 2 (1993): 378.

American literary history. Indeed, Rowlandson's story soon became the prototype of works concerned with Indian captivity. The text's abiding popularity and influence are symptomatic, underscoring the extent to which European America clings to obfuscating visions of its own history. Rowlandson's and all subsequent captivity narratives serve as lenses through which to view the Indian wars of the seventeenth, eighteenth, and nineteenth centuries, the foundational events of European-American history. They thus provide "a major vehicle for reflecting upon the meaning of the European occupation of the captured space of the New World,"[14] and as a result, they help to define American national identity itself.[15] Rowlandson's narrative, like others of its genre, attempted to justify the bloody conquest of Natives rebelling against colonial authority (a function that is frequently overlooked or underemphasized in criticism). For my purposes, the text's importance derives from the particular ways it represents the relationship between Native America and European America as well as its influence on twentieth-century forms of going native.

The opening pages of *The Soveraignty and Goodness of GOD* explicitly site the narrative in the colonial context of King Philip's War. Symptomatically, the Puritan cleric Increase Mather, who edited the book and wrote a preface,[16] expresses ambivalence about ethical issues involved in the conflict and Puritan claims to the contested land; he de-

---

[14] Gary L. Ebersole, *Captured by Texts: Puritan to Postmodern Images of Indian Captivity* (Charlottesville: University Press of Virginia, 1995), 3.

[15] See Sacvan Bercovitch, *The Puritan Origins of the American Self* (New Haven: Yale University Press, 1975), and Myra Jehlen, *American Incarnation: The Individual, the Nation, and the Continent* (Cambridge: Harvard University Press, 1986). Benedict Anderson describes Rowlandson's text as a nationalist narrative in "Exodus," *Critical Inquiry* 20 (winter 1994): 314–27. Indian captivity becomes a visual genre as well, for American artists (like their literary counterparts) have been obsessed with this subject since the early colonial period. One of the most famous depictions of the captive female is John Vanderlyn's 1804 painting, *Death of Jane McCrea*. The late nineteenth century saw a resurgence of interest in the captivity theme by painters such as Irving Couse, Frederic Remington, and Henry Farny. Currently, paintings and sculptures of hapless captives decorate museums, government offices, and public spaces in the nation's capitol.

[16] A number of critics have raised the question of the extent to which male editors distorted women's accounts of their captivities, suggesting that narratives such as Rowlandson's simultaneously reinscribe and challenge patriarchal structures; see, for example, Christopher Castiglia, *Bound and Determined: Captivity, Culture-Crossing, and White Womanhood from Mary Rowlandson to Patty Hearst* (Chicago: University of Chicago Press, 1996). While this may be the case, this divisiveness appears not to extend to the dynamics of racial conquest. On this issue, it is possible to identify a relatively coherent colonial position borne out by the course of American history. Rowlandson's narrative articulates this position without apparent ambivalence or dissension.

scribes how the Narragansetts "were for the second time beaten up, by the Forces of the united Colonies, who thereupon soon betook themselves to flight, and were all the next day pursued by the English, some overtaken and destroyed."[17] These opening lines, then, cast the circumstances surrounding King Philip's War, or at least this particular phase of it, as stemming from an English offensive. Another passage, following this one by only a few lines, reinforces the sense that it was the Indians who were the victims of aggression: "The Narrhagansets were now driven quite from their own Country, and all their provisions there hoarded up... [and] were now reduced to extream straits, and so necessitated to take the first and best opportunity for supply, and very glad, no doubt, of such an opportunity as this, to provide for themselves, and make spoil of the English at once... [and thus] fell with mighty force and fury upon Lancaster."[18] Not only do these passages foreground English aggression, they explain the Narragansett attack on Lancaster as a response to it. Oddly, then, the narrative raises at the outset questions about the validity of the English position and, by extension, even their presence on Indian land (by, for example, describing the displacement of the Indians from their "own Country").

These opening passages, in other words, articulate some of the text's central anxieties about the colonial culture's presence and practices in the "new world." However, if the narrative raises questions about the defensibility of English actions, it immediately attempts to assuage those doubts. It is, for instance, remarkable that the passages cited above often rely on the passive voice ("the Narrhagansets... were for the second time beaten up... [and] not driven quite from their own Country"), thus both raising and deflecting questions about English accountability. More obviously significant in this regard, though, is the passage located between the two cited above. Here, Mather's preface points out "the causless enmity of these Barbarians, against the English, and the malicious and revengefull spirit of these Heathen."[19] Having given cause for Indian "enmity," the text then retracts its explanation and condemns the Indians' action, describing the attack not only as "causless" but "malicious" as well. The main portion of the text follows suit by casting the event as explicable only by the Indians' innate malevolence. Rowlandson's story in fact commences with a horrific description of the attack in which the

[17] Increase Mather, Preface to the 1682 edition of Mary Rowlandson, *The Sovereignty and Goodness of GOD, Together With the Faithfulness of His Promises Displayed; Being a Narrative Of the Captivity and Restauration of Mrs. Mary Rowlandson...*, reprinted in *Narratives of the Indian Wars 1675–1699*, ed. Charles H. Lincoln (New York: Charles Scribner's Sons, 1913), 112.
[18] Ibid., 113.
[19] Idem.

"murtherous wretches" descend upon her town, setting it ablaze and slaughtering many of its inhabitants. It was, she contended, "the dolefullest day that ever mine eyes saw."[20] Highlighting in this way the savagery of the Indians' attack, the narrative thus contradicts the opening lines of the preface, casting the English as the Narragansetts' victims rather than as colonial aggressors. The narrative thereby attempts to establish the validity (even the inevitability) of the conquest, even as it inverts the power relations at work. The powerless figure of the female captive, signifying the national body, similarly belies the fact of colonial aggression.[21]

Another important way the text accomplishes this work is to cast English relations with the Indians in Biblical terms. The narrative frames Rowlandson's captivity as a conversion experience (or, better, as a reconversion, for her religious failure was backsliding), and her restoration to Lancaster as an indicator of spiritual redemption. In Mather's words, the narrative thus provides evidence of "the holy, powerfull, and gracious providence of God," and he likens Rowlandson's afflictions to those of the Biblical figures "Joseph, David and Daniel."[22] Passages from scripture punctuate Mather's preface as well as Rowlandson's narrative, reinforcing the impression that Rowlandson's experience embodies the archetypal struggle between good and evil.[23] Specifically, the Biblical frame redefines what is at stake in King Philip's War (and, by implication, in the broader historical relations between the colonists and the Natives) by moving the event from the political to the spiritual realm. In these terms, while Rowlandson enjoys an association with God's chosen ones in the Bible, the Indians embody the fall from grace. The opening pages of the narrative thus set up a startlingly clear distinction between the Narragansetts and the Puritans. These Indians are "ravenous Beasts," "hell-hounds," and "black creatures in the night"

---

[20] Mary Rowlandson, *The Soveraignty and Goodness of GOD...* , reprinted in *Narratives of the Indian Wars 1675–1699*, ed. Charles H. Lincoln (New York: Charles Scribner's Sons, 1913), 118. Hereafter cited by page number in the text.

[21] See Lauren Berlant, *The Anatomy of National Fantasy: Hawthorne, Utopia, and Everyday Life* (Chicago: University of Chicago Press, 1991).

[22] Mather, Preface to the 1682 edition of Rowlandson, 114.

[23] A good deal of critical work on *The Soveraignty and Goodness of GOD* examines the narrative's Biblical frame, seen through the lens of Puritan theology, that allows the articulation of frequently contradictory Puritan conceptions of the subject, the community, and their role in history. Emblematic works include Mitchell Breitwieser, *American Puritanism and the Defense of Mourning: Religion, Grief, and Ethnology in Mary White Rowlandson's Captivity Narrative* (Madison: University of Wisconsin Press, 1990), and Tara Fitzpatrick, "The Figure of Captivity: The Cultural Work of the Puritan Captivity Narrative," *American Literary History* 3, 1 (1991): 1–25.

whose encampment is "a lively resemblance of Hell" (121). This distinction clearly reflects on the historical dynamics of colonialism, leaving no doubt about what the outcome of the war should be. In this framework, in one critic's words, "wherever the Indian opposed the Puritan, there Satan opposed God," a logic that helped convince the Puritans of their "divine right to Indian lands."[24]

Rowlandson's captivity, her journey into the world of the "diabolical" Indians, thus figures as a descent into hell. It is an experience designed to test and to strengthen her faith, and ultimately to secure her difference from the Indians. Structured as a series of "removes" from Lancaster, the narrative shows the hapless captive moving "up and down" the wilderness, a spatial mapping that carries obvious moral implications. It reflects, for one thing, the state of her faith in God during her tribulations. This journey into the world of the Narragansetts, culminating in her restoration to Lancaster, is thus ultimately a confrontation with her own sinful nature. Even the fact of her captivity, it seems, results from her own misdeeds. As she recalls numerous sins, she sees how "righteous it was with God to cut off the thread of my life, and cast me out of his presence for ever" (124). But importantly, the captivity also provides a necessary opportunity for reconversion. Affliction after affliction—the death of her young daughter Sarah as well as countless cruelties heaped upon her by the Indians—threaten to drag her deeper into the depths, but scripture restores her. She cites numerous Biblical verses, most often passages designed to buoy failing faith, some promising deliverance, and others showing parallels between her own afflictions and those of Biblical characters such as Job (128–29). The Indians, figured as Satanic creatures, actually play a crucial role in Rowlandson's spiritual journey by providing a means for testing her faith and, in the end, illustrating God's providence in redeeming her. The figure of the female captive, as a symbol of Puritan society, thus provides a necessary means of redrawing the boundaries between the Puritans and the Indians. In the end, Rowlandson's foray into the Native world strengthens Puritan piety and consolidates colonial identity.

The narrative, however, cannot sustain these rigid boundaries between the Puritans and the Indians for the duration of the story. Rowlandson's relationship with the Natives changes as the ordeal progresses, reflecting the very real threat that the colonists, far from Europe, might acculturate to Native ways.[25] While the opening passages set

---

[24] Pearce, *Savagism and Civilization*, 21–22.
[25] Richard Slotkin, *Regeneration through Violence: The Mythology of the American Frontier, 1600–1860* (Middletown, Conn.: Wesleyan University Press, 1973), 98, 100.

up a stark contrast between Indians and Puritans, this distinction begins to break down as Rowlandson travels farther and farther into the wilderness. In fact, as the story proceeds, Rowlandson's behavior even begins to mirror that of the Narragansetts. The most obvious change occurs in her attitude toward Indian food, which reflects her relation to the culture in general. While during the early days of her captivity she finds it "very hard to get down their filthy trash," by the third week Narragansett fare seems to her "sweet and savoury." Soon, she even begins to compare these foods to English delicacies (131, 137). Her behavior and perceptions change in more overtly significant ways as well. She enters her captors' economy, bartering her sewing for food and other necessities, a behavior that signifies her potential to integrate into Narragansett society. She also begins to share her afflictions with the Indians, weeping openly and taking comfort in her captors' assurances. Most strikingly, she even starts to repeat the actions that she has condemned. For instance, she professes relief when her mistress's baby dies, leaving more room in the tent. At another point, she steals a horse hoof from a child captive in order to assuage her own hunger. These acts copy her account of the Narragansetts' treatment of her.

The narrative, in other words, indicates that Rowlandson might indeed go native, a possibility suggested by the Puritans' particular conception of the Natives. Though figured as brutish, Satanic creatures, Indians were not imagined as being *essentially* different from the English. They were, rather, creatures fallen from grace. Thus they served as "a symbol of what men might become if they lived far from God's word," of what the Puritans must not—but could—become.[26] Rowlandson's story shows the consequences of slipping too far from God in the striking figure of another captive. She meets this woman during the third remove when she finds herself encamped among nine other English captives. Rowlandson's "warning" is a woman much life herself. Though pregnant and accompanied by a young child, this woman is intent on escape. The nearest English town, however, is thirty miles away, making success virtually impossible. Together, she and Rowlandson consult scripture about her best course of action. Although the Bible they use opens to a passage that seems to advise waiting, Rowlandson's companion does not heed it. Instead, she persists in begging the Indians to let her return home. For her foolishness, she meets a frightful fate. The Indians strip her, dance around her in a "hellish manner," knock her and the child on the head, and then place them in a fire (128–29). Thus perishing in flames, she meets the fate that is surely overdetermined for a Christian who fails to heed the word of God.

[26] Pearce, *Savagism and Civilization*, 21.

As circumstances overwhelm her, Rowlandson must struggle against sharing the other captive's fate. The dangers awaiting a fallen Christian become even clearer a few pages after the story of the woman's execution. Here, Rowlandson tells how an Indian woman throws ashes in her eyes, resulting in her temporary blindness. While the text represents the incident merely as another instance of Indian cruelty, its implications are obvious. Her blindness reflects on her spiritual state:

> And here I cannot but remember how many times sitting in their Wigwams, and musing on things past, I should suddenly leap up and run out, as if I had been at home, forgetting where I was, and what my condition was.... About this time I began to think that all my hopes of Restoration would come to nothing. I thought of the English Army, and hoped for their coming, and being taken by them, but that failed.... Then also I took my Bible to read, but I found no comfort there neither, which many times I was wont to find. (141)

Three events—Rowlandson's forgetting that she is not at home among the "heathens," her loss of confidence in the English army (figured, remember, as the instrument of providence), and her failure to find meaning in the Bible—manifest a loss of faith in God that echoes that shown by Rowlandson's hapless companion. That woman, perishing as she does in the flames of hell-fire, thus functions as Rowlandson's alter ego, the prospect that she, too, will lose faith and die a fallen Christian. Paradoxically, not only do these "errors" bring her dangerously near the fate of the fallen Christian, they also bring her nearer to the Narragansetts themselves, since these Indians collectively embody a "fallen spiritual condition."[27] The figure of the fallen captive immersed in fire in fact explicitly recalls images of the Indians, described at the narrative's outset as "hell-hounds" whose encampment bears "a lively resemblance of hell." The way the text then links the ill-fated captive with Rowlandson suggests the very real possibility that she will find a home among the heathens—the possibility, in other words, that she will go native.

At the same time, going native also plays an important role in Rowlandson's spiritual redemption. As she recounts it in the narrative, her eleven weeks with the Indians before she is ransomed and returned home served to "scourge and chasten" her and to show that "our whole dependence must be upon [God]" (167). While her likeness to the Indi-

[27] Pearce, *Savagism and Civilization*, 25.

ans in the middle of the narrative shows her fallibility, her restoration serves as a mark of her salvation. Thus, at the conclusion of the story, *The Soveraignty and Goodness of GOD* redraws the boundaries separating the Puritans from the Indians by contrasting the "merciless and cruel Heathen" with the "pittiful, tender-hearted and compassionate Christians" (162). Rowlandson's story demonstrates God's providence in other ways as well. Her endurance of the ordeal shows God's "wonderfull power and might, in carrying of us through so many difficulties, in returning us in safety, and suffering none to hurt us" (166). As an opportunity for confronting and overcoming sin, Rowlandson's foray into the wilderness thus serves as a necessary ritual of redemption, a means of testing one's faith that distinguishes the fallen from God's chosen. When in the middle of the narrative she ponders God's motivation in sustaining the Indians—"I cannot but take notice of the strange providence of God in preserving the heathen" (131)—she raises an issue she resolves by the end of her ordeal: "I can but admire to see the wonderfull providence of God in preserving the heathen for farther affliction to our poor Countrey," and a bit later: "now our perverse and evil carriages in the sight of the Lord, have so offended him, that instead of turning his hand against them, the Lord feeds and nourishes them up to be a scourge to the whole Land" (159–60). These imagined Indians thus serve both as reflections of Puritan sinfulness, living embodiments of the fall from grace, and the source of affliction necessary to bring the errant ones back into the fold. Rowlandson's experience later helped in the spiritual reconversion of other Puritans as well, as she served as a public witness of God's grace. In this way, Indians in the text define and regenerate colonial society.

Going native serves another purpose here as well, this one more obviously related to the context of the war that frames the narrative. *The Soveraignty and Goodness of GOD* demonstrates "the strange providence of God, in turning things about when the Indians was at the highest, and the English at the lowest," a turn of events destined to occur in the case of the war as well (160). Inevitably, then, the narrative focus returns to the war. Rowlandson concludes with a series of observations made during her "afflicted time," many of them pertaining to wartime strategies: the English army's lost opportunities to destroy the enemy, its slowness and dullness in the eyes of the Indians, and the means Indians used to survive while under attack. That the text concludes with comments on the war suggests that military conquest is its fundamental concern. Moreover, Rowlandson's spiritual victory promised that the English army would similarly be victorious over the Indians. By providing the rescue of white females as justification for the conquest, Rowlandson's capture and redemption also gained recruits for the war against the Indians. In the end, the outcome of King Philip's War bore out the colonists' faith as English soldiers killed thousands of Indians, burning villages and crops in their wake. One observer's description of a massacre in which soldiers killed six hundred Indians resonates strongly with Rowlandson's narration of the Narragansett attack on Lancaster: soldiers "ran amok, killing the wounded men, women, and children indiscriminately, firing the camp, burning the Indians alive or dead in their huts." The Puritans, however, assumed no responsibility for the parallel atrocities or for the subsequent capture and sale of Indian women and children into the Caribbean slave trade. Nor did they see these actions as evidence of the devil's work. Rather, they explained them as "God's will."[28]

Rowlandson's captivity narrative, then, serves a number of crucial colonizing functions. The text defines Indians in Christian terms, as the Puritans' baser selves fallen from grace, and gives them a necessary role in Christian redemption. By going native and then returning to the Puritan fold, Rowlandson enacts and affirms this process of redemption. This is a role, moreover, that suggests the Puritans' superiority and justifies—even renders inevitable—their conquest of the Natives. At the same time, the text conceals the nature of this conquest by showing the Puritans, represented by the female captive, as the Indians' victims. Yet there is another important way in which the cultural work of representation contributes to that of military conquest. Just as the English army, during King Philip's War and throughout the colonial period, aimed to contain Native peoples in a literal way, so did the mechanisms of representation enact a kind of ideological containment. Specifically, by casting Indians as counterimages of ideal Puritans, the text controls and neutralizes the ideological challenge posed by cultural differences. In addition, the way that Rowlandson interpreted her encounter with the Natives as an internal drama, as an encounter with her own sinful nature, manifests a very literal form of containment. Thus, in the narrative, Indians support rather than question the Puritan worldview.

Nevertheless, the text also articulates contradictions in its representations of Indians. There are several points in the story in which the Indians fail to fit the "diabolical" roles assigned to them. While Rowlandson recounts the cruelties of the Natives, for instance, so too does she at times recount their kindnesses. It is the Natives whom she must thank for the Bible she reads during her captivity; they also give her food, provide comfortable places to sleep, and on occasion manifest profound

[28] Stannard, *American Holocaust*, 115–16. See also Richard Slotkin and James K. Folson, eds., *So Dreadful a Judgment: Puritan Responses to King Philip's War, 1676–1677* (Middletown, Conn.: Wesleyan University Press, 1978).

sympathy for her and her children. That such supposedly bloodthirsty and demonic creatures should exhibit compassion seems puzzling because these descriptions counter the text's other descriptions of Indian savagery. More striking, though, are the moments when the Indians move uncomfortably close to "Englishness"—for example, when she mistakes Indians approaching on horseback for Englishmen, when she compares one of the wives of King Philip (the Native leader also called Metacomet) to "a severe and proud Dame" like "any of the Gentry of the land," and when she encounters the utterly unheathen Praying Indians (148, 150, 152). True, after each of these revelations, Rowlandson carefully obscures the similarities—noting, for example, the "vast difference between the lovely faces of Christians, and the foul looks of those Heathens" on horseback. My point is not that Rowlandson approaches a dispassionate understanding of cultural difference. On the contrary, these moments—like the depictions of Indians as Satanic figures—remain delimited by a Eurocentric frame of reference. Rather, the fact that Rowlandson's Indians in the end fail to conform completely to the roles she assigns them clearly shows the text's ideological work and thus questions the text's project of accounting for and justifying conquest.

Nevertheless, *The Sovereignty and Goodness of GOD* provided a plot that has been repeated over and over again in subsequent accounts of relations between whites and Natives. However, in the years following the completion of the military conquest, the period under scrutiny in this book, the relationship between the captivity paradigm and going native has changed. By redrawing the boundaries between the Puritans and the Natives, Rowlandson's narrative affirmed European-American superiority and justified the ongoing military campaigns. After the completion of the conquest, by contrast, going native has served to conceal historical differences between Native America and European America, and in some cases even to elide their identities in a more permanent way. These events thus both articulate and deny white Americans' responsibility for—and indeed, even the fact of—the conquest. At the same time, Natives have assumed a more complicated role in the captivity plot by directly providing European Americans with rescue (physical or spiritual) and even redemption. The New Age in particular has seen a resurgence of interest in such captivity narratives, which frequently serve as the framework for New Agers' voyages into the worlds of non-Western others.[29] In part because these works utilize the

[29] Another emblematic text is Marlo Morgan's *Mutant Message Down Under* (New York: HarperCollins, 1991). I am grateful to Patricia Penn Hilden for bringing this pattern to my attention.

conventions of the most colonial of genres, the captivity narrative, these twentieth-century forms of going native betray their complicity in the history of conquest and contemporary racial subjugation despite their claims to the contrary.

CAPTIVITY IN THE NEW AGE

In 1981, three centuries after the initial appearance of Mary Rowlandson's captivity narrative, Lynn Andrews published *Medicine Woman,* a book she claims is an autobiographical account of her experiences with Native spiritual teachers. The author of several acclaimed and best-selling works bearing such otherworldly titles as *Jaguar Woman, Star Woman,* and *Flight of the Seventh Moon,* Andrews pens narratives catering to the New Age fascination with Native America. Her works, in fact, have positioned her as one of the foremost New Age spokespersons. In these books and on highly paid speaking tours, she teaches what she describes as the Indian "Medicine Way." Her authority to teach derives in part from the experiences she describes in *Medicine Woman,* her fourth book in which she goes native by learning "traditional" secrets about the "red road of womanhood" from Cree elders. Like her other books, this one caters to the women's market, specifically to those readers who look to other cultures in search of alternative gender models. Yet despite the popularity of her work, Andrews's career has been marked by controversy, most often in Native circles. Native activists and leaders have publicly and vigorously criticized Andrews for the fakery of her "Indian" message as well as for her impropriety in positioning herself as a teacher of Native spirituality.[30] These protests, however, have had little effect. Nor has her popularity suffered. One after another, her books have landed at the top of various bestseller lists, earning her both substantial wealth and the role, however absurd, of spokesperson for Native America.

While her apparently sympathetic portraits of Native peoples and spiritual beliefs win Andrews a wide readership, on closer examination the politics of her works prove complex. Although both Andrews and her readers claim her stories differ from representations of Indian "savages" characterizing the era of conquest, her works actually rely on colonial conventions. *Medicine Woman* is symptomatic. In both its content and its structure, in fact, the "autobiography" replicates many aspects of Rowlandson's *The Soveraignty and Goodness of GOD.* Like her literary ancestor, Andrews travels into the wilderness and encounters Indians

[30] See, for example, Rose, "The Great Pretenders," 415.

whom she initially labels "savage" and "diabolical." They oblige her purposes by keeping her there against her will. Quickly, however, readers discover that her experiences with these Natives will differ markedly (though temporarily) from Rowlandson's descriptions. While Rowlandson's Native world embodied a Christian's fall from grace, Andrews, by contrast, grows into a "higher" spiritual knowledge lacking in her own society. For her, going native thus provides the positive key to spiritual redemption where Rowlandson found only its negative. This difference, however, only obscures *Medicine Woman*'s relationship to Rowlandson's narrative and, by implication, the complicity of the New Age in the history of conquest. The parallels between the two texts again become clear when both protagonists attain spiritual redemption as a result of their forays into the Native world. Moreover, Andrews, like her predecessor, uses conversion and redemption to justify her appropriation of Native possessions (in this case, both things and beliefs). At the same time, however, both texts obfuscate the fact of this conquest by reversing these power relations, specifically by rendering the female captive as the hapless "victim" of the Natives rather than as an agent of colonial aggression.

Yet while the Puritans strove to differentiate themselves from the Indians, Andrews's effort to go native reflects this captive's very contemporary desire to occupy the cultural space of her Indian teachers. The narrative thus reflects a difference in the relations between Natives and European Americans in these two historical periods. Rowlandson's contemporaries sought to attain Indian land and disdained those Native cultural practices that did not provide furs, land, food, or other forms of material profit. By contrast, in the New Age, culture—especially spiritual knowledge—comprises the last domain of conquest. *Medicine Woman* complicates Rowlandson's narrative in other ways. Drawn to Cree country by her fascination with Indian culture (in particular, her desire to collect a Native basket), Andrews is later kept there against her will when her teachers subject her to a series of terrifying rituals. The text thus shows the double meaning of captivity in the New Age, signifying here both the power to captivate and to hold captive. This ambiguity, moreover, reflects the complicated racial dynamics of the New Age movement, which is characterized by a fascination with racial and cultural otherness and, paradoxically, by an insistence on white racial dominance that it attempts to conceal by showing Natives as the possessors of power.

Like Rowlandson's narrative, which begins by describing English aggression toward Indians during King Philip's War, *Medicine Woman* opens with a scene that clearly shows the power of European America over Native America. The form this power takes, however, reflects the particular dynamics of colonial desire in the New Age. While attending an opening at a posh Los Angeles art gallery, Andrews stumbles upon an oddly out-of-place photograph of an American Indian marriage basket. Images of the basket later appear in her dreams, and she becomes obsessed with obtaining it. Collecting, in fact, is one of her passions, a preoccupation that articulates the imperialist impulse to possess the nonwhite world and harks back to the colonial compulsion to acquire another Indian possession, land. Indeed, Andrews explicitly points to the politics of collecting early in the text, when she likens her own assemblage of objects to collections of "primitive art" in museums—collections enabled by conquest and the display of which manifests the Western world's imperial might.[31] "I looked around my living room. It was like sitting in the center of a combination African village and American Indian museum. Over the years I had relentlessly gathered a priceless collection of Congolese ancestral figures, magical fetishes and war gods, Navajo blankets, and baskets from all over North America and Guatemala. The room was magical, full of the poetry and power of ancient primitive traditions."[32]

Andrews's description of her home, later described by a friend as the "Beverly Hills wigwam," is telling in several respects. Not only does it evoke a history of Western racial violence, it also attests to the power of hegemonic culture to transform the meanings of these "priceless" Native things into signifiers of capitalism. It thus accomplishes the same ideological containment of difference manifested in Rowlandson's narrative. Important, too, is the fact that these objects (figures, fetishes, and war gods) represent culture ("the poetry and power of ancient primitive traditions"). This "priceless" collection "relentlessly" acquired thus betrays both the collector's economic privilege and her sense of entitlement to own these artifacts (and, by implication, to own their originating cultures). By collecting them, Andrews both dispossesses these cultures and foreshadows a larger colonial displacement of Natives she will enact later in the narrative. In fact, a quest for power explicitly compels Andrews to scour the world in search of artifacts and motivates her pursuit of the marriage basket. The basket soon becomes an obsession; she even claims, "never had I felt so compelled to acquire an object" (6). Yet, as the narrative progresses, Andrews conceals the politically charged nature of her search under an apparently more benign motivation: the

[31] See Patricia Penn Hilden and Shari M. Huhndorf, "Performing 'Indian' in the National Museum of the American Indian," *Social Identities* 5, 2 (1999): 161–83; and Hilden, "Race for Sale: Narratives of Possession in Two 'Ethnic' Museums," forthcoming in *TDR: The Drama Review*.

[32] Lynn V. Andrews, *Medicine Woman* (New York: Harper and Row, 1981), 6. Hereafter cited by page number in the text.

search for spiritual knowledge (another signifier of Native culture). Her hunt for the basket soon takes the form of another European appropriation from the traditional Native world, a "vision quest." This journey ultimately accomplishes her transformation into a self-described "medicine woman," an owner of and spokesperson for Native culture.

Andrews's quest for spiritual regeneration, then, echoes Rowlandson's journey toward redemption in the wilderness. In *Medicine Woman,* however, Native peoples play rather different roles in the captive's transformation. In the earlier text, the Narragansetts exemplify the fall from grace that threatens the errant Puritan. Here, by contrast, Indians provide models for Andrews to emulate. In this way, the narrative attempts to reverse the relationship between Native America and European America articulated in its opening scenes, and it thus reveals its will to colonial power as a source of anxiety. In this way, too, it parallels its predecessor narrative. While Andrews's collections clearly manifest this power, the next part of the story shows the Natives' superiority, for they are seen to possess the wisdom necessary to save the white world, a world in dire need of salvation. Given to excess, extravagance, and spiritual bankruptcy, the inhabitants of Hollywood (Andrews's home) lead lives devoted to "the struggle to amass a fortune." In the end, they can only look forward to their "last years spent in a malaise of bitterness and self-destruction" (11). Native society, by contrast, is enmeshed in ancient traditions and wisdom "lost" in the modern West.[35] It thus seems to provide Hollywood's only hope for redemption.

By following directions offered by dreams and "spirit guides," Andrews finally discovers that the coveted marriage basket can be found on the Cree reserve in Canada. At this point, the narrative takes a significant turn. While in the beginning Indians appear completely different from European Americans, the text now refigures these cultural relations in order to allow Andrews to cross these cultural boundaries. The narrative accomplishes this task by temporarily making gender rather than race or culture the focus of the drama. This shift in focus further conceals the dynamics of colonialism in the story. Until this point, Andrews's desire to acquire the basket has explicitly manifested colonial desire, the dominant culture's compulsion to own the possessions of the colonized. Now, however, her motivations appear to change to a desire to help Native women. Arriving on the reserve, where a "medicine teacher" named Agnes Whistling Elk inexplicably awaits

---

[35] It should be noted, however, that this rendering of Indians as the West's others bears little relation to any Native reality. The Indian world Andrews imagines comprises a variety of disparate, frequently unrelated, and often absurdly fake images and practices, ostensibly drawn from cultures ranging from the Northern Plains to Central America.

her, Andrews finds that the basket is at the center of a highly gendered struggle between Agnes (a Native woman who embodies the "red road of womanhood") and Red Dog (a white man who represents archetypal maleness). This battle, moreover, is cast as a spiritual battle between good and evil that resonates strongly with the theological drama at the heart of Rowlandson's narrative. Here, however, the terms are reversed as the Native women (initially, at least) occupy the position of good. Having introduced this conflict, the narrative proceeds to redefine the importance of the basket. Formerly symbolizing "culture" ("the poetry and power of ancient primitive traditions"), the basket now signifies "the ancient way of woman" (38). The use of the singular form here— woman rather than women—implies that Andrews and the Cree women share a fundamental sameness transcending racial and cultural differences. This, the text suggests, enables Andrews to enter the world of these Indian women unproblematically. The ability to cross racial and cultural borders freely is a privilege of whiteness, but here the text masks this racial privilege by making gender differences more fundamental.

Their shared gender identity becomes clear during a ritual Andrews undergoes at the hands of Native women elders soon after her arrival. Here, too, parallels with conventional captivity narratives become clear. Agnes leads her new apprentice through the woods in the middle of the night to a "luminous tipi." The Native women strip her of her clothing, insisting "you must face the grandparents naked." This highly sexualized scene resonates with the threat of rape in conventional captivity narratives, and this reinforces the suggestion that Andrews is at the mercy of her captors. This scene, however, differs in an important way from more conventional captivities. Since the sexuality takes homoerotic form, the narrative raises and then assuages anxieties about miscegenation—in other words, it guarantees the integrity of whiteness. Yet even as it prevents these Natives from violating the captive's body (and, by extension, compromising whiteness), the narrative foregrounds Andrews's ability to cross these same racial boundaries for her own purposes. Again, the scene uses gender to justify her ability to do so, thus further concealing the power relations at work. Naked, Andrews confronts six Indian women elders wrapped in blankets sitting around a fire. When she expresses her desire to obtain the basket, the women promise to dream and to pray for her. Later, Agnes explains the significance of the ordeal. "Are you a woman when you are naked?" she queries, "Do you have a vagina?...Do you menstruate?...Last night we had to make sure" (35, 44–45). In the narrative's terms, stripping Andrews of her clothing also apparently strips her of her European-American identity. It thus forges a bond between white and Indian women based on biological facts (read here as synonymous with gender). This scene, set in a real Native dwelling, also rewrites the opening scene where Andrews surveys the collection of exotic artifacts in her "Beverly Hills wigwam." Here, Andrews herself serves as the desired, exotic object of the gaze as the Native women examine her naked body, and this underscores the narrative's attempts to reverse the power relations at work in the story.

Andrews's interpretation of racial and cultural differences as less important than gender differences typifies much recent cultural criticism, including some key analyses of captivity narratives. In *Bound and Determined*, for instance, Christopher Castiglia contends that captivity narratives

> refuse to be static texts endorsing essential, unchanging identities and hence fixed social hierarchies of race and gender. Rather, the captivity narratives persistently explore generic and cultural changes, divisions, and differences occasioned by the captives' cultural crossing.... [W]hite women have consistently used accounts of captivity to transgress and transform the boundaries of genre in order to accomplish their own ends, even—perhaps especially—when they contradict the desires of their white countrymen.... [W]omen writers, in narrating their captivities, have blurred the line between fact and fiction in order to revise gender scripts and increase women's social mobility.[34]

Castiglia further argues that in many captivity narratives, women challenge gender hierarchies specifically by "defining themselves as primarily 'female,' therefore sharing identity with other women across racial difference, in opposition to men." By identifying with Native women in this way, white women gain "more mobility, more social prominence, and more economic participation than they had in their home cultures."[35]

While it may be true that some captivity narratives do challenge (usually implicitly) conventional gender roles, Castiglia's error lies in assuming that women's cross-racial identifications (which he unconvincingly contends refute "the binary logic of civilized/savage") constitute an anticolonial or antiracist position. Instead, as *Medicine Woman* demonstrates, these identifications actually articulate a form of white dominance while they use gender identification to conceal it. In this regard, the fact that Castiglia's book investigates narratives by white

[34] Castiglia, *Bound and Determined,* 4–5.
[35] Ibid., 8–9.

women is symptomatic. Culture crossing—the ability to journey into another culture for the purposes of redefining oneself and bettering one's own position—is most certainly a privilege of whiteness. Moreover, as Castiglia's argument makes clear, it is white women who benefit from these acts; it is they (rather than Native women, for example) who gain "mobility, more social prominence, and more economic participation" in their own cultures. Thus, this act itself comprises an act of dominance by inventing an "other" to serve one's own needs. Such a compulsion to transcend social boundaries, "to coordinate the differentiations of the world into a single ideology," in one critic's words, "is intimately linked to its capacity to subordinate other peoples to its values."[36] Castiglia's investment in this thesis motivates what I see as a serious misreading of Rowlandson's narrative in particular as a "resistance to" instead of an expression of "the power investments of white society."[37] His thesis, however, demonstrates the argument I am making here: that going native—in this case, through cross-cultural gender identification—participates in the process of conquest even as it denies its complicity.

Like some of the narratives Castiglia analyzes, *Medicine Woman* uses gender identification as a form of culture crossing, but here the colonial implications of this act are startlingly obvious. Upon discovering that the "true" meaning of the basket is "the ancient way of woman," Andrews finds herself drawn into the struggle for its possession. Red Dog, a powerful medicine man, has stolen the basket from Agnes. This event carries vast implications: "the basket was woven by dreamers and represented an unspeakable void—the womb in woman. . . . Agnes said that men have taken the void and said it was theirs, and that as a result our mother earth is now in a state of great imbalance" (57). Red Dog's possession of the basket thus signals his power over women. By pointing out the power Red Dog gains by owning the basket, the narrative simultaneously expresses and resolves anxieties about the implications of Andrews's own desire to possess. On the one hand, it suggests that her own possession of the basket would represent a similar kind of power over Indians. At the same time, however, because the basket now serves as a symbol of universal womanhood, her possession of it is both justifiable and necessary. Thus, Andrews's position vis-à-vis the dynamics of oppression has now changed. Her economic and cultural privilege move to the background as the narrative positions her as a victim (along with the Native women) of a patriarchal plot. In these

[36] Dean MacCannell, *The Tourist: A New Theory of the Leisure Class* (New York: Schocken Books, 1976), 13.
[37] Castiglia, *Bound and Determined*, 50.

terms, the effort to acquire the marriage basket seems noble, even heroic. By attaining the basket, Andrews—who serves as "the symbol of all women" since all women are "woman" (156)—will regain on behalf of these women the power that has been stolen from them by men.

The text conceals Andrews's racial dominance and privilege in another way as well, and this provides a more explicit parallel with conventional captivity narratives. When Andrews becomes sidetracked from her goal of stealing the basket by becoming infatuated with Red Dog, her teacher, Agnes, holds Andrews captive in her cabin in an effort to "cure" her. In another sexualized scene, Agnes binds Andrews's wrists and feet to her bed "as if she were bulldogging a calf" (153). She keeps her there until Andrews agrees to do her bidding by retrieving the basket. Not only does the helplessness of the captive reverse the power relations between these parties, but Agnes's efforts to cure her reinforce the notion that Andrews is acting on the Natives' behalf in seeking the basket. The remainder of the story describes the symbolically charged effort to steal the marriage basket from the demonic Red Dog. And herein lies another rescue story. The marriage basket, symbolizing womanhood, explicitly evokes the figure of the female captive. It, too, must be rescued from the Native world and returned to the white world (its location at the beginning of the story). The liberation of this captive—which literally delivers a Native possession into white hands—will mark the triumph of good over evil. In this way, *Medicine Woman* resonates with the conclusion of Rowlandson's narrative, which similarly showed the appropriation of Native land as the work of God.

Yet while *Medicine Woman* attempts to conceal the exploitation of Native America through cross-cultural gender identification, it nonetheless betrays a racial dynamic. The narrative, at times, explicitly supports European-American dominance. This becomes particularly obvious in Andrews's contest with Red Dog. The competition is ostensibly a spiritual one, with the opponents deriving their power from so-called Native beliefs and practices. Importantly, however, both Red Dog and Andrews are racially white. Red Dog initially came to the reservation as a priest, but soon he grew interested in Native life. Agnes then took him as her apprentice. In the process, "[he] learned as much as any man can learn. He knows the native world as well as anyone, and he can do anything he wants.... [H]e is made out of power" (46). Red Dog finally grew strong enough to steal the marriage basket from Agnes, who is unable to take it back. The task of reclaiming the basket awaits Andrews, who also quickly grows more powerful than her teacher. Not only do the European-American characters occupy center stage in the drama to "own" Indian culture, but they do so because of their superiority—stunningly, their superior knowledge of the Native world.

Medicine Woman manifests white dominance in other ways, which at times explicitly evoke the history of conquest that the narrative generally seeks to conceal. Andrews, for instance, is drawn to the basket not by her own will but rather by *destiny,* a highly resonant term that recurs several times. Early in the story, Agnes instructs Andrews to "follow [her] destiny" in acquiring the knowledge to steal the basket; later, Andrews realizes that "somehow my will was being fed, that it would begin to control and propel me toward a strange destiny" (42, 53). This motivation further deemphasizes Andrews's agency in seeking the basket, and it also carries important historical associations. The word echoes that most American of phrases, "manifest destiny," the notion that white possession of Native land was inevitable and even ordained by God. This association is reinforced by the nature of Andrews's quest to *steal* the basket and so to acquire *power.* Her terms as well as her actions thus recall the military conquest of Native America. Remarkably, in an uncharacteristic moment, the text makes these parallels even clearer when it refers directly to the conquest. During one of her lessons on spiritual power, Agnes tells the following story:

> That old way was a good way, a sweet way. Then everything in the world changed abruptly. It is said that a man came to a Dakota village, the first white man anyone ever saw, and everyone was curious.... The white man tried to tell everyone his stomach was about to touch his backbone—he was hungry.... In those days, I have to tell you, fat was very scarce. Fat was the most valued and important part of any animal.... [A] woman gave the white man a knife and pointed to the deer that were hanging nearby. That man rushed up and cut the fat away from every deer and ate it. That was the first white man we ever saw, and those Dakota called him wasichu, which means takes-the-fat. The medicine people looked at that white man with the deer oil running down his face, then looked at one another. They knew it was all over, and they were right. The long knives came and took much more than deer fat. (102–3)

What the Indians retained after the military conquest, Agnes concludes, was "medicine" or "true knowledge," adding that "Red Dog is [now] the master of all those lost arts" (104). By narrating this sequence of events, the text defines Red Dog's possession of Native knowledge, as well as Andrews's attempts to wrest it from him, as a form of cultural theft related to European America's historical dispossession of Native peoples. It cements this association in another way as well. The description harks back to an earlier moment in the narrative in which we see Andrews butchering a deer, an event that links her metonymically to the colonizing "wasichu" in this story. These links with colonial history become even more obvious in another atypical moment, when Ruby Plenty Chiefs, Agnes's companion, challenges Red Dog's presence on Cree land: "What are you doing on the reserve anyway? Why don't you live with other white people?" Red Dog replies: "It's none of your business where I live.... I can live any damn place I want to" (179). This exchange solidifies the association of Red Dog's and Andrews's cultural theft with other dimensions of conquest, including the theft of Native land in the past as well as in the present. Yet even as the text repeats these colonial paradigms, it also rewrites them in an important way. The text both draws upon and transforms highly gendered colonial discourses wherein European men appropriated "virgin land" and penetrated the "wilderness," formulations that resonate with the literal rape of Native women. By making Andrews the agent of conquest and the "owner" of the Indian marriage basket, explicitly described as a "womb," the narrative shows her repeating the behavior of colonizing white men. *Medicine Woman* thus further establishes that texts that challenge patriarchy (or purport to) can also reinforce white dominance.[38]

While the text thus articulates the complicity of its own project in the domination of Native America, it quickly proceeds to justify it. Although Andrews acknowledges her goal of obtaining the basket as theft, Agnes (the text's utterly un-Native "Indian" voice) supports Andrews's efforts. Not only does she "want [Andrews] to have the marriage basket more than anything" (138) but, incredibly, she also casts Andrews's acquisitiveness as a traditional "Indian" quality:

> Stealing was one method for a high warrior to excel and become a medicine person.... Pretend that you have to confront me for power.... You are stronger than I am, and I know it. I am honored. I cry and beg the Great Spirit to take care of you and give you even more power. You have come from the enemy lodge and I am honored. A medicine woman is always honored by the successor. Teachers want their knowledge to be stolen. That's the way it used to be. And that's the way it still is. (102)

In her words and in her own apparent inability to steal the basket, Agnes acknowledges Andrews's "superiority" to her and even affirms the goodness of colonization and dispossession. In legitimizing the theft

---

[38] Though important, the question of whether Andrews's notions do in fact challenge patriarchy is not central to my concerns here. It is worth noting, however, that her extreme gender essentialism would doubtless give many feminists pause.

of the basket, she also legitimizes the related historical dispossession of Native peoples. This occurs elsewhere in the text. At several points, for example, Agnes mistakes Andrews for her own child, a daughter she had lost years before, implying that Andrews is Agnes's natural heir. In another sexualized moment recalling the blood-bonding scene in *Gone to Texas,* Agnes even slashes her palm with a knife, wetting Andrews's body with her own blood and literalizing their blood ties. In the story, Andrews does indeed steal the basket in a dramatic ritual symbolizing the empowerment of all women (although, paradoxically, it also shows Agnes's disempowerment). Interestingly, though, at the end of the text, the basket—first signifying "Indianness" and then the "power of woman"—is now restored to its original meaning as a symbol of Native culture. This is possible since Andrews's quest has rid itself of the guilt of cultural conquest. With the coveted marriage basket in tow, she returns to Beverly Hills, charged with the responsibility of giving the "spirit world" to "her [European-American] people." This ending, too, resonates with Rowlandson's, whose reconversion in the Native world served as a source of witnessing and of Puritan spiritual regeneration.

Andrews's errand into the wilderness, she claims, enables her to function as "a bridge between the Indian world and the white world" and entitles her to speak on behalf of Native America (111). She can do so because her theft of the basket means that she (along with, by implication, European America) possesses "Indianness." In this way, Rowlandson's and Andrews's narratives accomplish similar cultural work with regard to racial conquest. Both enact a very literal kind of dispossession of Native peoples while using the captivity paradigm to obfuscate and justify the power relations between European America and Native America. But Andrews's experience has another important dimension: she claims that her journey into the Native world transformed her into a "medicine woman." This change in her identity begins in the middle of the story, when she undergoes a ceremony orchestrated by Agnes and her companion, Ruby Plenty Chiefs. Andrews describes the sensations she experienced while Agnes shook her ceremonial rattle: "The awareness of my physical being had disappeared. I looked down on the two women, and then I was them." This moment marks a "new birth," completed when she donned Agnes's buckskin clothing and became a "new woman" (92, 116). Thus Andrews not only "owns" Native culture, signified by the basket, but by going native actually occupies the cultural space and even the identities of her Indian teachers.

While Rowlandson's narrative concludes by redrawing the boundaries between European America and Native America, *Medicine Woman* dissolves these boundaries by showing Andrews permanently going native.

Although these differences reflect the particularities of racial subjugation in the colonial period and in the New Age, the effects are similar. By making culture (in this particular case, material and spiritual culture) constitute Native identity and then by taking possession of this identity, Andrews both displaces and dispossesses Native peoples. Since she now embodies the Indian wisdom that can save the white world, she also renders their existence unnecessary. Native peoples have not disappeared, however, nor have they acquiesced to these manifestations of colonial power. Indeed, especially in the so-called New Age, contemporary Native peoples represent the relationships between Native America and European America in ways that rewrite colonial narratives and, in so doing, challenge these appropriations.

OTHER VOICES, OTHER STORIES

Captives' narratives, then, have conventionally articulated and justified European America's conquest of Native America, and this pattern extends to New Age practices of going native. Yet some texts by Native writers also draw upon the genre's conventions, in these cases to challenge colonizing discourses. Many of the countless Natives captured during the centuries of conquest have provided accounts of their experiences that oppose the imaginings of the dominant European America culture and reveal its suppressed violent histories. As we saw in Chapter 2, during his captivity Minik wrote letters that contradicted popular Arctic representations and revealed the effects of colonialism that explorers' accounts concealed. Native writers of fiction and autobiography have also rewritten captivity narrative conventions for similar purposes.[39] One important example is Leslie Marmon Silko's novel *Gardens in the Dunes*. The novel takes us back to the turn of the twentieth century, the period in which we began our story. While world's fairs and fraternal organizations of that era celebrated U.S. imperial might, including the military conquest of Native America, they purposely left the stories of the victims untold. These suppressed histories provide one theme of *Gardens*. In the novel, Indigo, the young Native protagonist, spends part of her life in captivity in the white world, and her experiences there provide a counternarrative to the ones offered by Rowlandson and Andrews. *Gardens* also reflects on the New Age fascination with Indianness as some of its characters seek to collect Native

[39] While many works by Native writers function as reverse captivity narratives, particularly striking examples include D'Arcy McNickle's novel *The Surrounded* (1936; reprint, Albuquerque: University of New Mexico Press, 1992) and Zitkala-Sa's narration of her boarding school experience in *American Indian Stories* (1921; reprint, Lincoln: University of Nebraska Press, 1985).

objects as well as Native spiritual knowledge—in other words, to go native. Whereas discourses associated with going native conceal their complicity in cultural domination, Silko's narrative clearly shows their deadly consequences for Native peoples. At the same time, Silko's novel challenges the conventional narratives of Natives' "disappearance" upon which going native depends. Although Indigo is plagued by death, poverty, and tragic loss, she tells the story of a Native person's survival in a changing world.

In *Gardens in the Dunes,* Indigo is captured and taken from her home in the Arizona desert. What makes this captivity different from conventional narratives is that this captive is an Indian girl, and her "remove" takes her into the white world. The story begins with Indigo and Sister Salt of the fictional Sand Lizard tribe losing both their mother and grandmother, their only living relatives. Mama disappears after joining some Ghost Dancers in Needles, a nearby town, and Grandma dies shortly thereafter. While searching for food, the girls are captured by police, agents of the federal government on a mission to combat the "Indian problem." The police turn the girls over to the local Indian agent, another government emissary, who promptly decides their fates. Sister Salt will go to a nearby reservation, and Indigo will go to the Sherman Institute, a federal Indian boarding school in Riverside, California. These events refer directly to different dimensions of the conquest of Native America. The military campaign against Natives dispossessed them of their lands and confined them to reservations, a history the novel repeats in Sister Salt's story. In the latter part of the nineteenth century, the federal government then began its attempts to assimilate the survivors, in part through the boarding school policy, and Indigo's story reenacts this part of the conquest. By taking as its frame this history of conquest, *Gardens* relies on captivity narrative conventions. But Silko overturns these conventions by foregrounding the violence of the conquest. Like other Natives during the boarding school years, Indigo encounters absolute horror in the school, where she witnesses Indian children die of disease, abuse, and heartbreak.[40] Consequently, she becomes one of the

[40] Native accounts of the boarding school experience include Louise Erdrich's poem "Indian Boarding School: The Runaways," in *Native American Literature: An Anthology,* ed. Lawana Trout (Lincolnwood, Ill.: NTC Publishing Group, 1999), 624–25; Francis LaFlesche's autobiography, *The Middle Five: Indian Schoolboys of the Omaha Tribe* (1900; reprint, Lincoln: University of Nebraska Press, 1978); K. Tsianina Lomawaima, *They Called It Prairie Light: The Story of Chilocco Indian School* (Lincoln: University of Nebraska Press, 1994); Luther Standing Bear's account of his experience at Carlisle in *My People the Sioux* (1928; reprint, Lincoln: University of Nebraska Press, 1975); and Zitkala-Sa's (Gertrude Bonnin's) autobiographical section of *American Indian Stories.*

countless Indian runaways. The story of Indigo—her name associated with Indio or Indians—thus represents a much broader history. Like all of Silko's novels, *Gardens* has many layers and subplots, but it is Indigo's story in particular that concerns us here.

Indigo's flight from the boarding school begins another, parallel captivity. During her journey, Indigo is discovered and recaptured by a white couple, Edward and Hattie, who then confine her in their home. Their home physically resembles the boarding school, thus solidifying the similarities of these captivities. The couple soon become fascinated with Indigo and opt to keep her for a time. *Gardens in the Dunes*, like *Medicine Woman,* thus associates captivation (European America's fascination with Natives) and captivity, but Silko's texts underscores the destructiveness of both impulses. This connection becomes explicit when, after an unsuccessful attempt to return Indigo to the boarding school (now deserted for the summer holiday), Edward and Hattie decide to take her on a journey to the East Coast and then on to Europe. An unwilling traveler, longing for home, Indigo again tries to escape, this time by jumping from the train as it passes through Arizona. To her great dismay, she fails. Indigo thus reluctantly commences another journey into the white world, a journey that conventional narratives (including many of those analyzed in this book) tell us will inevitably result in death for the Native. Indigo's story, however, turns out differently. A journey from west to east, it reverses the direction of conventional frontier narratives (such as Frederick Jackson Turner's) of the "settlement" of North America. It is also a journey backward in time to white America's European origins. These reversals point to the way this story will rewrite—even undo—these conventional colonial narratives. Instead of meeting her fate in the white world, Indigo will find the tools necessary for her own survival and, by implication, the survival of Native America. Like Rowlandson and Andrews, in other words, Indigo finds in her captivity a source of salvation. This time, though, it is the Native world that benefits from the journey in a way that challenges rather than reinscribes European-American dominance.

In fact, the ability to engage and learn from the white world—as Indigo must during her experience as a captive—proves integral to Native survival. This is true in part because these experiences enable her to understand the colonial dynamic that has shaped her life. These historical lessons commence upon Indigo's arrival in the East. At the group's first stop in New York City, Indigo's eyes immediately settle on a frightening sight: exotic circus animals, locked in cages, are being unloaded from the train. This event resonates with several others in the book. The parallel with Indigo's own captivity is obvious. Later in the story, she encounters some Matinnecock Indians, whose dispossession and confinement to a small reservation on Long Island similarly resemble the animals' captivity. Upon her arrival in England, she views a former slave market, the site of yet another horrifying history of captivity. Together, these events attest to a series of intertwined histories that show Europeans' compulsion to dominate the world. Yet, of the three travelers, Indigo alone can make the connections between these events and her own experience as a captive. Seeing the slave markets, Indigo relates the Sand Lizard tribe's very recent experiences with slave hunters. Hattie's disbelief—"Oh Indigo! There are no slave hunters anymore!"[41]—is symptomatic. Although she is well meaning, Hattie here articulates white America's denial of both its history of conquest and racial subjugation in the present. *Gardens* thus recovers several concealed histories, but it is the colonization of Native America that proves the narrative's most central concern as it shows its white characters forgetting and even repeating this violent past.

Hattie, as a character in the novel, not only displays European America's historical amnesia but also elucidates the connections between contemporary colonial domination and going native. Her fascination with Indigo and her research interests are compelled by linked quests to attain pre-Christian spiritual knowledge and to recover non-patriarchal traditions. In this way, her interests resonate with Andrews's New Ageism in *Medicine Woman*. Moreover, like Andrews's project, Hattie's search proves destructive for the Indians, despite her intentions. Hattie's story begins before she meets Indigo. Highly educated and independent, Hattie inhabits late-nineteenth-century society uneasily, finding few stimulating paths open to women. Her marriage to Edward, motivated by convenience rather than by love, comes relatively late in her life, and it follows a disastrous episode in her scholarly career. While pursuing a degree at Vassar, Hattie had undertaken a master's thesis on the feminine principle in the Gnostic tradition. Her research had unearthed overwhelming evidence of the powerful roles women played in the early church, one of the suppressed histories described in the novel. In the end, the thesis committee rejected her work, claiming her sources were unreliable (although they were later authenticated). In *Gardens* this event, followed by a sexual assault on Hat-tie by a fellow student, demonstrates both the violence of patriarchy and its ability to write the past on its own terms. (Ironically, though, this is an activity Hattie unwittingly engages in herself on behalf of the white world by disbelieving Indigo's stories about Sand Lizard history, and this contradiction underscores

[41] Silko, *Gardens in the Dunes* (New York: Simon and Schuster, 1999), 233.

the complex relations of race and gender that also come to bear on Andrews's text.)

Though deterred from continuing her scholarly pursuits, Hattie remains driven by her quest to recover the feminine principle in alternative historical and spiritual traditions. Her journey to the eastern United States and Europe, accompanied by Indigo and Edward, provides an important opportunity to indulge this fascination. In Europe, the travelers tour a series of gardens, and there they unearth artifacts of powerful female figures originating in pre-Christian pagan traditions. Together, these female-centered traditions represent a better world for women than the one Hattie inhabits. Not only do these fertility images point to what she longs for in her personal life (she wants to have a child, but she and Edward never consummate their marriage, a fact that suggests the sterility of the white world in the novel). Images of powerful women also highlight her own powerlessness, which becomes even more obvious as the narrative progresses. After months spent touring gardens, the travelers eventually return home. Compelled by the child's pleas, Hattie pledges to return Indigo to her home in the desert. In Arizona, after she has reunited Indigo with Sister Salt, a carriage driver viciously attacks Hattie, raping her and fracturing her skull. The punishment is symbolic, and it recalls the events surrounding the failure of her thesis. The rape clearly shows male dominance, while the fractured skull indicates that her intelligence and her scholarly pursuits are unacceptable in a patriarchal world.

Emotionally unable to part with Indigo and confronted with the intransigence of patriarchy, Hattie then attempts to go native by seeking a haven in the home of the Sand Lizard sisters. In this way, Hattie repeats Andrews's behaviors in *Medicine Woman*. The narrative in *Gardens* takes a different turn, however. The former text, like the other forms of going native I have analyzed, conceals the effects of going native on the Indian world and its implication in the history of conquest. *Gardens*, by contrast, foregrounds these effects and this connection. Hattie's presence among the Indians draws the unwelcome and harmful attention of the authorities, including the police who captured Indigo and Sister Salt at the outset (events that recalled the broader history of colonization). They erroneously blame the Natives for the attack on Hattie, and they eagerly seek other reasons to persecute them. Recognizing the harm caused by her presence, Hattie leaves the reservation and eventually returns to England. Silko thus both indicates the colonizing effects of going native and urges those in search of alternative traditions to turn to their own pasts to solve their society's problems.[42]

[42] Here, Silko echoes Sherman Alexie's argument in "White Men Can't Drum."

Gardens in the Dunes further underscores the colonizing impulses of going native by drawing parallels between Hattie's Indian fascinations and those of her husband, Edward. A scholar and collector, Edward travels the world in search of specimens of various sorts (in this, his enterprise mirrors Andrews's love of collecting). We find him first in the jungles of South America illegally gathering rare orchids for American markets, where "orchid mania" results in the near extinction of species that had once lavishly decorated the region's riverbanks.[43] Edward's lifelong dream is "to discover a new plant species that would bear his name."[44] In this, he resembles Adam in the Garden of Eden (one of the many gardens suggested by the novel's title), asserting his mastery over nature through the act of naming. Edward also resembles another figure we have encountered before: the traveler/discoverer asserting his dominance and ownership of Native lands and peoples. His collecting, too, is linked to the work of these other figures in its connection to the near extinction of the fictional Sand Lizard people. Silko has made this history explicit in an interview: "I had this idea about these two sisters, and I knew right away that they weren't Pueblo people. I knew that they were from the Colorado River....So many of the cultures along the Colorado River were completely wiped out. There's no trace of them left. And it was done by gold miners and ranchers. They didn't even have to use the Army on them. Just the good upstanding Arizona territory, the good old boys, slaughtered all these tribes of people that are just gone forever."[45]

In the novel, Edward's hunting of specimens obviously parallels the Arizonans' hunting of the Native peoples, and both acts result in the extinction of their objects. This link becomes even clearer in Edward's first encounter with Indigo: "Edward continued to search through his library for ethnological reports on the desert Indians. He was intrigued with the notion that the child might be the last remnant of a tribe now extinct, perhaps a tribe never before studied by anthropologists....Edward asked Hattie to bring the girl up to his study."[46] Edward, in other words, views Indigo as one of his rare specimens. The novel underscores this connection as Indigo often finds herself in places where Edward stores his specimens, places like his study—where his desk, "massive as a throne," contains collector's tools (such as chemicals for preserving dead specimens, maps, and dried leaves)—or the greenhouse with its

---

[43] Silko, *Gardens in the Dunes,* 131.
[44] Ibid., 80.
[45] Ellen Arnold, "Listening to the Spirits: An Interview with Leslie Marmon Silko," *SAIL* 10, 3 (1998): 3.
[46] Silko, *Gardens in the Dunes,* 113.

"strange skeletons and dried remains of plants all lined up in rows on the floor."[47] The novel's narrative and imagery both point to the deadly effects of Edward's fascinations, just as they show their similarities to Hattie's interests.

While *Gardens* thus challenges popular narratives by pointing out the parallel effects of these twin fascinations—collecting and going native—on the Native world, so too does it rewrite colonial discourse in the fate it assigns these characters. As we have seen, in conventional narratives, contact with whites and modernity spells death for the Natives, a seemingly inevitable fate. In *Gardens,* by contrast, it is not the Natives but rather the collector who perishes, a victim of his own avarice. After his return from Europe, greed compels Edward to enter a partnership with the lecherous Dr. Gates. Together, the partners plan to mine a meteor crater in Arizona. Edward falls ill while engaged in this project, and eventually he dies. While the narrative foreshadows this event when earlier a tarot card reader prophesies that "greed will be punished," greed in fact comprises only part of the reason for Edward's demise. Edward's collecting is to blame for his fate in another way. Disturbing ancient artifacts from across the Americas and Europe carries a price. Edward's fate, in fact, is foretold on two other occasions. First, when Edward attempts to collect meteorites from the "Black Indian" of Tampico, she commands, "You cannot buy them but you will pay!"[48] Later, ancient Celtic curse tablets unearthed during an archeological dig reveal an inscription that warns against removing items from the temple. For anyone who fails to return these objects, it predicts childlessness and ill health, fates that eventually befall Edward. Significantly, Hattie shares these same ailments, although she ultimately survives while Edward does not. Thus the novel reinforces the link between Edward's nefarious collecting practices and Hattie's admittedly well-intentioned desires to go native. More generally, it condemns white America's colonizing impulses and challenges its right to "own" the world. Furthermore, by pointing to the fates of those who indulge in these activities, the novel deconstructs the notion of "progress," a commonplace rationale for European America's appropriation of Nativeness.[49]

---

[47] Ibid., 78, 105. In an interview, Silko actually makes explicit the association between the plant collector and other colonials, noting that historically plant collectors followed the conquistadors and the missionaries. See Arnold, "Listening to the Spirits," 3.

[48] Silko, *Gardens in the Dunes,* 90.

[49] See also Silko's previous novel, *Almanac of the Dead* (New York: Simon and Schuster, 1991), which renders a hard-hitting critique of capitalism and its relation to the colonial history of the Americas.

While other captivities conclude by showing a regenerated white world, *Gardens in the Dunes* thus describes European America's fate as a result of its misdeeds. At the same time, by assigning Indigo a very different end, it challenges white America's self-serving myth of the vanishing Native, a myth that further justifies white America's ownership of all things Native. Unlike most other narratives and events analyzed in this book, *Gardens* does not show Indigo perishing as a result of her contact with the white world. Rather, during her captivity, Indigo gains knowledge that enables her to survive and to help the Sand Lizard people resist further colonization. The novel thus challenges another key paradigm upon which going native depends, wherein Native America is white America's opposite and remains irremediably mired in the past.

That the Natives' survival depends upon change and adaptation first becomes apparent at the beginning of the novel, when the Native characters engage in the Ghost Dance. This is a significant historical reference. A widespread revivalist and resistance movement, the Ghost Dance movement swept the West in the latter part of the nineteenth century. It was in an effort to suppress the movement (and Native resistance more generally) that soldiers slaughtered Indians in the Wounded Knee massacre of 1890. In Native America, the Ghost Dance movement and the violent suppression of it signify the entire history of conquest and Native resistance. In *Gardens,* Silko's framing of these events explicitly conveys these meanings: "Jesus promised Wovoka [the Paiute prophet and leader of the movement] that if the Paiutes and all the other Indians danced this dance, then the used-up land would be made whole again..., then they would be able to visit their dear ones and beloved ancestors...[and] great storms would purify the Earth of her destroyers." The "Earth's rebirth," the novel continues, would "dry up all the white people and all the Indians who followed the white man's ways."[50] Ironically, though, the Ghost Dance provides a means of resistance in part because of (rather than despite) its syncretic nature. Historically, the Ghost Dance movement drew upon Christianity (the figure of the Messiah is one example of Christianity's influence) as well as upon Native traditions and the visions of Native prophets. It thus inaugurates the story with the notion that this syncretism is essential to Native survival, an idea that becomes even clearer at the novel's conclusion.

Significantly, Indigo believes she is following the path of the Messiah and his family on her own trek through Europe, since she assumes they traveled eastward after disappearing from Needles. While in Europe,

[50] Silko, *Gardens in the Dunes,* 25.

she too gathers objects and knowledge from European cultures. This activity resonates with the syncretism of the Ghost Dance and thus links Indigo's activities with Native resistance and survival. During her voyage, for instance, she gathers seeds from the gardens she tours and learns new cultivation techniques. Like Edward, then, Indigo is a collector, but her practices prove strikingly different. Edward collects orchid specimens and cultural objects out of greed and a desire for mastery. His collecting is associated with death (which is why "strange skeletons and dried remains of plants" line his greenhouse), and this death suggests the demise of the Natives. Indigo's plant specimens, by contrast, bring life to the Sand Lizard people when she returns to the Arizona desert. Her story—her capture, her immersion in a foreign world, and her return—thus follows the structure of conventional captivities. The ending, too, replicates these conventions, but this time by narrating the regeneration of the Native world rather than that of whites. Indigo's specimens contribute to this regeneration in a very literal way. Upon her return, she plants her seeds and specimens, and these yield necessary food to sustain Indigo, Sister Salt, and their friends. As was the case with the Ghost Dance, elements imported from European cultures are associated with Native survival. Remember, too, that Edward's collecting metonymically links the fates of Natives peoples and species of plants. That the Sand Lizard people reside in gardens—the gardens in the dunes—supports this association. The growth of plants thus symbolizes the continuity of Native life even as it reverses this entropic colonial narrative. In *Gardens*, other foreign imports also support Native survival. Indigo brings with her two animals: a parrot she calls Rainbow and a monkey named Linnaeus. The novel links Rainbow to the figure of Minerva, and he thus signifies wisdom. Linnaeus, on the other hand, clearly suggests scientific knowledge. *Gardens*, then, shows that objects and knowledge from the white world, if used for Native purposes, support rather than threaten Native survival.

Indigo's story, then, does not illustrate a case of going nonnative. Rather, Indigo returns home to an exclusively Native world, and this implies the endurance (rather than the stereotypical demise) of that world. Yet, in making change and adaptation of other cultural elements necessary to the Natives' survival, *Gardens* defies static and essentialist notions of Native identity (in part through its use of trickster figures like Linnaeus). Rowlandson's and Andrews's narratives, as we have seen, close by reasserting white dominance and essentializing cultural differences. Their rendering of Natives as others who are irremediably mired in the past suggests that Native peoples cannot negotiate the modern, white world. At the same time, this paradigm enables Indianness to function in conventional narratives as a source of white regeneration. *Gardens,* on the other hand, resists this paradigm and the two possibilities that conventional representations leave open for Native peoples in the modern world: disappearance or assimilation. The novel offers another alternative, one that more accurately reflects Native realities. Indigo and her friends innovatively combine traditions and modern ways, past and present, thus resisting the primitivizing tendencies of mainstream representations. The closing Ghost Dance scenes further affirm that syncretism of this sort is necessary for survival. The form of the narrative follows this pattern as well, since Silko employs and refigures the conventions of the captivity narrative, historically a genre linked to the process of conquest, to tell another story about the history and future of Native peoples in the Americas.

Indigo, moreover, is not the only character who unites disparate worlds for these purposes. Sister Salt also returns to the gardens with a child she calls the "black grandfather." This baby serves as an emblem for contemporary Native life. His name refers both to his race (his father is African American) and to Sister Salt's conviction that he is the girls' "old grandfather's soul returned."[51] As a figure who is racially mixed and who unites past and present, the child is the ultimate crosser of racial and temporal boundaries (as we have seen, an activity that generally articulates the privileges of whiteness). He is a character who remains rooted in the Native past while adapting to the changing world. Neither locked in the historical past nor portrayed as European America's "other," the black grandfather challenges the representations of Native America upon which going native, in the forms I have described it, depends. He is also a survivor. He was born prematurely, and many had predicted his death (just as dominant cultural narratives predict, over and over, the disappearance of Native Americans). Like the other Indians in Silko's story, however, he survives despite these predictions. He is also a teller of stories, and he begins speaking to his mother when he is still in her womb about events in the past and the future. The black grandfather, in other words, represents a viable, contemporary Native presence and the persistence of Native voices.

[51] Ibid., 468.

CONCLUSION

Rituals of Citizenship: Going Native and Contemporary American Identity

IN NOVEMBER 1994, slightly more than a century after the World's Columbian Exposition commenced in Chicago, another national exhibition opened to great fanfare, this time in New York City. Visitors had long awaited the chance to visit the highly publicized National Museum of the American Indian's George Gustav Heye Center, the newest addition to the Smithsonian Institution. The New York Heye Center provides one of two NMAI exhibition facilities; the second one, currently under construction, will join the other Smithsonian museums on the Mall in Washington, D.C. This new museum, like its nineteenth-century predecessors, explicitly reflects on the nation's past, yet it also seeks to distance itself from colonial history. In planning the inaugural exhibits, NMAI's organizers sought to break the colonial conventions of ethnographic displays. Western collections of "primitive" artifacts, critics point out, originate in histories of imperial conquests. Displaying these objects in Western institutions—the imperial centers—rearticulates these histories and power relations. Bearing these problems in mind, NMAI's organizers promised that their institution would be a "museum different," one that would convey Native peoples' histories and worldviews on their own terms.[1] These promises, along with publicity about the nature of NMAI's collections, drew large crowds to the inaugural exhibit in 1994, and the museum remains one of New York City's favorite tourist attractions. Despite officials' claims, however, the exhibits bear a complicated and disturbing relationship to white America's history of colonizing Native peoples. These displays show that more than a century after the completion of the military conquest, reenacting the colonization of Native America by going native remains an important ritual of European-American national identity.

---

[1] See Hilden, "Race for Sale," for a discussion of the "new museology" and a more detailed analysis of NMAI's complicated responses to this body of critical work.

It is, in part, the particular history of this collection, especially the story of its acquisition, that raises problems. Before the Smithsonian acquired these objects in the 1980s, they were the property of the George Gustav Heye Foundation, whose founder had amassed the vast collection largely through his personal efforts. From the turn of the century to the late 1920s, the avaricious Heye scoured Native America, now devastated in the wake of the conquest, for cultural artifacts.[2] He gathered a stunning 4.5 million objects. It was, very literally, the conquest that enabled Heye's collecting. Poverty stricken, their communities shattered, and in some cases tormented by cultural shame (the internal mechanism of colonialism), many of the survivors of America's holocaust sold objects that had long been cherished by Native families and nations. Those artifacts that Heye could not purchase he stole, even resorting on occasion to grave-robbing. Their loss recalls other devastating losses—of the millions of people who perished, of land, of other forms of culture. To many Native people, then, Heye's collection represents a broad and terrible history of death and destruction.

Decades later, in the 1980s, only 1.2 million of these objects remained in the Heye collection. (Rumors suggest that many of the "missing" objects had been stolen or illegally sold.) Nevertheless, the collection comprised one of the largest of its kind. It thus caught the eye of Smithsonian officials, who eventually arranged to acquire it when the Heye Foundation found itself in financial trouble. One possibility was to return the collection to Native nations, many of which have established their own museums that counter conventional representations of Native America.[3] But the idea that these objects properly belong to the people who made them seems not to have occurred to the Smithsonian's representatives.[4] Instead, they became part of "America's" collection. The collection now belongs to the Smithso-

[2] My knowledge of Heye is based on the work of Dean Curtis Bear Claw, who compellingly explores the relationship between collecting and other colonial practices in a film in progress and in an unpublished paper titled "Rethinking the Roaring Twenties: Sacred Objects, Crow Society and New York Collectors," presented, appropriately, at the National Museum of the American Indian, Smithsonian Institution, 12 November 1995.

[3] There are now dozens of museums and cultural centers that are organized by Native peoples. A few prominent examples include the Alaska Native Heritage Center, the Museum at Warm Springs, the U'mista Cultural Centre, and the Kwagiulth Museum and Cultural Centre.

[4] Filmmaker Chris Eyre made this point shortly after the opening of the museum. See Hilden and Huhndorf, "Performing 'Indian.'"

nian, that most American institution, a fact that implies European America's ownership of Native America. Colonial dominance also finds expression in NMAI's exhibits. Predictably, the Heye Center does not acknowledge the troubling history of the collection; indeed, it celebrates Heye's rapacious collecting. At the same time, the conquest is reenacted daily by the museum's visitors, who gaze upon these displays of Nativeness much as their predecessors had a century earlier, finding there both entertainment and confirmation of white America's dominance.

These displays serve another purpose as well, one that shows that going native—another means of possessing Native America and obscuring the conquest—remains an integral part of this ritual of American identity. Despite the museum's claims to respond to Native peoples' concerns, New Age spectacles offering spiritual regeneration to nonnatives find a prominent place here. For example, visitors are invited to step inside a "sacred circle" drawn on the floor and surrounded by an aura of light; those who do, a placard promises, can share an "Indian" experience by "acknowledg[ing] [their] part in Creation." While this display shows the dominant culture's flight from modernity, a nearby exhibit refigures colonial history in ways consistent with other forms of going native. Here, we find a boarding school classroom, another display of Indian captivity reminiscent of similar scenes at the Philadelphia Centennial Exposition and the World's Columbian Exposition. At these world's fairs, the boarding school exhibits showed the "benefits" of white civilization for Natives by concealing the heartbreaking experiences that drove Native children to commit suicide and to run away repeatedly. No troubling histories mar viewers' experiences of NMAI's exhibit either. In fact, this boarding school classroom is startlingly cheerful. Dolls and other playthings fill the display cases while instructional tools point to the more serious—yet still benign—aspects of boarding school education.

Yet there is an important difference between NMAI's boarding school exhibit and its predecessors. While the World's Columbian Exhibition featured a "live" exhibit with real Native children, no Native people occupy these desks. (Were they to do so, they might contest white America's suppression of its terrible history as well as its ownership of its collections.) But this exhibit is "live" in another way. In the Indian education display, the museum encourages visitors to sit in the children's desks and to perform the "Indian" experience, even providing crayons, paper, and other playthings to ensure their amusement. Like other forms of going native over the last century, this performance obscures the relations between the colonizers and the colonized, in this case by inviting visitors literally to occupy Natives' places and histories. That the National Museum of the American Indian, the newest addition to the Smithsonian Institution—*America*'s museum—should stage this exhibit is symptomatic. It shows that going native, an act that both articulates and denies white America's history of conquest, remains an integral performance of national identity.

Bibliography

Alexie, Sherman. *Indian Killer.* New York: Atlantic Monthly Press, 1996.
——. *Reservation Blues.* New York: Warner Books, 1995.
——. "White Men Can't Drum." *New York Times Magazine,* 4 October 1992, 30–31.
Anderson, Benedict. "Exodus." *Critical Inquiry* 20 (winter 1994): 314–27.
Anderson, William L. Introduction to *Cherokee Removal: Before and After,* ed. Anderson, vii–xvi. Athens: University of Georgia Press, 1991.
Andrews, Lynn V. *Medicine Woman.* New York: Harper and Row, 1981.
Arnold, Ellen. "Listening to the Spirits: An Interview with Leslie Marmon Silko." *SAIL* 10, 3 (1998): 1–33.
Ashcroft, Bill, Gareth Griffiths, and Helen Tiffin. *The Empire Writes Back: Theory and Practice in Post-Colonial Literatures.* New York: Routledge, 1989.
Axtell, James. *The Invasion Within: The Contest of Cultures in Colonial North America.* New York: Oxford University Press, 1985.
Baden-Powell, Sir Robert. *Scouting for Boys.* London: C. Arthur Pearson, 1924.
Badger, R. Reid. *The Great American Fair: The World's Columbian Exposition and American Culture.* Chicago: Nelson Hall, 1979.
Baird, Robert. "Going Indian: Discovery, Adoption, and Renaming toward a 'True American' from *Deerslayer* to *Dances With Wolves.*" In *Dressing in Feathers: The Construction of the Indian in American Popular Culture,* ed. S. Elizabeth Baird, 195–209. Boulder: Westview, 1996.
Balikci, Asen. "Anthropology, Film and the Arctic Peoples." *Anthropology Today* 5, 2 (1989): 4–10.
Bancroft, H. H. *The Book of the Fair: An Historical and Descriptive Presentation of the Columbian Exposition at Chicago in 1893.* Vol. 1. Reprint, New York: Bounty Books, n.d.
Barsam, Richard. *The Vision of Robert Flaherty: The Artist as Myth and Film-maker.* Bloomington: Indiana University Press, 1988.
Bear Claw, Dean Curtis. "Rethinking the Roaring Twenties: Sacred Objects, Crow Society and New York Collectors." Paper presented at the National Museum of the American Indian, Smithsonian Institution, Washington, D.C., 1995.
Bederman, Gail. *Manliness and Civilization: A Cultural History of Gender and Race in the United States, 1880–1917.* Chicago: University of Chicago Press, 1995.

Bennett, Tony. *The Birth of the Museum: History, Theory, Politics*. London: Routledge, 1995.

——. "Popular Culture and 'the Turn to Gramsci.'" In *Cultural Theory and Popular Culture*, ed. John Storey, 222–29. London: Harvester Wheatsheaf, 1994.

Bercovitch, Sacvan. *The Puritan Origins of the American Self*. New Haven: Yale University Press, 1975.

Berkhofer, Robert F., Jr. *The White Man's Indian: Images of the American Indian from Columbus to the Present*. New York: Alfred A. Knopf, 1978.

Berlant, Lauren. *The Anatomy of National Fantasy: Hawthorne, Utopia, and Everyday Life*. Chicago: University of Chicago Press, 1991.

Bhabha, Homi K. "Introduction: Narrating the Nation." In *Nation and Narration*, ed. Bhabha, 1–7. London: Routledge, 1990.

Bieder, Robert E. "The Grand Order of the Iroquois: Influences on Lewis Henry Morgan's Ethnology." *Ethnohistory* 27, 4 (1980): 349–61.

Bloom, Lisa. *Gender on Ice: American Ideologies of Polar Expeditions*. Minneapolis: University of Minnesota Press, 1993.

Bogdan, Robert. *Freak Show: Presenting Human Oddities for Amusement and Profit*. Chicago: University of Chicago Press, 1988.

Boy Scouts of America: The Official Handbook for Boys. 15th ed. Garden City, N.Y.: Doubleday, Page, 1916.

Breitbart, Eric. *A World on Display: Photographs from the St. Louis World's Fair, 1904*. Albuquerque: University of New Mexico Press, 1997.

Breitwieser, Mitchell. *American Puritanism and the Defense of Mourning: Religion, Grief, and Ethnology in Mary White Rowlandson's Captivity Narrative*. Madison: University of Wisconsin Press, 1990.

Buel, J. W. *The Magic City: A Massive Portfolio of Original Photographic Views of the Great World's Fair*. Philadelphia: Historical Publishing, 1894.

Cameron, William E., ed. *History of the World's Columbian Exposition*. 2d ed. Chicago: Columbian History Company, 1893.

Carnes, Mark C. "Iron John in the Gilded Age." *American Heritage*, September 1993, 37–45.

——. *Secret Ritual and Manhood in Victorian America*. New Haven: Yale University Press, 1989.

Carter, Dan T. "Southern History, American Fiction: The Secret Life of Southwestern Novelist Forrest Carter." In *Rewriting the South: History and Fiction*, ed. Lothar Honnighausen and Valeria Gennaro Lerda, 286–304. Francke Verlag: Tubingen, 1993.

Carter, Forrest. *The Education of Little Tree*. 1976. Reprint, Albuquerque: University of New Mexico Press, 1986.

——. *Gone to Texas*. In *Josey Wales: Two Westerns by Forrest Carter*. Reprint, Albuquerque: University of New Mexico Press, 1989.

——. *The Vengeance Trail of Josey Wales*. In *Josey Wales: Two Westerns by Forrest Carter*. Reprint, Albuquerque: University of New Mexico Press, 1989.

Castiglia, Christopher. *Bound and Determined: Captivity, Culture-Crossing, and White Womanhood from Mary Rowlandson to Patty Hearst*. Chicago: University of Chicago Press, 1996.

Christopher, Robert J. "Through Canada's Northland: The Arctic Photography of Robert J. Flaherty." In *Imaging the Arctic*, ed. J. C. H. King and Henrietta Lidchi, 181–89. Seattle: University of Washington Press, 1988.

Churchill, Ward. *A Little Matter of Genocide: Holocaust and Denial in the Americas 1492 to the Present*. San Francisco: City Lights Books, 1997.

——. "Lawrence of South Dakota: *Dances with Wolves* and the Maintenance of American Empire." In *Fantasies of the Master Race: Literature, Cinema and the Colonization of American Indians*. Monroe, Maine: Common Courage, 1992.

The City of Palaces: Picturesque World's Fair. Chicago: W. B. Conkey, 1894.

Clayton, Lawrence. Afterword to *Josey Wales: Two Westerns by Forrest Carter*. Albuquerque: University of New Mexico Press, 1989.

Collins, Henry B. "History of Research before 1945." In *The Arctic*, ed. David Damas, 1–16. Vol. 5 of *Handbook of North American Indians*, ed. William E. Sturtevant. Washington: Smithsonian Institution Press, 1984.

Cornelius, Laura. *Our Democracy and the American Indian*. Kansas City: Burton Publishing Company, 1920.

Costner, Kevin, dir. *Dances with Wolves*. Orion Pictures, 1990.

Damas, David. Introduction to *The Arctic*, ed. Damas, 1–7. Vol. 5 of *Handbook of North American Indians*, ed. William E. Sturtevant. Washington: Smithsonian Institution Press, 1984.

Deloria, Philip J. *Playing Indian*. New Haven: Yale University Press, 1998.

Deloria, Vine, Jr. *Custer Died for Your Sins: An Indian Manifesto*. Norman: University of Oklahoma Press, 1988.

——. "Foreword: American Fantasy." In *The Pretend Indians: Images of Native Americans in the Movies*, ed. Gretchen M. Bataille and Charles L. P. Silet, xi–xiii. Ames: Iowa State University Press, 1980.

Dilworth, Leah. *Imagining Indians in the Southwest: Persistent Visions of a Primitive Past*. Washington, D.C.: Smithsonian Institution Press, 1996.

Drinnon, Richard. *Facing West: The Metaphysics of Indian-Hating and Empire-Building*. Minneapolis: University of Minnesota Press, 1980.

Ebersole, Gary L. *Captured by Texts: Puritan to Postmodern Images of Indian Captivity*. Charlottesville: University Press of Virginia, 1995.

Ellwood, Robert, and Harry B. Partin. *Religious and Spiritual Groups in Modern America*. Englewood Cliffs, N.J.: Prentice Hall, 1988.

Erdrich, Louise. "Indian Boarding School: The Runaways." In *Native American Literature: An Anthology*, ed. Lawana Trout, 624–25. Lincolnwood, Ill.: NTC Publishing Group, 1999.

Fabian, Johannes. *Time and the Other: How Anthropology Makes Its Object*. New York: Columbia University Press, 1983.

Fair, Alan. "The Beast in the Jungle: Mailer, Eastlake and the Narrating of Vietnam." In *Tell Me Lies about Vietnam: Cultural Battles for the Meaning of the War*, ed. Alf Louvre and Jeffrey Walsh, 62–72. Philadelphia: Open University Press, 1988.

Faragher, John Mack. "'A Nation Thrown Back upon Itself': Frederick Jackson Turner and the Frontier." In *Rereading Frederick Jackson Turner*. New York: Henry Holt, 1994.

Fellman, Michael. *Inside War: The Guerrilla Conflict in Missouri during the American Civil War*. New York: Oxford University Press, 1989.

Fienup-Riordan, Ann. *Freeze Frame: Alaska Eskimos in the Movies*. Seattle: University of Washington Press, 1995.

Fitzhugh, Percy Keese. *The Boys' Book of Scouts*. New York: Thomas Y. Crowell, 1917.

Fitzpatrick, Tara. "The Figure of Captivity: The Cultural Work of the Puritan Captivity Narrative." *American Literary History* 3, 1 (1991): 1–25.

Flaherty, Robert J. *My Eskimo Friends: "Nanook of the North"*. Garden City, N.Y.: Doubleday, Page, 1924.

———, dir. *Nanook of the North*. Revillon Frères, 1922.

Flaste, Richard. "American Indians: Still a Stereotype to Many Children." In *American Indian Stereotypes in the World of Children: A Reader and Bibliography*, ed. Arlene B. Hirschfelder, 3–6. Metuchen, N.J.: Scarecrow, 1982.

Forbes, Jack D. "Frontiers in American History and the Role of the Frontier Historian." *Ethnohistory* 15 (spring 1968): 203–35.

Freuchen, Peter. *Book of the Eskimos*. Cleveland: World Publishing, 1961.

———. *Eskimo*. New York: Horace Liveright, 1931.

Friedenberg, Richard, dir. *The Education of Little Tree*. Paramount Pictures, 1997.

Galantiere, Lewis. Introduction to *Kabloona*. New York: Time-Life Books, 1980.

Gilbert, James. *Perfect Cities: Chicago's Utopias of 1893*. Chicago: University of Chicago Press, 1991.

Green, Rayna. "The Tribe Called Wannabee: Playing Indian in America and Europe." *Folklore* 99 (1988): 30–55.

Greenhalgh, Paul. *Ephemeral Vistas: The Expositions Universelles, Great Exhibitions and World's Fairs, 1851–1939*. Manchester: Manchester University Press, 1988.

Griffith, D. W., dir. *The Birth of a Nation*. Epoch Producing, 1915.

Gubar, Susan. *Racechanges: White Skin, Black Face in American Culture*. New York: Oxford University Press, 1997.

Hale, Janet Campbell. *Bloodlines: Odyssey of a Native Daughter*. New York: HarperPerennial, 1993.

Hall, G. Stanley. "Civilization and Savagery." *Proceedings of the Massachusetts Historical Society*. 2d ser. Boston: Massachusetts Historical Society, 1903.

Hall, Stuart. "Gramsci's Relevance for the Study of Race and Ethnicity." In *Stuart Hall: Critical Dialogues in Cultural Studies*, ed. David Morley and Kuan-Hsing Chen, 411–40. London: Routledge, 1996.

———. "Notes on Deconstructing 'the Popular.'" In *Cultural Theory and Popular Culture*, ed. John Storey, 455–66. London: Harvester Wheatsheaf, 1994.

Handbook of the World's Columbian Exposition. Chicago: Rand McNally, 1893.

Hannaford, Ivan. *Race: The History of an Idea in the West*. Baltimore: Johns Hopkins University Press, 1996.

Haraway, Donna. "Teddy Bear Patriarchy." In *Primate Visions: Gender, Race, and Nature in the World of Modern Science*. New York: Routledge, 1989.

Harper, Kenn. *Give Me My Father's Body: The Life of Minik, the New York Eskimo*. Iqaluit, N.W.T., Canada: Blacklead Books, 1986.

Heelas, Paul. *The New Age Movement: The Celebration of the Self and the Sacralization of Modernity*. Oxford: Blackwell, 1996.

Henson, Matthew. *A Black Explorer at the North Pole*. 1912. Reprint, Lincoln: University of Nebraska Press, 1989.

Higham, John. "The Reorientation of American Culture in the 1890s." In *The Origins of Modern Consciousness*, ed. John Weiss, 25–48. Detroit: Wayne State University Press, 1965.

——. *Strangers in the Land: Patterns of American Nativism, 1860–1925*. New Brunswick, N.J.: Rutgers University Press, 1988.

Hilden, Patricia Penn. "Race for Sale: Narratives of Possession in Two 'Ethnic' Museums." Forthcoming in *TDR: The Drama Review*.

——. *When Nickels Were Indians: An Urban, Mixed-Blood Story*. Washington, D.C.: Smithsonian Institution Press, 1995.

Hilden, Patricia Penn, and Shari M. Huhndorf. "Performing 'Indian' in the National Museum of the American Indian." *Social Identities* 5, 2 (1999): 161–83.

Hinsley, Curtis M. "The World as Marketplace: Commodification of the Exotic at the World's Columbian Exposition, Chicago, 1893." In *Exhibiting Cultures: The Poetics and Politics of Museum Display*, ed. Ivan Karp and Steven D. Lavine, 344–65. Washington, D.C.: Smithsonian Institution Press, 1991.

Ingram, J. S. *The Centennial Exposition, Described and Illustrated*. Philadelphia: Hubbard Bros., 1876.

Jehlen, Myra. *American Incarnation: The Individual, the Nation, and the Continent*. Cambridge: Harvard University Press, 1986.

Jennings, Francis. *The Invasion of America: Indians, Colonialism, and the Cant of Conquest*. Chapel Hill: University of North Carolina Press, 1975.

Kammen, Michael. *Mystic Chords of Memory: The Transformation of Tradition in American Culture*. New York: Vintage, 1991.

Kaplan, Amy. "'Left Alone with America': The Absence of Empire in the Study of American Culture." In *Cultures of United States Imperialism*, ed. Amy Kaplan and Donald E. Pease, 3–21. Durham: Duke University Press, 1993.

——. "Romancing the Empire: The Embodiment of American Masculinity in the Popular Historical Novel of the 1890s." *American Literary History* 3 (December 1990): 659–90.

Kaplan, Caren. *Questions of Travel: Postmodern Discourses of Displacement*. Durham: Duke University Press, 1996.

Kimmel, Michael. "Baseball and the Reconstitution of American Masculinity, 1880–1920." In *Cooperstown Symposium on Baseball and the American Culture (1989)*, ed. Alvin L. Hall, 281–97. Westport, Conn.: Meckler Publishing, 1991.

——. *Manhood in America: A Cultural History*. New York: The Free Press, 1996.

Kroeber, Theodora. *Ishi in Two Worlds: A Biography of the Last Wild Indian in North America*. Berkeley: University of California Press, 1961.

LaFlesche, Francis. *The Middle Five: Indian Schoolboys of the Omaha Tribe.* 1900. Reprint, Lincoln: University of Nebraska Press, 1978.

Lake, Ahnna, Linda Peerce, Jacqueline Gremaud, Jacques Leroux, Guy Tessier, with Asen Balikci. "Le stéréotype des Eskimaux chez les élèves du niveau primaire." *Etudes/Inuit/Studies* 8, 2 (1984): 141–43.

League of Women Voters. "Children's Impressions of American Indians: A Survey of Suburban Kindergarten and Fifth Grade Children: Conclusion." In *American Indian Stereotypes in the World of Children: A Reader and Bibliography,* ed. Arlene B. Hirschfelder, 7–14. Metuchen, N.J.: Scarecrow, 1982.

Lears, T. J. Jackson. "From Salvation to Self-Realization: Advertising and the Therapeutic Roots of the Consumer Culture, 1880–1930." In *The Culture of Consumption: Critical Essays in American History, 1880–1930,* ed. Richard Wightman Fox and T. J. Jackson Lears, 1–38. New York: Pantheon Books, 1983.

——. *No Place of Grace: Antimodernism and the Transformation of American Culture, 1880–1920.* Chicago: University of Chicago Press, 1981.

Limerick, Patricia Nelson. "The Adventures of the Frontier in the Twentieth Century." In *The Frontier in American Culture: An Exhibition at the Newberry Library, August 26, 1994–January 7, 1995,* ed. James R. Grossman, 66–102. Berkeley: University of California Press, 1994.

——. *The Legacy of Conquest: The Unbroken Past of the American West.* New York: W. W. Norton, 1987.

Lipsitz, George. "Mardi Gras Indians: Carnival and Counter-Narrative in Black New Orleans." In *Time Passages: Collective Memory and American Popular Culture.* Minneapolis: University of Minnesota Press, 1990.

——. "The Possessive Investment in Whiteness: Racialized Social Democracy and the 'White' Problem in American Studies." *American Quarterly* 47, 3 (1995): 369–87.

Lomawaima, K. Tsianina. *They Called It Prairie Light: The Story of Chilocco Indian School.* Lincoln: University of Nebraska Press, 1994.

London, Jack. *The Call of the Wild.* New York, Bantam Books, 1981.

Lott, Eric. *Love and Theft: Blackface Minstrelsy and the American Working Class.* New York: Oxford University Press, 1993.

Lutz, Catherine A., and Jane L. Collins. *Reading National Geographic.* Chicago: University of Chicago Press, 1993.

MacCannell, Dean. *The Tourist: A New Theory of the Leisure Class.* New York: Schocken Books, 1976.

MacDonald, Robert H. *Sons of the Empire: The Frontier and the Boy Scout Movement, 1890–1918.* Toronto: University of Toronto Press, 1993.

Macleod, David I. *Building Character in the American Boy: The Boy Scouts, YMCA, and Their Forerunners, 1870–1920.* Madison: University of Wisconsin Press, 1983.

Macy, Terry, and Daniel Hart, dirs. *White Shamans and Plastic Medicine Men.* Native Voices Public Television, 1995. Videocassette.

Mander, Jerry. *In the Absence of the Sacred: The Failure of Technology and the Survival of the Indian Nations.* San Francisco: Sierra Club Books, 1991.

Marcuse, Herbert. *An Essay on Liberation.* Boston: Beacon, 1969.

Marten, James. *Texas Divided: Loyalty and Dissent in the Lone Star State 1856–1874*. Lexington: University of Kentucky Press, 1990.

Masayesva, Victor, dir. *Imagining Indians*. IS Productions, 1992.

Massot, Claude, dir. *Nanook Revisited*. Ima Productions, 1990.

Mather, Increase. Preface to the 1682 edition of Mary Rowlandson, *The Sovereignty and Goodness of GOD, Together With the Faithfulness of His Promises Displayed; Being a Narrative Of the Captivity and Restauration of Mrs. Mary Rowlandson. . . .* In *Narratives of the Indian Wars 1675–1699*, ed. Charles H. Lincoln, 112–17. New York: Charles Scribner's Sons, 1913.

Matthiessen, Peter. "Survival of the Hunter." *New Yorker*, 24 April 1995, 67–77.

McGaa, Ed [Eagle Man, pseud.]. *Rainbow Tribe: Ordinary People Journeying on the Red Road*. San Francisco: HarperCollins, 1992.

McLoughlin, William G. *Cherokee Renascence in the New Republic*. Princeton: Princeton University Press, 1986.

McNickle, D'Arcy. *Native American Tribalism: Indian Survivals and Renewals*. New York: Oxford University Press, 1973.

——. *The Surrounded*. 1936. Reprint, Albuquerque: University of New Mexico Press, 1992.

——. *Wind from an Enemy Sky*. 1978. Reprint, Albuquerque: University of New Mexico Press, 1995.

Mead, Margaret. *People and Places*. Cleveland: World Publishing, 1959.

Mechling, Jay. "'Playing Indian' and the Search for Authenticity in Modern White America." In *Prospects 5*, ed. Jack Salzman, 17–34. New York: Burt Franklin, 1980.

Melton, J. Gordon. "A History of the New Age Movement." In *Not Necessarily the New Age: Critical Essays*, ed. Robert Basil, 35–53. Buffalo: Prometheus Books, 1988.

Meyer, Karl E. *The Art Museum: Power, Money, Ethics*. New York: William Morrow, 1979.

Michaels, Walter Benn. *Our America: Nativism, Modernism, and Pluralism*. Durham: Duke University Press, 1995.

Mitchell, Lee Clark. *Westerns: Making the Man in Fiction and Film*. Chicago: University of Chicago Press, 1996.

Mooney, James. *The Ghost-Dance Religion and the Sioux Outbreak of 1890*. Chicago: University of Chicago Press, 1965.

Morgan, Lewis Henry. *Ancient Society, or Researches in the Lines of Human Progress from Savagery through Barbarism to Civilization*. New York: Henry Holt, 1878.

Morgan, Marlo. *Mutant Message Down Under*. New York: HarperCollins, 1991.

Morrison, Toni. *Playing in the Dark: Whiteness and the Literary Imagination*. Cambridge: Harvard University Press, 1992.

Mulvey, Laura. "Visual Pleasure and Narrative Cinema." In *Film Theory and Criticism: Introductory Readings,* 3d ed., ed. Gerald Mast and Marshall Cohen, 833–44. New York: Oxford University Press, 1985.

Murray, William D. *The History of the Boy Scouts of America*. New York: Boy Scouts of America, 1937.

Namias, June. *White Captives: Gender and Ethnicity on the American Frontier.* Chapel Hill: University of North Carolina Press, 1993.

Nansen, Fridtjof. Introduction to *People of the Twilight*, by Diamond Jenness. Chicago: University of Chicago Press, 1959.

Nash, Roderick. *Wilderness and the American Mind.* New Haven: Yale University Press, 1982.

Nelson, Ralph, dir. *Soldier Blue.* Avco-Embassy, 1970.

Nemerov, Alex. "Doing the 'Old America': The Image of the American West, 1880–1920." In *The West as America: Reinterpreting Images of the Frontier, 1820–1920,* ed. William H. Truettner, 284–343. Washington, D.C.: Smithsonian Institution Press, 1991.

North, Michael. *The Dialect of Modernism: Race, Language and Twentieth-Century Literature.* New York: Oxford University Press, 1994.

Norton, Frank H., ed. *Frank Leslie's Illustrated Historical Register of the Centennial Exposition 1876.* New York: Frank Leslie's Publishing House, 1877.

Ortiz, Simon. *From Sand Creek.* Oak Park: Thunder's Mouth, 1981.

Oswalt, Wendell H. *Eskimos and Explorers.* Novato, Calif.: Chandler & Sharp, 1979.

Panzer, Mary. "Panning 'The West as America': or, Why One Exhibition Did Not Strike Gold." *Radical History Review* 52 (winter 1992): 105–13.

Paskievich, John, dir. *If Only I Were an Indian.* Zimma Pictures with the National Film Board of Canada, 1995.

Pearce, Roy Harvey. *Savagism and Civilization: A Study of the Indian and the American Mind.* Berkeley: University of California Press, 1988.

———. "The Significances of the Captivity Narrative." *American Literature* 19, 1 (1947): 1–20.

Peary, Robert. *The North Pole: Its Discovery in 1909 under the Auspices of the Peary Arctic Club.* New York: Frederick A. Stokes, 1910.

———. "The Value of Arctic Exploration." *National Geographic Magazine* 14, 12 (1903): 429–56.

Perdue, Theda. "The Conflict Within: Cherokees and Removal." In *Cherokee Removal: Before and After,* ed. William L. Anderson, 55–74. Athens: University of Georgia Press, 1991.

———. *Slavery and the Evolution of Cherokee Society 1540–1866.* Knoxville: University of Tennessee Press, 1979.

Poisey, David, and William Hansen. *Starting Fire with Gunpowder.* Tamarack Productions, 1991.

Poncins, Gontran de. *Kabloona.* New York: Time-Life Books, 1980.

Pratt, Mary Louise. *Imperial Eyes: Travel Writing and Acculturation.* New York: Routledge, 1992.

Rony, Fatimah Tobing. *The Third Eye: Race, Cinema, and Ethnographic Spectacle.* Durham: Duke University Press, 1996.

Roosevelt, Theodore. "The Strenuous Life." In *The Roosevelt Book: Selections from the Writings of Theodore Roosevelt,* ed. Robert Bridges, 21–29. New York: Charles Scribner's Sons, 1914.

———. *The Winning of the West.* 4 vols. New York: G. P. Putnam's Sons, 1889–96.

Rosaldo, Renato. *Culture and Truth: The Remaking of Social Analysis.* Boston: Beacon, 1989.

Rose, Wendy. "The Great Pretenders: Further Reflections on White Shamanism." In *The State of Native America: Genocide, Colonization, and Resistance,* ed. M. Annette Jaimes, 403–22. Boston: South End, 1992.

Rosenthal, Michael. *The Character Factory: Baden-Powell and the Origins of
the Boy Scout Movement.* New York: Pantheon Books, 1984.

Ross, Andrew. *Strange Weather: Culture, Science and Technology in the Age of
Limits.* London: Verso, 1991.

Roszak, Theodore. *The Making of a Counter Culture: Reflections on the Technocratic Society and Its Youthful Opposition.* Garden City, N.Y.: Doubleday,
1969.

Rotha, Paul, and Basil Wright. *The Innocent Eye: The Life of Robert J. Flaherty.* New York: Harcourt, Brace and World, 1963.

Rowlandson, Mary. *The Soveraignty and Goodness of GOD, Together With the
Faithfulness of His Promises Displayed; Being a Narrative Of the Captivity
and Restauration of Mrs. Mary Rowlandson....* Reprinted in *Narratives of
the Indian Wars 1675–1699,* ed. Charles H. Lincoln, 118–67. New York:
Charles Scribner's Sons, 1913.

Rozwenc, Edwin C., and Thomas Bender. *The Making of American Society.*
Vol. 2. New York: Alfred A. Knopf, 1973.

Rydell, Robert. *All the World's a Fair: Visions of Empire at American International Expositions, 1876–1916.* Chicago: University of Chicago Press,
1984.

———. *World of Fairs: The Century-of-Progress Expositions.* Chicago: University of Chicago Press, 1993.

Said, Edward W. *Culture and Imperialism.* New York: Alfred A. Knopf, 1994.

Saldívar, José David. *The Dialectics of Our America: Genealogy, Cultural Critique, and Literary History.* Durham: Duke University Press, 1991.

Scheckel, Susan. *The Insistence of the Indian: Race and Nationalism in
Nineteenth-Century American Culture.* Princeton: Princeton University
Press, 1998.

Schultz, J.W. *My Life as an Indian.* 1907. Reprint, New York: Fawcett Columbine, 1981.

Seals, David. "The New Custerism." *The Nation,* 13 May 1991, 634–39.

Seltzer, Mark. *Bodies and Machines.* London: Routledge, 1992.

Senungetuk, Joseph. *Give or Take a Century: An Eskimo Chronicle.* San Francisco: Indian Historian Press, 1971.

Shaw, Christopher. "A Theft of Spirit?" *New Age Journal,* July/August 1995,
84–92.

Shohat, Ella. "Gender and Culture of Empire: Toward a Feminist Ethnography of the Cinema." *Quarterly Review of Film and Video* 13, 1–3 (1991):
45–84.

Silko, Leslie Marmon. *Almanac of the Dead.* New York: Simon and Schuster,
1991.

———. *Gardens in the Dunes.* New York: Simon and Schuster, 1999.

Slotkin, Richard. *The Fatal Environment: The Myth of the Frontier in the Age
of Industrialization, 1800–1890.* New York: Atheneum, 1985.

———. *Gunfighter Nation: The Myth of the Frontier in Twentieth-Century
America.* New York: Atheneum, 1992.

———. *Regeneration through Violence: The Mythology of the American Frontier, 1600–1860*. Middletown, Conn.: Wesleyan University Press, 1973.

Slotkin, Richard, and James K. Folson, eds. *So Dreadful a Judgment: Puritan Responses to King Philip's War, 1676–1677*. Middletown, Conn.: Wesleyan University Press, 1978.

Smith, Andrea. "For All Those Who Were Indian in a Former Life." *Cultural Studies Quarterly*, winter 1994, 70–71.

Smith, Paul Chaat and Robert Allen Warrior. *Like a Hurricane: The Indian Movement from Alcatraz to Wounded Knee*. New York: The New Press, 1996.

Smith, Susan, dir. *Sweating Indian Style*. Women Make Movies, 1994.

Spurr, David. *The Rhetoric of Empire: Colonial Discourse in Journalism, Travel Writing, and Imperial Administration*. Durham: Duke University Press, 1993.

Standing Bear, Luther. *My People the Sioux*. 1928. Reprint, Lincoln: University of Nebraska Press, 1975.

Stannard, David E. *American Holocaust: The Conquest of the New World*. New York: Oxford University Press, 1992.

Stefansson, Vilhjalmur. *My Life with the Eskimo*. New York: Macmillan, 1943.

Steiner, Stan. *The New Indians*. New York: Harper & Row, 1968.

Stern, Julie. "To Represent Afflicted Time: Mourning as Historiography." *American Literary History* 5, 2 (summer 1993): 378–88.

Strickland, Rennard. "Sharing Little Tree." Foreword to *The Education of Little Tree*, by Forrest Carter. Albuquerque: University of New Mexico Press, 1991.

Sturtevant, William C., and David B. Quinn. "This New Prey: Eskimos in Europe in 1567, 1576, and 1577." In *Indians and Europe: An Interdisciplinary Collection of Essays*, ed. Christian F. Feest, 61–140. Aachen: Rader Verlag, 1987.

Tagg, John. *The Burden of Representation: Photographies and Histories*. Amherst: University of Massachusetts Press, 1988.

Tompkins, Jane. "Saving Our Lives: *Dances with Wolves*, Iron John, and the Search for a New Masculinity." In *Eloquent Obsessions: Writing Cultural Criticism*, ed. Marianna Torgovnick, 96–106. Durham: Duke University Press, 1994.

———. *West of Everything: The Inner Life of Westerns*. New York: Oxford University Press, 1992.

Torgovnick, Marianna. *Gone Primitive: Savage Intellects, Modern Lives*. Chicago: University of Chicago Press, 1990.

———. *Primitive Passions: Men, Women, and the Quest for Ecstasy*. New York: Alfred A. Knopf, 1997.

Trachtenberg, Alan. *The Incorporation of America: Culture and Society in the Gilded Age*. New York: Hill and Wang, 1982.

Trelease, Allen W. *White Terror: The Ku Klux Klan Conspiracy and Southern Reconstruction*. New York: Harper and Row, 1971.

Trennert, Robert A., Jr. "A Grand Failure: The Centennial Indian Exhibition of 1876." *Prologue*, summer 1974, 118–29.

Turner, Frederick Jackson. "The Significance of the Frontier in American History." In *Rereading Frederick Jackson Turner*, ed. John Mack Faragher. New York: Henry Holt, 1994.

Tyler, Edward Burnett. *Primitive Culture.* 1873. Reprint, New York: Harper and Row, 1958.

Van Dyke, W. S., dir. *Eskimo.* MGM, 1934.

Wade, Wyn Craig. *The Fiery Cross: The Ku Klux Klan in America.* New York: Simon & Schuster, 1987.

Wald, Priscilla. *Constituting Americans: Cultural Anxiety and Narrative Form.* Durham: Duke University Press, 1995.

Warren, Allen. "Citizens of the Empire: Baden-Powell, Scouts and Guides and an Imperial Ideal, 1900–40." In *Imperialism and Popular Culture*, ed. John M. MacKenzie, 232–56. Manchester: Manchester University Press, 1986.

A Week at the Fair Illustrating the Exhibits and Wonders of the World's Columbian Exposition. Chicago: Rand McNally, 1893.

Whitt, Laurie Anne. "Cultural Imperialism and the Marketing of Native America." *American Indian Culture and Research Journal* 19, 3 (1995): 1–32.

York, Michael. *The Emerging Network: A Sociology of the New Age and Neo-Pagan Movements.* Lanham, Md.: Rowman & Littlefield, 1995.

Zitkala-Sa [Gertrude Bonnin]. *American Indian Stories.* 1921. Reprint, Lincoln: University of Nebraska Press, 1985.

Zolla, Elemire. *The Writer and the Shaman: A Morphology of the American Indian.* Trans. Raymond Rosenthal. New York: Harcourt Brace Jovanovich, 1973.

Index